"This smart analysis focuses on historical cases in which there have been disagreements between the US and its European allies in order to draw conclusions about the actors' evolving identities and the changing relationships that have resulted in the wake of the Cold War and 9/11. The author asks critical questions about these cases that she takes pains to answer. Scholars and practitioners can learn from these lessons of the past and the important insights Simoni draws for the future."

—Joyce P. Kaufman, *Whittier College*

"Painstakingly researched and elegantly written, Serena Simoni's work makes us reexamine our assumptions about transatlantic relations and the causes of post-Cold War differences. Hers are persuasive, original, and often surprising findings about perceptions and foreign policy-making in Washington, London, Paris, and Berlin."

—Robert English, *University of Southern California*

Understanding Transatlantic Relations

In light of the Arab Spring and after days of public quarreling that highlighted the divisions among NATO's members on an agreement to give command of the "no-fly" zone in Libya to the alliance, it is evident that the United States is having problems engaging with its European allies and partners. Why is this happening?

Breaking away from the conventional way to study transatlantic relations, Serena Simoni uses a constructivist theoretical lens to argue that the transatlantic partners' changing identities since the early 1990s have influenced their political interests and, as a consequence, their national security policies. Contemporary divergences are a notable by-product of these transformations. By focusing on cases of disagreement (i.e., NATO's enlargement, the International Criminal Court, and Debt Relief for Africa), this book shows how since the 1990s, the United States has started to see itself as the actor carrying the international defense burden, while the European Union has developed an image of itself as the actor in charge of humanitarian efforts, which generally entails diplomacy rather than military efforts. Contemporary cases of disagreement as the Arab Spring, Libya, and Foreign Assistance in Africa illustrate how redefined national identities continue to alter the course of transatlantic relations.

Understanding Transatlantic Relations provides a more accurate examination of the future of transatlantic relations and offers an understanding of those issues that the United States and Europe would consider important enough to justify their cooperation.

Serena Simoni is Assistant Professor of Political Science at Samford University, Birmingham, Alabama.

Routledge Advances in International Relations and Global Politics

For a full list of titles in this series, please visit www.routledge.com

Understanding Transatlantic Relations

Whither the West?

Serena Simoni

NEW YORK AND LONDON

First published 2013
by Routledge
711 Third Avenue, New York, NY 10017

Simultaneously published in the UK
by Routledge
2 Park Square, Milton Park, Abingdon, Oxfordshire OX14 4RN

First issued in paperback 2015

*Routledge is an imprint of the Taylor & Francis Group,
an informa business*

Library of Congress Cataloging-in-Publication Data

Simoni, Serena.
    Understanding transatlantic relations : whither the West? / Serena Simoni.
        pages cm — (Routledge advances in international relations and global
politics; 107)
    1. Europe—Foreign relations—United States.   2. United States—Foreign
relations—Europe.   I. Title.
    D1065.U5S45   2013
    327.4073—dc23
    2012051132

ISBN13: 978-1-138-94303-2 (pbk)
ISBN13: 978-0-415-50159-0 (hbk)

Typeset in Sabon
by Apex CoVantage, LLC

Contents

PART IV
Conclusion

Figures and Tables

Acknowledgments

This book could not have been written without the generous support of the School of International Relations (SIR) at USC and the Howard College of Arts and Sciences at Samford University. Their financial assistance and their flexibility allowed me the means and the time for research and writing. In particular, at SIR, I am grateful to Hayward Alker for his initial enthusiastic reaction to my project, and to Robert English, Steven Ross and Steven Lamy for their comments at the early stages of this manuscript. At Samford, my gratitude goes to David Chapman and Fred Shepherd: I could not have hoped for better and more understanding colleagues. It is thanks to their generosity that I had the assistance of three wonderful students: Devon Arnold, Thomas Espy and Cara Wilson.

For their patience in answering my many questions, I want to thank Ambassador Marisa Lino, former director of the Bologna Center of the Paul H. Nitze School of Advanced International Studies (SAIS), Johns Hopkins University; Stephen Flanagan, Henry A. Kissinger chair in Diplomacy and National Security at the Center for Strategic and International Studies (CSIS); Kurt Volker, former U.S. ambassador to NATO, senior advisor to the Atlantic Council, and senior fellow with the Center for Transatlantic Relations at Johns Hopkins University's School of Advanced International Studies in Washington; and François Rivasseau, the deputy head of the Delegation of the European Union. A special debt of gratitude I owe to President José María Aznar, former prime minister of Spain, for his valuable advice and constant encouragement.

And finally, to Carlo Chiarenza, who shared my life during the long process of writing, rewriting and revising, I am forever grateful for the gift of his love, for his patience in reading the many drafts of my manuscript and, of course, for his cooking.

Part I

Historical Context and Theories of Transatlantic Relations

1 Introduction

In the light of the Arab Spring and after days of public quarreling, which highlighted the divisions among NATO's members on an agreement to give command of the "no-fly" zone in Libya to the alliance, it is evident that the United States is having problems engaging with its European allies and partners. The question is why is this happening?

International relations practitioners and policy makers on both sides of the Atlantic have tended to dismiss potentially poisonous crises in transatlantic relations that could lead to a significant change in those relations (e.g., the Suez crisis, the Gaullist challenge, criticism of the Vietnam War, the clashes caused by Reagan's policies of the early 1980s). Those transatlantic disagreements were considered little family squabbles, which would not cause major long-term problems, for, as the Latin locution states, *Ubi Maior Minor Cessat*. Certainly, in the East-West confrontation, America and Europe had no alternative but to collaborate in order to counter the threat of the Soviet Union. As it was initially conceived, this was a relationship predominantly focused on a military dimension, but that dimension soon broadened to encapsulate economic and political elements, which were underscored by values common to both sides. Differences, therefore, were resolved and discrepancies settled. The end of the Cold War, however, changed the international system and brought about two fundamental transitional phases in the transatlantic relationship: the first was in 1991–2001, the second in 2001–2011.

The first cracks in U.S.-European relations began to appear in 1989. German reunification had been a common goal for most of the Cold War, but when it became a reality, Americans and Europeans were divided in their vision of the new scenario. For better or for worse, faithful to their old notion of "keeping the Germans down," the Europeans were not much thrilled with the prospect of German unification, nor were they pleased with the George H. W. Bush administration's support for it. The British Prime Minister, Margaret Thatcher, perceived it as potentially causing the destabilization of Eastern Europe.[1] In 1990, the president of France, Francoise Mitterrand, said that he would "fly off to Mars" if Germany were to reunite.[2] Indeed, on this issue the Europeans were closer to the Soviet Union's negative view.[3]

The Soviets seemed to have two approaches: either to block Germany's re-unification with the support of the UK and France; or, if that plan did not work, to prevent Germany from joining NATO.[4] But in the end, Americans obtained what they wanted: a united Germany integrated into NATO.[5]

The extent to which these differences are the source and outcome of change in the international context is the subject of this book. In order to investigate this question, I have analyzed the processes that link contexts and actions in the development of a sense of identity and the effect that a shifting identity has on subsequent actions and contexts. *This book intends to contribute to previous analyses that have focused on the process of identity as the product of constant interaction with the international context*; and I, like others, reject the idea that the state or its leaders purposely opt for a specific identity and impose it nationally and internationally.[6] Consequently, in my empirical research, I have examined transatlantic divisions in six post-Cold War and post-9/11 cases where the United States and its European allies disagreed on three main areas of cooperation as articulated in the New Transatlantic Agenda: promoting peace, promoting stability, and promoting development around the world.[7]

Fundamentally, this book investigates *why the United States and its European allies have problems engaging with each other*. While there are studies that address crises and change in the transatlantic relationship, there is no single volume that analyzes them in a comparative framework and from a perspective concerned with creating a conceptual lens with which to study the relationship. This, I believe, is an effective way to proceed in a field that has traditionally lacked conceptual approaches and has focused almost entirely on military-security issues. This volume examines whether new identities are emerging and whether these identities are changing American and European interests.

Each chapter analyzes a case in which there was disagreement (NATO's enlargement, the International Criminal Court, Debt Relief for Africa, the Arab Spring, Libya, and Foreign Assistance) and tests the notion of constructivism and its suitability for explaining transatlantic relations.

The traditional conceptual approaches, which dominate current analyses of the transatlantic relationship, are fairly standard. Neorealists and neoliberals have completed studies of Euro-American relations based on power politics and on the role of institutions.[8] However, such analyses cannot offer an adequate account of the disagreements between the United States and Europe, because they do not take into consideration the effects of identities on interests and on behavior. I will demonstrate how in the 1990s, after the fall of the Soviet Union; and in the 2000s, in the aftermath of 9/11, identities redefined interests in the transatlantic relationship. In six case studies, this book examines the evolution of context, interest and identity during the two periods mentioned above: 1991–2001 and 2001–2011. In the first period, there was no perceived common enemy that could catalyze the partners, and in the second, Islamic terrorism was construed as the new common threat. The world-shattering context created by 9/11 has strongly affected American and European identity and interests and consequently their relationship. The post-9/11 context propelled to the fore old discussions and reemphasized an imminent danger as the catalyst of transatlantic relations. These accounts, however, add little to our understanding because they assume that the substance of those interests is unchanging and comprises some mixture of the need for survival, power, wealth, and security. To the contrary, from a constructivist theoretical approach, I argue that interests are not fixed or given and that social relations influence interests, not material resources. As Hurd puts it, "what distinguishes a specifically *constructivist* story on interests is that the influences on interest formations are *social*."[9] In essence, a constructivist would argue that the transatlantic partners' current preoccupation with Iran's development of nuclear weapons is a response to the social relationship between the West and Iran, rather than to nuclear weapons per se. This constructivist focus leads to a larger issue: the relationship between structures and agents. Structures are institutions and shared meanings that form the international context in which states act. Agents are the actors who work within such an international context. Ultimately, going back to the example of Iran, the hostile relationship between the West and Iran is not fixed and stable, but is rather the product of continuous interactions between the West and Iran, and among these two entities and their social context. These exchanges may harden the relation of hostility, or they may alter it. Additionally, they may change the larger social structures in which agents exist, including norms and other forms of shared meaning regarding interests or threats.[10]

In this context, structures and states are mutually constituted. Hence, the actions that states undertake contribute to the formation of international norms and institutions and such norms and institutions influence, shape and socialize states. What is even more important, both structures and states can be redefined in the process. In studying transatlantic relations during the last 20 years, it is clear that the United States and Europe have shifted their behavior in response to changing structures; and, in so doing, international norms and institutions have simultaneously influenced the interests and behavior of the United States and Europe. Contemporary divergences are thus a notable by-product of these transformations.

The constructivist approach does not entail any particular method of analysis. To the contrary, constructivists are divided into two camps: a positivist camp and post-positivist one, divided by a controversy over epistemology and the use of scientific methods in the study of international relations. Positivists argue that the socially constructed international system comprises patterns that can be generalized and falsified.[11] In this view, objective laws govern patterns of behavior and of social interactions. The study of world politics is thus aimed at explaining the cause-effect relationships, which are independent from the observer.[12]

Post-positivists, to the contrary, maintain that there is no single objective reality, but a multiplicity of perspectives that challenge any classification. Therefore, when studying international relations it is impossible to separate "causes" and "effects." What one can do is recognize that social laws are "inherently contingent," not natural and objective.[13] Thus, social inquiry should be concerned with how discourses and practices shape international politics and interactions between states.[14] In line with such a methodological view, this book will attempt to interpret *in what way the mutual constitution of social meanings and states redefine interests and behavior, and, how in the process, it changes structures and agents.* Such an examination analyzes social practices as constitutive of policies and advances the scholarship in international relations on identity, social practices and norms.[15]

I. INTERESTS, IDENTITY, CONTEXT AND ACTION IN INTERNATIONAL RELATIONS

In order to move forward, it is necessary to establish the usage of the concepts of interest, identity, context and action.

Just to be clear, I am not questioning the notion that states are self-interested. States do indeed seek power, security and wealth, but the question remains as to how states conceptualize their interests. As Martha Finnermore asked in her seminal work, *National Interests in International Society*: "how do states know what they want?"[16] In order to answer this question, constructivists challenge the common assumption held by many realists, liberals, and Marxists in international relations: that interests are a consequence of material sources.[17] In essence, going back to my example, they challenge the idea that the West's preoccupation with Iran's nuclear program derives entirely from its possible acquisition of nuclear weapons. The possession of material sources alone does not explain why the West is not worried if Israel retains nuclear capabilities. It follows that it is not merely military capabilities that shape the interests of the states. Rather, identities underpin interests.

Military capability is certainly critical in dealing with external threats, but the conceptualization of whom and what must be protected determines what weapons to acquire; in other words, it determines interests. Furthermore, when neorealists argue that, given the anarchic structure of the international system, each state seeks to survive,[18] they suggest that "survival" is the fundamental interest. Theorizing survival as the fundamental interest, however, presupposes an identity, or a self, to be preserved.[19] At this point the question becomes how do states know who they are? Constructivists respond that the social structures of the international system create states as actors with certain identities and interests. It follows that interests and identities are socially created.

Constructivists who study alliances explain that shared identity (e.g., the Western identity) makes states willing to go beyond just bearing the cost to protect themselves. Moreover, it makes states keen to invest in collective security. In this book, I will be advancing a different although not incompatible argument: *if the collective "Self" shrinks, so does the willingness to work together toward collective security.*

The claim that international institutions can transform state interests is central to neoliberal challenges to the realist assumption that "process" (i.e., interaction and learning among states) cannot fundamentally affect system "structure" or the context (i.e., anarchy and the distribution of capabilities).

Constructivist scholarship points to ways in which the identities and interests of states are socially constructed by knowledgeable practice, or action.[20] Alexander Wendt, in the well-known article, "Anarchy is What States Make of It: The Social Construction of Power Politics," builds a bridge between constructivism and neoliberalism by developing a theory of identity- and interest-formation in support of the neoliberal claim that international institutions can transform states' interests.[21] He focuses on the realist view of anarchy, which determines states' behavior. For realists, the anarchic system is necessarily a self-help system, which justifies a lack of interest in the processes of identity and interest formation.[22]

Conversely, Wendt claims that self-help is not a function of anarchy but of process and, as such, is itself an institution that determines the meaning of anarchy and the distribution of power for state action.[23]

In other words, the self-help environment is socially created by states' interactions. "Self-help" can be transformed by practices of sovereignty, by an evolution of cooperation, and by critical strategic practice. It follows that anarchy, and thus the international system, is, as Wendt argues, what states make of it.

This reasoning is germane to my definitions of interests, identity, context and action.

Interests. Interests are not a set of fixed and innate concerns, and the structure that determines the behavior of the states does not depend on material factors such as the distribution of power, or geography. Instead, ideas and norms constrain and construct the ways in which states define their interests.

Identity. The concept of identity is the perception of the state's "self." That is, states and their leaders develop an understanding of their state's "self" or its identity. This understanding determines the behavior of the states within the international system. In other words, states' identity produces states' interests. However, identity is created socially by interactions with other states within the international system. The behavior of the state is the consequence of such relations. It is not produced by factors external to the system. Rather, it is endogenous to both the system and its relations.[24]

Context. The context, or international structure, is the normative structure within which states operate. This structure is fluid and constantly changing, a characteristic that depends on changes in meanings. For example, the emergence of new human rights norms, the dialectical construction of new enemies, the emergence of new security and economic discourses all change the meaning of whom and what should be protected. These factors may produce a broad change in the system, which in turn transforms the relations between states. In the case of the end of the Cold War, the change in meaning altered the relationship between the United States and Europe (and, of course, Russia). As a result, interactions with Russia, which under the previous structure were impossible, became conceivable. Likewise, with the change of the post-Cold War normative structure, the relationship between the United States and Europe also began to evolve.

Action. Action is the behavior(s), practice(s) or "knowledgeable" practices of the states within the international system. Action depends on the normative context and, contingently, it changes norms, values and perceptions. States are simultaneously producers of meaning (practices and actions) and "products" produced by meaningful practices. In essence, actions are produced by states, but such actions change the international system and transform the identity of the individual states and thus their interests.

Transatlantic relations since 1991 reveal the co-constitution of identity and interests at its starkest. In this book, I set out to do the following: develop a conceptual lens with which to study the transatlantic relationship; examine how changing identities have shaped interests in the United States and in Europe; provide a rebuttal of neorealist and neoliberal accounts of disagreements in transatlantic relations; and advance constructivist scholarship in international relations.

By focusing on cases of disagreement this book shows how since the 1990s, the United States has started to see itself as the actor carrying the burden of international defense while the European Union has developed an image of itself as the actor in charge of humanitarian efforts, which generally entail diplomacy rather than military efforts. Focusing on more contemporary cases of disagreement as the Arab Spring, Libya, and Foreign Assistance in Africa, the second part of the book shows how redefined national identities continue to alter the course of transatlantic relations.

Before turning to an overview of the post-Cold War and the post-9/11 empirical cases examined in the book, it is necessary to clarify why these cases have been selected. Transatlantic relations have been problematic since the end of the Cold War: examples include the United States' refusal to sign the Convention on the Prohibition of the Use, Stockpiling, Production and Transfer of Anti-Personnel Mines and on Their Destruction (Ottawa Treaty, 1997); the U.S. Senate's refusal to ratify the Comprehensive Test Ban Treaty to stop all nuclear testing (1999); the U.S.'s abandonment of the Kyoto global warming treaty (Kyoto Protocol, 1997) aimed at reducing the emission of greenhouse gases (2001); the U.S.' abandonment of the 1972 Anti-Ballistic Missile treaty as well as the rejection of the 1972 Biological Weapons Convention (2001). However, there are three cases of

U.S.-European disagreement that are the object of extensive debate in terms of their impact on transatlantic relations: NATO's 1999 first enlargement at the Washington Summit, which admitted three new members (Hungary, Poland, and the Czech Republic); the establishment of the International Criminal Court in Rome in 1998, for which treaty 120 states voted in favor, while 7 states voted against it (the United States, Israel, Iraq, Libya, People's Republic of China, Qatar, Yemen); and the agreement for debt relief for Africa in 1999 in Cologne at the G8 Summit, at which the United States and Europe pledged joint proposals to help relieve the burden of debt and poverty. The manner in which their efforts were triggered, however, was remarkably different.

The secondary literature on these cases, mainly in the field of international relations and international law, tends to be divided on two key issues: first, did the disappearance of the common enemy lead to a crisis in U.S.-European relations? And, second, can common norms, interests and values still hold the transatlantic partners together?

II. ORGANIZATION OF THE CASE STUDY MATERIAL

These questions are examined in the first three case studies through an analysis of the justifications and motivations that American and European policy makers offered to explain their actions. After a brief discussion of how the political and security context of the relationship was transformed by the end of the Cold War, I examine the different attitudes towards global governance as well as the U.S. interaction with Europe bilaterally and multilaterally. Chapter 3 assesses the extent to which traditional approaches to transatlantic relations (neorealism and neoliberalism) explained the disputes of the 1990s and sets the stage for an identity-based account, which interprets changes of interests and behavior. Chapter 4 examines why the United States moved forward on NATO's enlargement, why the Europeans opposed it, and how these tensions were resolved. In the end, Europeans accepted the three Eastern European countries, and I consider the reasons for this. Part of the explanation for accepting the American strategic vision is the development of an identity, which encompassed the commonly held Western principle of the protection of human rights. This case reveals that within a post-Cold War security context, American and European identities were resocialized through the recognition of a new norm: humanitarian intervention. Chapter 5 investigates why, given the commitment to human rights, the creation of the International Criminal Court was particularly contentious. I reflect on the idea that under a different interpretation of international justice, sharing a common norm for punishing the conduct of war criminals can still produce opposing interests and behaviors. Chapter 6 takes on the transatlantic commitment to promote development around the world and focuses on the debt relief for Africa. This indicates that both the United States and Europe agreed on the need to solve the unsustainable debt burden. The key question here is how distinct social values have stirred such common interests. Once again, identity appears to be the main factor in generating these interests.

The importance of analyzing the justifications and the public accounts of the policy makers of the post-Cold War cases is that it offers the basis for a comparative analysis of the post-9/11 cases of disagreements. The rest of the book shows that in the post-9/11 phase, there is a persistent propensity for divergence and tension, even in the presence of a newly perceived common enemy, shared norms, and occasional collective interests. Chapter 7 takes up the Arab Spring and analyzes why the transatlantic partners have been doubtful as to what to do. Both the United States and Europe welcomed the Arab Spring and hoped democracy and freedom would spread in the region. Yet Europe feared massive refugee and migration problems while the United States sought minimal involvement. The so-called Obama doctrine of "leading from behind" served this purpose in Libya. Likewise, the allies dreaded the possibility of Islamists taking power with undesirable consequences (i.e., oil supply cutoffs, the development of WMDs programs, breaching agreements with Israel). Given common concerns, the question is why did the allies not develop a common transatlantic policy to promote peace and stability in the region? The answer is that they do not share a common understanding of security. The Europeans tend to operate through institutions rather than by building military capabilities as the United States does. This challenges the indivisibility of transatlantic security; but, as I argue, the transatlantic partners' changing identities are influencing their political interests and, as a consequence, their national security policies.

Given the long history of transatlantic relations and given their shared values (i.e., democracy and capitalism), one would have expected that at a pivotal moment like the uprising in Libya, Europe and the United States would have found agreement, maybe even unity, on how to deal with the crisis. Chapter 8 considers whether the showdown that took place between February and October 2011 in Libya demonstrates serious problems in transatlantic relations. The United States and Europe encountered great difficulties in finding a common position on Libya and therefore, I claim, they set in motion a redefinition of their relations. Post-Cold War transatlantic relations are the consequence of a broad structural change, which has led to an all-encompassing change in the normative structure, in the identity and the practices of the transatlantic allies.

Chapter 9 analyzes how the global financial crisis is affecting both European defense and its foreign assistance capabilities. The largest international aid donors are the European Union and its member states. European soft power and leadership are the consequences of Europe's Official Development Assistance (ODA). The Organization for Economic Cooperation and Development (OECD) estimated that the 15 European member countries of the OECD secured $67.1 billion in ODA in 2009. This total increases to $80.5 if we add the $13.4 billion from the EU institutions. For the same period, the United States spent $28.7 billion in ODA. Yet, according to some pundits, the ongoing economic and financial crisis could lead to a deeper political crisis.[25] Is there any evidence to suggest that a reduction in foreign aid will further strain the transatlantic partnership? I contend that a European reduction in aid commitments and implementation could lead to new frictions in its relations with the United States. Likewise, a reduction in the ODA budget will perhaps also redefine Europe's identity and its national security.

The concluding chapter of the book embarks on these issues by reflecting on the effects of identity and change and on the consequences that these changes will have on transatlantic polices. I will elaborate on different theories and their explanations on the future of said relations, and I will reflect on the lessons learned. Nonetheless, as I have anticipated, these relations will remain uncertain as long as there is an enduring transatlantic values gap.

2   The Changing Security Context

I. THE END OF THE COLD WAR AND THE NEW POLITICAL AND SECURITY CONTEXT

The end of the Cold War brought with it extraordinary expectations for a "new world order" that would be inherently less antagonistic and essentially more cooperative. The fall of the Berlin Wall in 1989, followed by the collapse of the Soviet Union in 1991, gave the West real reasons to celebrate. Finally, the division that had characterized the political geography of Europe was no more. Besides, the unification of Germany also coincided with the end of the USSR. This completely unexpected event marked the end of a system that could, at a minimum, have led to a Russian invasion; and, more perilously, to a Third World War. Still, moments of transition are by nature complex and entrenched with uncertainties. Accordingly, while George H. W. Bush optimistically hoped for a "new world order ... in which nations recognize the shared responsibility for freedom and justice,"[1] the Chinese government was massacring students protesting in Tiananmen Square, and Saddam Hussein was invading and occupying Kuwait.

The changes, which occurred in the first two years of the presidency of George H. W. Bush, 1989–1991, are particularly relevant to our understanding of transatlantic relations vis-à-vis changes in the security context. Such changes in effect had the potential to destroy the transatlantic solidarity, which had been continuing to build during the previous 40 years. In effect, a European security system for a whole and free Europe, where security was indivisible, could have demolished the political-military transatlantic alliance.[2]

Additionally, the new reality could have pushed both Europe and the United States to construct new political, security and even economic, architectures. This, however, did not happen. On the contrary, the transition period produced greater transatlantic solidarity, although somewhat marred by some moments of somber disagreements, which we are still experiencing today. The reason for this solidarity is to be found in the change of the security context, which led to a redefinition of identity and interests across the Atlantic.

The Unification of Germany and Its Integration into NATO

The first unexpected political/security change that the transatlantic partners confronted was the unification of Germany. Indeed, among the allies, the reaction to the possibility of a united Germany was mixed. After all, Germany was still perceived as potentially dangerous. Nonetheless, Germany went ahead with its plans for reunification. The strategy of the West German Chancellor, Helmut Kohl, to unify Germany was very well received among Germans, and there was a clear sense that the people were embracing the political reconstruction of their country.[3] The elections held in the German Democratic Republic expressed such a sentiment, one that was matched in the German Federal Republic. Policy makers on both sides therefore moved forward to bring about a rapid reunification. The two Germanys in 1990 signed an agreement for a monetary, economic and social unification, and thus the Deutschmark became their official currency. This was a historical moment, one that Chancellor Kohl called "a first decisive step on the path to unity."[4] The transition, however, has not been a complete success, and to some extent the growth of far-right movements in Germany has much to do with a disillusioned generation, which had placed great hopes in the unification. In the early 1990s, Chancellor Helmut Kohl had to confront much social unrest. Germany is economically the most powerful state in the union, but over the course of the years (and even today) it has faced numerous economic and social problems, caused mostly by the cultural differences developed in its two separate halves during the Cold War.

To be sure, not all the transatlantic allies rejoiced at the idea of a unified Germany. Some feared that it would be a destabilizing factor in Europe. That was, for example, how British Prime Minister Margaret Thatcher perceived it.[5] The president of France, Francois Mitterrand, promised he would move to Mars were Germany to be unified.[6] Other, non-NATO members (i.e., Russia) were not thrilled about this prospect either.[7] But the United States was very enthusiastic about the idea. Notwithstanding the concerns of the British and the French (as well as the Italian among others), President Bush did all he could to ensure the reunification of Germany as well as its integration within the alliance.[8] So did President Bill Clinton.[9] In a way, the unification of Germany caused a restructuring of the transatlantic relations within NATO and, more importantly, brought about the first "enlargement" of the alliance. In effect, after 1989, the major question became that of whether a united Germany should be integrated into the alliance. The Federal Republic of Germany (FRG) had joined NATO in 1955, but the reunification presented the problem of whether the former German Democratic Republic should join the FRG in its membership of NATO. With the diplomatic support of the United States, an agreement was reached as to how to proceed on the question of German unification vis-à-vis the international context. The negotiation was called 2+4, which meant that the discussions were to take place between the two Germanys and the four occupying powers (the

United States, the United Kingdom, France and Russia).[10] Other European countries were thus excluded from the talks. The discussion was focused principally on the role of Germany within NATO. In the end, and with the consent of both the French and the British, the prevailing plan was to keep Germany within NATO in order to avoid it becoming so powerful as to be capable, eventually, of building an alternative architecture to that of the alliance. This solution solved everybody's concerns about a united Germany. Those who were worried about potential instability due to the unification of Germany and its integration into NATO could, in fact, rest assured that, as NATO's first secretary general, Lord Ismay, famously said, "the Germans were down, the Americans in and the Russian out."[11] In essence, with this adjustment, NATO would still make secure the integrity of Europe, soon to become a "whole" Europe, by restraining Germany, engaging the United States and precluding Russia.

II. TRANSATLANTIC PARTNERS AND GLOBAL GOVERNANCE

Desert Storm and Transatlantic "Out-of-Area" Cooperation

Not only was it in the heart of Europe that dramatic political changes were occurring that would challenge the solidarity of the transatlantic alliance, new realities were also developing outside the Atlantic area. In a way, the old system as they knew it and to which they had adapted was shifting, and grappling with the new reality was not an easy task. In addition to the unification of Germany and the problems such an event created vis-à-vis NATO, in August 1990, Saddam Hussein's army invaded Kuwait, an oil-producing country, and, historically, a province of Iraq.[12] Iraq hoped to solve its economic and, possibly, its military problems with this invasion. After all, Kuwait's production of oil was enormous, and with the revenues obtained from successfully seizing Kuwait, the Iraqi government could have paid off its debts. Furthermore, a victory over Kuwait would have restored national pride, which had been badly damaged by the Iran-Iraq war. It was also possible that Saddam Hussein thought that the West, preoccupied with the German transition and its position within NATO, would turn a blind eye to his actions. But the West did pay attention to what was happening in Kuwait, and the transatlantic allies reacted to the invasion by forming a coalition that for the first time dealt with an issue that was "out-of-area": that is, out of the "transatlantic" area. This is hugely relevant, because the changing international system, with a shift in the security realm, led the allies to form a multinational coalition.

   The international condemnation of Iraq produced several UN Security Council resolutions.[13] Iraq's assets were frozen, and economic sanctions were imposed. Then a multilateral coalition was created, led by the United

States, named Operation Desert Storm. The coalition had the goal of liberating Kuwait and of reestablishing the status quo ante. In November 1990, Security Council Resolution 678 gave an ultimatum to Iraq. If Saddam Hussein did not remove Iraqi troops from Kuwaiti territory, the multilateral, U.S.-led coalition, was authorized to do so. On January 15th, 1991, Operation Desert Storm began by launching attacks against Iraqi targets, and after both air and ground attacks, on February 27, Kuwait was liberated and the Sabah royal family was restored as the legitimate authority of that country.[14] But even though coalition forces had penetrated Iraqi territory, they left without removing Saddam Hussein from power. Operation Desert Storm was perceived as a great victory for the West. Indeed, it was a U.S.-led operation, but many NATO countries participated in the military effort: the United Kingdom, Italy, Spain and France, to name but a few. Germany also participated, though its effort was substantially more financial.

The relevance of the Gulf War in the new context should be clear. It propelled the United States to act as the primary security actor in a shifting political and military context. It also showed the willingness of the United States to cooperate in multilateral efforts; and, most important, it revived transatlantic relations in a period of transition. Furthermore, it pulled the transatlantic partners together to face new crises, even if those crises happened outside the geopolitically defined transatlantic area. A few years later, the events in Yugoslavia would further enhance transatlantic cooperation through a redefinition of the allies' identity and interests.

The Conflict in the Balkans

For almost a century, turmoil in the Balkans has been a source of concern for Europeans. After all, tensions in this part of the world engendered two world wars, and at the beginning of the 1990s, the Balkans were again experiencing political unrest. Europeans and Americans confronted that unrest with trepidation, particularly because it was happening in a transitional moment: during the collapse of the Soviet Union, the unification of Germany and the Gulf War. In effect, when on June 25, 1990, Slovenia and Croatia declared their independence from Yugoslavia, the federal army, composed mainly of Serbs, responded militarily to the separationist attempts of the two former Yugoslav republics, thus creating thousands of refugees, especially among Croatians.[15] The Americans and the Europeans were not prepared for this crisis. The U.S. administration let it be known that it regretted the unilateral action of Croatia and Slovenia and warned that the situation could become dangerous. But in May 1992, only three months later, the European allies recognized both countries as independent republics.[16] The Europeans, for their part, had seen an opportunity to exercise diplomacy and, finally, to solve a crisis in their own backyard on their own, and they grabbed it. They wanted to avoid military intervention; they favored diplomacy, both to avoid casualties and because NATO, at least theoretically, could not have been employed since the Balkans were outside the Atlantic area. In fact, EU officials began working on a cease-fire right away, but it soon became clear that the situation was unmanageable.[17] The rise of nationalism and internal economic problems as well as the attempts of Slobodan Milosevic to control Yugoslavia actually prompted the breakup of the country. The war continued through most of 1992 and, finally in December, a cease-fire was negotiated and supervised by UN peacekeepers.

But the turmoil was not yet over, and when the war spread to Bosnia-Herzegovina it had even more devastating effects. If the war in Croatia had caused the killing of 10,000 people and the displacement of 500,000, the war in Bosnia generated 2 million refugees and 140,000 dead or missing. The vicious war between Bosnian Serbs, Bosnian Croats and Bosniaks (Bosnian Muslims) caused the death of 11,000 people in Sarajevo alone.[18]

When in October 1991, Bosnia, following the example of Slovenia and Croatia, declared its independence, the international community rapidly accepted the change. But the shelling of Sarajevo did not cease and continued almost without interruption for another year. In May 1992, the UN Security Council condemned the Serbs for the atrocities they had committed in Bosnia and, because the United States and Europe sided with the UN, they imposed economic and diplomatic sanctions against Serbia. It should be remembered that UN attempts to provide humanitarian assistance to the people of Sarajevo and to Muslims in general had been an utter failure. The Srebrenica massacre, 8,000 Bosniaks (men and boys) killed by the Serb army under the command of General Ratko Mladic, happened under the UN's watch.[19]

The story of the war in the Balkans is complex, but peace negotiations finally began in 1993. The first attempt to end the war in Bosnia was through the so-called Vance-Owen plan, which suggested a partition of the country into 10 tentatively homogeneous areas.[20] It seemed that this plan showed promise and might succeed, but in the end the Yugoslav Parliament rejected it. At that point it became clear that probably the only solution would be to partition the country based on military lines. This was indeed the starting point upon which work began in Dayton. Meanwhile, in 1994, the Washington Agreement ended the hostilities between Bosnian Croats and the Bosniaks. The two former rivals then joined forces against the Bosnian Serbs, who, supported by the Serbian government, were unrelenting in the fight to control the territory of Bosnia-Herzegovina. The Serbs seemed unstoppable and undaunted by the threat of NATO's retaliation. But after the massacres of Srebrenica and Zepa and the Sarajevo market massacre, NATO began air attacks, which lasted for 14 days. At that point the Serbs decided to join the negotiation table. Finally, after numerous diplomatic efforts and NATO's military intervention, the war ended with the signing of the Dayton Peace Accords in 1995.

The Balkans, however, were still unstable. In early 1997, an enduring desire for independence led the Kosovo Liberation Army to attack Serb military and police facilities. The Serbs were quick to respond to the KLA, so that tensions erupted into a full war. For years the Serbs had been inflexible at the idea of an independent Kosovo, because they traced that territory back to their history as a nation. In effect, in the Middle Ages, Kosovo was the cultural and administrative center of the Serbian state and, in the Serbian tradition, it never ceased to be their homeland; Serbs often refer to it as "Old Serbia."[21] Kosovars, however, who are primarily Albanians, saw in the breakup of the former Yugoslavia (and the West blaming the Serbs), their long-awaited opportunity for independence, and they tried to seize the moment. They hoped for NATO's intervention, since ultimately that was their only concrete chance to gain independence. The end of Sali Berisha's government in Albania enhanced the vigor of the KLA effort, but the West was still not very responsive. Finally, in 1998, the United States sent in Richard Holbrooke, the mastermind behind the Dayton Accords, to get the parties to agree to a cease-fire. Milosevic agreed to negotiations and at Rambouillet, near Paris, the Serbs and the Albanian Kosovars were pressed into reaching an agreement, but the Kosovars refused to accept a compromise that would keep Kosovo within Serbia.[22] The Serbs, for their part, did not want to lose control of Kosovo either. In the meantime, the NATO allies were not quite ready to undertake military action. But in 1999, the allies reached an agreement and began a bombing campaign that lasted for almost three months.[23] In June of 1999, NATO and FRY officials began talks for a Serbian withdrawal, NATO's bombing was suspended and its troops were deployed in Kosovo with the approval of the UN Security Council.

III. AFTER MAASTRICHT: THE RELATIONSHIP BETWEEN THE UNITED STATES AND THE EUROPEAN UNION

The end of the Cold War expedited the integration of Europe. The war in the Balkans had in many ways increased anxiety about a possible rise of nationalism in the old continent. After all, nationalism, or the exploitation of nationalism, had brought Fascism to Europe 60 years earlier. The collapse of the iron curtain could have boosted nationalist cries in the heart of Europe, in Germany for example. But the French president, François Mitterrand; and the German chancellor, Helmut Kohl, were aware of such a danger and were thus committed to deepening and strengthening European integration.[24] As so happened, in 1951, with the creation of the European Coal and Steel Community, France and Germany envisioned more integration to avoid potential instability in Europe. This time, however, the integration was more profound and included the idea of a European single currency. In effect, the 1992 Maastricht Treaty created a European Union that consisted of three pillars: the European Communities, Common Foreign and Security Policy (CFSP), and police and judicial cooperation in criminal matters (JHA).[25] It put forward the idea of European citizenship and gave birth to the economic and monetary union. The euro was launched on January 1, 1999, and it became the official currency of 11 European states: Belgium, Germany, Ireland, Spain, France, Italy, Luxembourg, the Netherlands, Austria, Portugal and Finland. The euro was initially only a currency for cashless payments and accounting purposes, but on January 1, 2002, banknotes and coins began circulating. Not all the European states, however, joined the monetary union, for example; Denmark and the United Kingdom managed to obtain an "opt-out" clause exempting them.

While the euro is certainly the more emblematic example of the deeper European integration that followed the end of the Cold War, the three pillars establishing the EU are also important to understanding the changing and the deepening of the relationships within continental Europe. The first pillar, which contains the European Community, the European Coal and Steel Community and the Euratom, is concerned with the question of the EU member states' shared sovereignty in the European institutions. The second pillar starts a CFSP and encompasses an intergovernmental decision-making process, which essentially relies on unanimity. The third pillar is about cooperation on justice and home affairs (JHA). The idea here is that the EU should protect European citizens when it comes to freedom, security and justice. In this case as well the decision-making process is intergovernmental. All three pillars clearly expanded cooperation and interdependency within Europe. Thus, in the early 1990s, Europe was increasingly becoming a united actor and in many respects a single player, so one would have expected some enthusiasm across the Atlantic. Even though it is most likely a legend the saying attributed to Henry Kissinger: "Whom do I call if I want to call Europe?" an actual number was about to be issued. Yet the U.S. reaction was somewhat subdued. The deepening and widening of European integration did not really make headlines. The Bush administration remarked that the EU was a good development and that both the United States and Europe would benefit from it.[26] In essence, he said that a strong and united Europe was in America's interests. The United States, however, did not seem to be too enthusiastic about it and probably the reason for that was that it felt that no matter how much Europe was integrated, the United States was still the most powerful world leader. Nonetheless, the creation of the European Union was remarkable and indeed had effects on the power relationship within NATO, as it will become clearer later in the book. The attempt to construct a European defense system as an alternative to the North Atlantic Alliance certainly challenged the cohesion of transatlantic relations. Additionally, Europe was becoming an impressive new actor, both economically and demographically.

IV. CONCLUSION

The events considered in this chapter constitute major changes in the international political context that occurred at the beginning of the post-Cold

War era. They are relevant in the context of this book because they set in motion a process of transformation of transatlantic relations, which led to tensions and to a redefinition of the allies' interests. Moreover, those changes led to a redefinition of the identity of the allies, a process that is still going on and that can, in fact, explain why there is often disagreement in transatlantic relations.

The collapse of the Soviet Union and the unification of Germany forced the allies to deal with the new political reality. After the fall of the Berlin Wall, it soon became evident that the allies differed in their opinions on the future of Germany as a united nation. France and the UK were not excited at the idea of, yet again, a powerful Germany. The United States, on the other hand, was not only pleased, it was actually eager to have a united Germany integrated within NATO. The discrepancy of their interests was undoubtedly due to the changing security context and the uncertainty that such revolution could have engendered. For some Europeans a unified Germany constituted a potential threat to the security, which had been patiently built over the years. For Americans, the new Germany was a strong ally that had to be included in the alliance.

In general, however, the early 1990s are important because they constitute a transitional period underlined with dramatic changes in the political system: the unification of Germany, its inclusion in NATO, Desert Storm, the conflict in the Balkans, the rise of a powerful Europe with the EU. Such changes could potentially provoke significant reevaluations of transatlantic relations, and in fact they did. The following chapters will analyze the redefinition of U.S.-European relations and the further changes that occurred in the international context as a result of that redefinition.

3   Theories of Transatlantic Relations

I. INTRODUCTION

Despite the fact that during the Cold War, transatlantic relations were marred by frequent disputes, during those years pundits and policy makers frequently rejected the hypothesis that such disagreements could lead to the dissolution of those relations. For example, they did not consider the Suez crisis, the Gaullist challenge, criticism of the Vietnam War or the clashes caused by Reagan's policies of the early 1980s to be serious enough to damage international relations. In fact, during the Cold War, the Euro-Atlantic partnership seemed almost unbreakable, and it was assumed that their alliance would endure as long as the United States and Europe had a common enemy (the USSR). The East-West rivalry did not seem to offer any alternatives for America and Europe but that of collaboration, in order to counter the threat of the Soviet Union. As it was initially conceived, this was a relationship predominantly focused on the military dimension, but one that soon broadened to encapsulate political and economic elements, a relationship in which differences were resolved and discrepancies settled.

However, with the disappearance of the common threat once posed by the then-Soviet Union, this strong partnership was shaken to its roots. The consequences of the removal of the threat once represented by the Soviet Union have been much debated among practitioners and scholars in terms of the future of transatlantic relations, in the light of changing priorities and the loss of the Cold War "glue."[1] The nature and dynamic of this evolving debate were epitomized by the U.S. decision to invade Iraq in 2003 and the open opposition to that decision of France and Germany, as well as the opposition of public opinion in the United Kingdom, Italy and Spain, three Western European governments that accommodated the Bush doctrine.[2]

The invasion of Iraq magnified concerns over the future of the Atlantic community. America appeared to be out of sync with some of its Western European partners, and major divisions among the Europeans seemed to further underline the possibility for a transatlantic separation. Was the conflict over Iraq the validation of John Mearsheimer's argument that, absent a common threat, the United States would withdraw from Europe and as a result Europe would fall back to power politics?[3] Or was it just another insignificant dispute that would leave unaltered transatlantic cooperation, even in the absence of a common threat?

This chapter examines the growing body of literature, which focuses on the policy disputes between the United States and Europe and constitutes an attempt to synthesize and rationalize the central argumentative positions taken in the debate on the future of transatlantic relations. In order to do this, it offers an overview of how studies concerning transatlantic relations are framed, and it identifies the underlying assumptions of those central argumentative positions. Rather than setting forth any set of specific hypotheses to be tested, this chapter constitutes the analytical framework that integrates the various approaches to thinking and writing about transatlantic relations and serves as a foundation for the analysis that follows in later chapters of the book. Furthermore, in opposition to those who tend to consider Atlantic relations as less theoretical,[4] in this chapter, I put forward the argument that there is in fact no shortage of theoretical vibrancy in the study of the relationship between the United States and Europe. To that extent, in this chapter, I also argue that the theories applied, mainly neorealism and neoliberalism, are less equipped than others, such as constructivism, to account for an ever-evolving transatlantic relationship. Accordingly, this chapter is divided into two parts: The first introduces the primary analytical frameworks that have been used to inscribe and transcribe transatlantic relations, neorealism and neoliberalism, and demonstrates what each of those theoretical accounts expected would happen to transatlantic relations with the end of the Cold War. It also offers a comparison of the contending neorealist and neoliberal arguments. Part 2 draws upon the shortcomings of the neorealist and neoliberal arguments and reflects on the usefulness of other theories, such as constructivism, to explain the evolution of transatlantic relations.

II. TRANSATLANTIC RELATIONS AND TRADITIONAL APPROACHES: NEOREALISM AND NEOLIBERALISM

In the two decades since the end of the Cold War, the debate on the likely future of transatlantic relations has continued to be lively. Articles and books have generally stressed that transatlantic relations are in a state of inevitable decline, although there is some dissent among those who hold this view.[5] An analysis of the debates in the decade that followed the end of the East-West rivalry reveals that the debates are theoretically grounded and that such theoretic understandings permeate the various discourses about the future of the Atlantic community. Moreover, questions about the future of transatlantic relations were not triggered exclusively by the war in Iraq in 2003. As I have already stated, their onset was in fact the collapse of the Soviet Union in 1991. Against this backdrop, it is useful to take a look at the proliferation of scholarly works on transatlantic relations prior to the political storm of 2003, in order to explicitly uncover some of the theoretical assumptions about transatlantic relations in a decade not defined by a perceived common threat, which had most likely driven the United States and Europe into a military-political-economic partnership.[6] Details about specific disagreements and U.S.-European policies regarding transatlantic relations before and after the invasion of Iraq can be found in the later chapters of this volume.

In public and academic circles experts have tended to rely on two well-established theories in attempting to understand the dynamics and realities of international relations: neorealism and neoliberalism.[7] An analysis of the debates on the future of transatlantic relations in the interim period between the end of the Cold War and 9/11 reveals that international relations scholars were sharply divided on the likely future of the Euro-American partnership. Neorealists, in fealty to their belief that balance of power politics is the main determinant of international relations, expected a worsening of Euro-American relations, while neoliberals, following their core belief in the power of institutions, maintained a more optimistic outlook.[8]

As stated earlier, neorealist academics such as John Mearsheimer and Stephen Walt have contended that the end of the Cold War removed the ideological "glue" that made for unity in transatlantic relations.[9] Most of those who endorse Mearsheimer's contention share a common set of basic assumptions associated with the realist position: namely, that states are the main actors in international relations, and their actions are motivated by their own survival.[10] In addition, the realist worldview also suggests that states can harm or even destroy one another. Furthermore, the realist position contends that the principle governing relations between states is anarchy (i.e., the absence of a central authority that regulates their interactions and therefore protects them if another state threatens or attacks them).[11] Finally, they share the belief that states live in an uncertain realm wherein they do not know the intentions and capabilities of other states. Therefore, they claim that states are constantly insecure, and war is always possible. Consequently, these scholars believe that security is one of the primary and continual concerns of the state.[12] Within this neorealist literature, one set of arguments largely employs the balance of power theory to offer an explanation of transatlantic relations vis-à-vis the end of the Cold War.[13] These theorists claim that states seek to balance the power of threatening states.[14]

Such acts of balancing can take the form of unilateral action or military cooperation, but attempts to balance power can also lead to other forms of cooperation, such as economic cooperation, because combined economic advantages gained by states would ultimately enhance their power overall. Correspondingly, the demise of a common external threat can undermine the types of cooperation, including military and economic, as described above. Within the dynamics of the latter scenario, neither military nor economic cooperation would be of overriding interest and could possibly be perceived as risky, since such a partnership could enhance the relative military power of one or the other partner, as a result of the economic gains achieved through the partnership.[15]

As stated earlier, the foundational premise behind neorealist explanations for the future of transatlantic relations, in particular their cooperative efforts, lies behind the perception of, and reaction to, a commonly perceived threat (Figure 3.1). Historically, they argue, the fear of the Soviet Union induced the United States and Europe to form a powerful military alliance, NATO. The economic cooperation between the transatlantic core states, they claim, was a consequence of their military collaboration. In short, NATO augmented their combined power. These theorists seem to agree that the overriding security interest kept the transatlantic core states together in a political alliance. In essence, during the Cold War, security interests superseded ideological divergences, which did indeed exist at the time.[16] Thus, the presence of the Soviet threat was seen as the leading cause for political unity. Some conceptualize transatlantic relations within a bipolar system[17] and further conceive the threat that had been constituted by the Soviet Union as the most important factor.[18]

It is worth noting that the neorealist argument has been very consistent over the course of the years. All neorealist scholars tend to agree that the end of the Cold War should have attenuated Euro-American military and economic cooperation (Figure 3.2). For example, John Mearsheimer, in his often-cited article "Back to the Future: Instability in Europe after the Cold War," argued that NATO would, at best, become an empty shell.[19] He went on to argue that if the Cold War came to a complete end, the United States would abandon Europe completely, thus provoking the end of a stable bipolar order.[20] Mearsheimer claimed that the stability of bipolarity would be replaced by the instability of a multipolar structure.[21] He maintained this pessimistic argument over the subsequent decade, suggesting that without the United States, or the American pacifier, Europe would revert to power politics with Germany as its military fulcrum.[22] This prediction of separation and rivalry is commonly shared within neorealist scholarship. Owen Harries, for example, in his article "The Collapse of the West," reinforced this point by arguing that the West could not endure the collapse of the Soviet Union, because the concept of the West was constructed out of "desperation and fear," not "natural affinities." In addition to the anticipated split of the military alliance, other neorealists such as Stephen Walt have argued that, given the absence of a common threat, there could also be an end to economic cooperation.[23] Along with other neorealists, Walt recognized that the United States and Europe were brought together by the fear of the Soviet threat; however, he further underlined that it was economic ties during the Cold War, which reinforced military cooperation.[24] In other words, the common threat induced economic cooperation, which produced economic gains that ultimately enhanced the combined powers of the partners. Conversely,

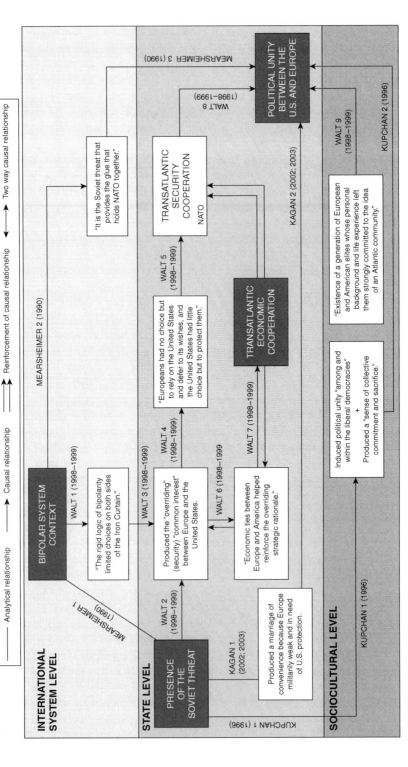

Figure 3.1 Neorealists. Cold War: Factors That Kept the United States and Europe Together

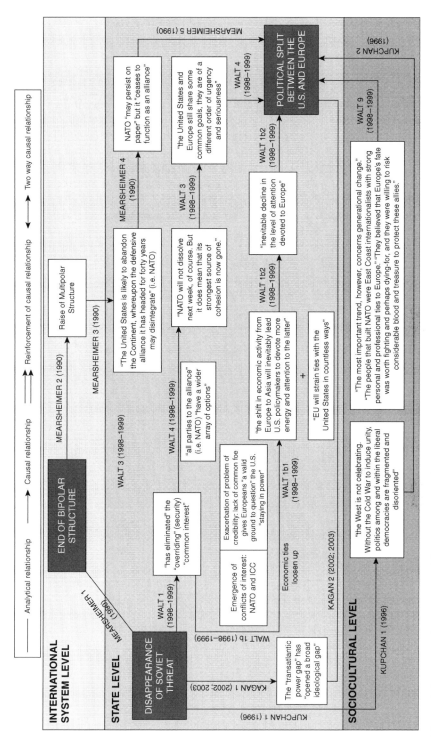

Figure 3.2 Neorealists. Post-Cold War: Factors That Are Pulling the United States and Europe Apart

Walt argued, the end of the Cold War would eliminate the overriding common security interest and consequently loosen economic ties as well.[25] In fact, Walt already saw the signs of this trend in the U.S. shift in economic activity from Europe to Asia; he warned that such a shift "will inevitably lead U.S. policymakers to devote more energy and attention to the latter [meaning Asia]."[26] In addition, the expansion of the European Union, he suggested, would create further tensions. The euro, Walt explained, had the potential to challenge the dollar as the principle international reserve currency.

A further element inducing fragmentation and disorientation in transatlantic relations is the decline of a sense of commitment to the Atlantic community.[27] Americans are no longer willing to sacrifice for Europe, Walt contends, because of a generational change. "The people that built NATO were East Coast internationalists with strong personal and professional ties to Europe. . . . They believed that Europe's fate was worth fighting and perhaps dying for, and they were willing to risk considerable blood and treasure to protect these allies."[28] But, he concludes, this is no longer the case. The end of the Cold War is thus producing a transatlantic split.

The aftermath of 9/11 and the ensuing debates over the legitimacy of attacking Iraq have produced relevant scholarly discussions that reduce the current "world disorder" to a division between the United States and Europe based, yet again, on military and economic reasons.[29]

Kagan writes,

> the U.S. is quicker to use military force, less patient with diplomacy, and more willing to coerce (or bribe) other nations in order to get a desired result. Europe, on the other hand, places greater emphasis on diplomacy, takes a much longer view of history and problem solving, and has greater faith in international law and cooperation.[30]

His highly controversial argument has been that on major strategic and international questions, "Americans are from Mars and Europeans are from Venus." Kagan argued that powerful states (i.e., the United States) see the world differently from weak states (i.e., Europe) because of their power difference.[31]

Kagan's generalization assumes that any change in the relationship between the allies is due to a shift in the balance of power. In his view, Europeans want to rebalance American hegemony by empowering international organizations. The assumption is that since Europe has been unable to influence the United States after 9/11, the Europeans deploy the inherent power of international organizations to balance against, and thus limit, American power.[32]

In addition to "power" and "weakness" as determinates of the behavior of states, Kagan explains that conceptions of power and power dynamics also influence how much power a particular state decides to pursue.[33] For

Kagan, Europeans have a Kantian vision of the world, in which force is unnecessary and counterproductive in solving disagreements. Conversely, Americans have a Hobbesian view and think that the world is a dangerous place, thus believing that states need to always keep the use force as an option.

A less catastrophic but nonetheless equally pessimistic view is that forwarded by Ronald Asmus and Kenneth Pollack, who observed that the emergence of new threats, such as terrorism, weapons of mass destruction, mass migration and rogue states would make the United States and Europe "rethink the purpose of the transatlantic relationship."[34] In essence, for Asmus and Pollack, the rise of a new threat will once again produce transatlantic political unity. Their conclusion, however, is not shared by all. For instance, Ivo Daalder disagrees with them and claims instead that 9/11 "reinforced America's strategic shift away from Europe."[35] The fundamental consequence of the end of the confrontation with the USSR, he argues, is that the security concerns of America and Europe diverged exponentially. America's focus was global, Europe's was local. In other words, while the United States engaged in global leadership, Europe concentrated on regional leadership in its immediate backyard (i.e., the former Soviet satellites in Eastern Europe). These differences, Daalder points out, only intensified over the course of the years and more particularly under the Bush administration. This sample of various positions, within the neorealist camp alone, helps to illustrate the level of theoretical disparity that continues to infuse the debate over the future of transatlantic relations. In the neorealist view, the overriding interest in preserving security was the building block of the transatlantic community.

Contrary to the neorealist position in fundamental ways, the argument of neoliberals was that the United States and Europe would continue to cooperate because, even in the absence of a common threat, the transatlantic partners shared security and economic interests, norms, values, political identities and membership in public institutions (Figure 3.3). These factors, they claimed, had been and would continue to be the basis of transatlantic cooperation and would reduce the likelihood of separation while continuing to encourage cooperation.[36] The assessment of neoliberals of the future of transatlantic relations was based on a threefold understanding of the shared constitutive elements, which, in their view, formed the Euro-American partnership, namely: (1) common security, (2) common economic interests, and (3) common values and political identity.

In the post-Cold War period, neoliberals claimed, transatlantic relations would still be characterized by military cooperation. In 1993, James Elles wrote that "Europe is America's natural partner by virtue of its actual military capability."[37] John Duffield, in an article published in 1994, stressed that there was still a solid consensus between the United States and Europe on the need to preserve NATO. The alliance, he emphasized, "continues to enjoy generally strong support from its member states."[38]

Robert Blackwill in 1999 wrote that "the two sides of the Atlantic continue to share enduring vital interests and face a common set of challenges both in Europe and beyond."[39] These challenges, he underlined, are many and diverse (i.e., slowing down the spread of weapons of mass destruction or avoiding the emergence of a hostile hegemony in Europe) and cannot be adequately addressed by either the United States or Europe alone. Thus, he concluded, the Euro-American partnership would endure even in a world without the specific threat of the Soviet Union. Joseph Nye also predicted that NATO would continue to play an important role because, for example, Europe had not been capable of solving the Balkan problem on its own.[40] In short, neoliberals contended that transatlantic relations had not been and would not be jeopardized by the collapse of the Soviet Union. These scholars tended to see the transatlantic axis as a concern for security, independent from other challenges the extant alliance might face, or had been built upon initially. This view was closer to the concept of the Deutschian North Atlantic area as a security community that developed a spirit of its own.[41]

The neoliberal argument, however, also points to common economic interests that will guarantee cooperation in the Atlantic community. James Elles identifies Europe and the United States as natural economic partners by virtue of their economic weight.[42] Daniel Deudney and John Ikenberry observe that "[t]he business of the West is business."[43] They claim that American and European societies are "permeated by market relations, mentalities and institutions" and, they add, "[a]s the importance of the markets grow in these societies, their characters converge."[44] Joseph Nye warns us not to listen too much to the "doom-sayers." He in fact underlines that "[w]hile American trade with Asia has surpassed the one with Europe, American trade with Europe is still more balanced."[45] He also points out that "American foreign investment in Europe still exceeds that in Asia."[46] Similarly, Anthony Blinken in 2001 emphasized that "American investment in Europe has increased seven-fold over the past six years."[47] This, in his view, was the sign of a strong relationship not weakened by the end of the East-West rivalry. Indeed, the current economic meltdown is emphasizing transatlantic

Figure 3.3   Neoliberals: Correlation Map of Post-Cold War Arguments

economic interdependence, and policy makers across the Atlantic seem to hold the view that cooperation is the only way to end the crisis. Therefore, the economic meltdown could be an element of unification. For example, at the London summit on April 2, 2009, the G20 announced that the leaders had committed to $1.1 trillion in new funds to increase the capital available to the International Monetary Fund (IMF). The goal was the revival in trade that was expected to lessen in 2009 for the first time in 30 years.[48] The G20, an institution that is heavily biased in terms of transatlantic membership, could be seen as bringing together the leaders of the world's major economies to take collective action to stabilize the global economy and rescue jobs.

Finally, neoliberals emphasize that shared norms, values, political identities and membership in common public institutions will continue to foster cooperation between the United States and Europe. Deudney and Ikenberry underline the fact that the West is "bound by a web of complex institutional links and associations" that created what they call "the spirit" of the West.[49] Such a "spirit," they claim, is made up of common norms, public mores, and political identities. Because the United States and Europe share this common "spirit," they are likely to keep cooperating within an international institutional framework. Thus, the transatlantic relationship, from the neoliberal perspective, seems likely to survive and to continue to be deeply embedded in international (transatlantic) regimes such as NATO, the G20 or the G7.[50]

Given this worldview, international institutions such as NATO embody common Western values and political identities, and since those institutions are also an integral part of U.S. and European domestic and international politics, an institution like NATO cannot be considered merely instrumental, but rather the cornerstone of Western cooperation. James Elles, for example, claims that there is no reason to be pessimistic about the future of transatlantic relations because the United States and Europe share the common values of democracy and a market economy.[51] Furthermore, he stresses that they have also created "mechanisms, procedures and institutional and personal relationships for coordinating positions and resolving differences."[52] Kupchan is of the same opinion when he claims, "shared norms are working together to produce the cohesiveness of the transatlantic community."[53] Joseph Nye identifies the transatlantic communality of values in democracy and human rights, and claims that the United States shares such values more thoroughly with Europe than with most other states.[54] Finally, Anthony Blinken argues that there is no value gap between Americans and Europeans and that "the U.S. and Europe are converging culturally."[55] As evidence, he observes that while American support for the death penalty is decreasing in the States, it is increasing in Europe. As a result of such observable social phenomenon, Blinken concludes, transatlantic values are converging, rather than diverging.[56] More recently, Tod Lindberg endorsed Blinken's argument by claiming that Americans

and Europeans share political and moral matters and similarity on public policy preferences as well.[57] In essence, disagreements among members
of the alliance take place within a larger framework of agreement about
"fundamental values." It is worth noticing that while in the last 20 years
many scholars have grappled with the question of the future of the transatlantic order, what emerges from the theoretical debates is a definition of
"transatlantic relations" that largely excludes Canada from such a political
order. In fact, all the authors in this review of the literature seem to have a
"narrow" idea of transatlantic relations, which is by and large confined to
the United States and Europe. Whether this can be interpreted as a sign of
cultural blindness remains to be verified; however, under any set of circum-
scribed arguments, Canada is certainly a leading actor in the transatlantic
community, and there appears to be no rational reason for her exclusion.
As is made clear in this discussion, neorealists and neoliberals have viewed
transatlantic relations from different perspectives and have reached almost
diametrically opposed conclusions about their future. From a neorealist perspective, the end of the Cold War was supposed to lead to the end of the
transatlantic security effort. For neoliberals, shared economic interests and
political identities (i.e., democracy and free market economies) as well as
membership in public institutions such as NATO, WTO, IMF and G7 continued to constitute a stable basis for transatlantic cooperation. The absence
of a common threat and the presence of such shared elements, neoliberals
have argued, decrease the likelihood of separation between the transatlantic
allies. As we will see, both theories have flaws.

Almost two decades of empirical records have shown that military cooperation between the United States and Europe has continued. Clearly, NATO
has survived the disappearance of the external threat that had prompted its
creation in the first place, and has remained the key political and security
organization for its members. However, subsequent to the disappearance
of the Soviet threat, each party has emphasized different means for achieving the newer and evolving goals of the alliance over time. Primarily, this
harmony within the alliance was accomplished by the allies' redefinition
of their transatlantic interests on humanitarian grounds. The Kosovo War
was a revealing example of the reshaped moral identity of the transatlantic
leaders.[58] The character of this "renovated West" is deeply normed or value
laden, since the frictions that occurred in the 1990s were reconciled through
a re-born sense of Western identity, which was developed on the unifying
principle of the protection of human rights.[59] Thus, even militarily, the unity
and self-identification of the post-Cold War West is adjudicated by the common perception that human rights must be defended.

However, in predicting the probability of a troubled transatlantic relationship, neorealists have also been reasonably accurate, and since the
1990s the transatlantic relationship has indeed been characterized by internal clashes. The United States and Europe have been at odds on security
issues, and these policy disagreements can justifiably be interpreted as a

political split. The flaw within the neorealist view rests, rather, in its inability to predict how the evolution of the identity of the allies affected their interests and norms. Consequentially, they failed to acknowledge that this process could contribute to avoiding a more serious split.

The empirical record (the Kyoto Protocol in 1997, the Ottawa Treaty in 1997, the Rome Statute in 1998 and most recently the invasion of Iraq in 2003) also highlights flaws in the neoliberal approach.[60] Such a premise, with its emphasis on cooperation based on shared values, is flawed for not having taken into account the evolution of transatlantic relations in the 1990s. In this case, an oversimplification in their theories has impeded neoliberals from explaining the disagreements, which have emerged in a post-Cold War world. Conversely, there is a need to draw attention to the conflicts within the relations. This is not inconsistent with my critique of the neorealists' analysis, because on a broader scale, while it is clear that both the United States and Europe do share the common value of protecting human rights, there are some fundamental differences as to how to prevent such violations and on how to punish those who violate such rights.[61]

Without an understanding of how changing norms of behavior influenced the redefinition of the West, even in terms of security issues, it is impossible to comprehend why those disagreements did not bring about a total split in transatlantic relations. In essence, while it is evident that the 1990s and the 2000s were and are years of change, characterized by disagreements between the transatlantic partners, change in the security context, identity, interests and behavior, such as the need to protect human rights, are redefining the West beyond the traditional commonalities of being capitalist democracies emphasized by neoliberals.

III. A CONSTRUCTIVIST APPROACH

Constructivist approaches provide alternative understandings of mainstream international relations issues by privileging the concept of "identity" in world politics and culture within international relations theory. One of the main questions for constructivists is "how much do structures constrain and enable the actions of actors, and how [far] can actors deviate from the constraints of structure."[62] Within the constructivist view of world politics, a "structure" is a set of unchangeable norms and principles that constrains the behavior of states. One of the critically important questions for constructivism is how a given action may or may not (correspondingly and/or simultaneously) reproduce both the state and the structure. For example, to the extent that Franco-German opposition to the invasion of Iraq was plausible because of France and Germany's identity as "middle powers," it also correspondingly constitutes France and Germany as "middle powers" because of their use of, and preference for, diplomacy. Conversely, with reference to the invasion of Iraq, nonmilitary intervention was an inconceivable option for the United States because of the conceptualization of U.S. identity as a "great power." Once again, correspondingly, it was the military intervention itself that reflexively constituted the United States as a great power.[63]

As Ted Hopf explains, "meaningful behavior, or action, is possible only within an inter-subjective social context. Actors develop their relations with, and understanding of, others through the media of norms and practices. In the absence of norms, exercises of power, or actions, would be devoid of meaning. Constitutive norms define an identity by specifying the actions that will cause Others to organize that identity and respond to it appropriately."[64]

Answering questions about the future of the Euro-American partnership requires the consideration of two factors: an understanding of the fluidity of transatlantic relations within the social context and an assessment of the ongoing debates on the future of the transatlantic relations.

Given what constructivism brings to our understanding of world politics, determining the future of transatlantic relations will require knowing more about the situation (i.e., culture, norms, institutions, procedure, rules, and social practices) that constitutes the United States and Europe as well as the inherent "structures" that define them. Therefore, we need to investigate the social practices of the United States and Europe as constitutive practices.[65] In short, we need to employ a constructivist approach, which will better enable us to predict the future of the partnership because the United States and Europe both behave and act within a prescribed social context. Consequently, an approach that considers these interactive exchanges or "inter-subjective" actions within a social context will give us insights into how their interests are changing and how changing interests are shaping their behavior.[66]

Given that for constructivists, "identity" has a very unique and specific meaning, it is crucial to consider U.S. and European political identity as discrete, and to investigate how their identity affects their behavior and consequently their relations. The identity of a state entails, as Ted Hopf puts it, "its preferences and consequent actions." And it is important to note further, that *each state defines others according to the identity it ascribes to them*. This process is rendered even more dynamic because the state also constructs its own identity through continuous daily practice. Indeed, the way the state perceives others and itself determines its self-identity, as well as its preferences, which ultimately result in actions the state will choose to exercise. In essence, if a state identifies itself as a "great power," it will have a different set of preferences or interests than the one that identifies itself as a middle power.[67] These types of considerations can enable us to understand why the United States and Europe seem to be headed in different directions. The Atlantic partners simply have different preferences that are due to self-defined identities within the larger international and transatlantic context. It is the social construction of their identity that determines diverging interests, not the gap of military capabilities, as Robert Kagan wants us to believe.

Lastly, we need to employ the constructivist approach because neorealism and neoliberalism seem to be inadequately equipped to explain the fluidity of the transatlantic partnership. A relationship that is changing and constantly evolving cannot be analyzed by theories that tend to explain and perceive international politics as static. Such an analysis is not able to capture elements of change because it does not conceive change as a constitutive factor. Constructivism, on the other hand, allows for an analysis of the interactions or *praxis*[68] of the United States and Europe within international institutions. Providing evidence for their behavior,[69] such an analysis would show the validity and usefulness of both the neorealist and neoliberal predictions for the future of the transatlantic relations. Further, it would tell us which predictions have thus far been more accurate and insightful and would expose the underlying general theoretical assumptions of each approach with respect to a transatlantic partnership between the two powers. Additionally, such an analysis would offer an understanding of what issues the United States and Europe would consider worthy of their cooperation, and would therefore allow for more accurate predictions on the future of transatlantic relations.

IV. CONCLUSIONS

This chapter has examined two of the most important and controversial theoretical approaches in the study of transatlantic relations—neorealism and neoliberalism—and has suggested an alternative theory for analyzing them: constructivism. The balance of power theory does not seem to be able to explain the preservation of NATO nor its enlargement, nor its new out-of-the-region missions. However, its long-term prediction regarding a troubled partnership thus far seems to hold true. Conversely, neoliberal theories seem to be able to explain NATO's persistence, but not how transatlantic relations are evolving and how the allies are often at odds. Neoliberals have led us to believe that there is almost a natural inclination to cooperation in the transatlantic arena. However, there is nothing truly 'natural' or innately predictable about international politics. International, as well as transatlantic, relations exist within a context that is socially constructed. In other words, the evolution of a state's identity carries onto the international arena and affects state relations because these changes in identity are constantly and correspondingly reformulating their interests. Furthermore, interactions between states also have an impact on both their identity and normative behavior; such behavior is also constitutive of identity. In this scenario, what needs to be analyzed is the evolution of American and European identity within the context of transatlantic relations, which can offer an explanation as to where the relationship is headed. We need to recognize change both in their relations and in their ever-evolving notions of self-identity. Thus, we need constructivism to analyze transatlantic relations because so far it is the only theory that can offer a dynamic account of them. Scholarly works on this subject will move forward the debate on the future of the Atlantic community and will enhance our knowledge of the explanatory power of theories.

Part II

Transatlantic Relations from the End of the Cold War to 9/11

4   NATO's Enlargement
The Implications of Developing a New Identity

I. INTRODUCTION

This chapter is devoted to analyzing the behavior of the United States and Europe within the context of new security issues in the post-Cold War period. In it I analyze how the development of a new identity affected the actions of both partners of the alliance and how, finally, these new identities have transformed the normative structure of the alliance. Essentially, I analyze how NATO has gradually adapted to the new security context. I first examine the disputes among NATO's members on whether to enlarge the alliance and on how to do so. Then I examine their reconciliation in concomitance with the Balkan wars, and more specifically the war in Kosovo, and, finally, I offer an explanation for the fact that the allies were able to overcome their differences and reach an agreement. This analysis shows that in the years that followed the end of the Cold War, the transatlantic allies redefined themselves through the advancement of new norms of international behavior. In particular, they revisited two well-established norms: the norm of noninterference in the internal affairs of other nation-states and the norm that prohibits the use of force without the authorization of the UN Security Council. Changing the normative context was justified and, later, legitimated, because of the necessity to use military force in order to stop gross violations of human rights. Thus, the identity of the allies in the post-Cold War period was redefined by the social practice of "humanitarian intervention." In effect, this new developing identity encompassed the common value of the protection of human rights, and this was possible because of the changing security context, related mainly to the events in the Balkans. The evolution of this new security context generated the fertile ground necessary for a change of behavior/action (intervention in civil wars) and thus identity (the West protects human rights). This, however, induced a further change of behavior/action (the use of force to protect such rights) and of the structural context (military intervention without the authorization of the UNSC has become a normative behavior).

The situation in the Balkans and the intervention in Kosovo epitomize the first transitional phase in the evolution of the transatlantic relationship.

Such an evolution, however, must be understood within the greater context of the shift in political and security priorities at the end of the Cold War and the emerging vision of a new strategic role for NATO. Civil wars usually create humanitarian emergencies, but until the wars in the Balkans, the principle of sovereignty was used as a shield to protect states from outside interference, mainly in the form of military intervention. Thus, theoretically, only the state had the critical power to deal with its internal political and security problems. With the intervention in the Balkans, however, the transatlantic allies recognized that it was of utmost importance to avoid any gross violation of human rights, and the principle of sovereignty was consequently overruled. Yet new international norms tend not to be accidental but rather originate, consciously or unconsciously, from the behavior of the actors involved, the actors generally being states. The salience of this point, within the context of this book, rests on the fact that the effort to modify international norms (i.e., nonintervention in civil wars without a UN mandate) was carried out successfully in Kosovo. Evidence from this chapter suggests that the transatlantic partners had difficulty finding a common position on the renovation of NATO for the new security context of the post-Cold War. Such difficulties, however, were overcome because of a resocialization of the allies through the establishment of a new norm: humanitarian intervention. Consequently, this chapter also sheds light on the reidentification of the transatlantic partners through their behavioral change.

II. NATO: FROM A POLITICAL-MILITARY ALLIANCE TO A VALUE-LADEN ALLIANCE

As I have argued in chapter 3, as soon as the Cold War was over, many in international relations claimed that the disappearance of the common threat (i.e., the USSR) would lead to a deep crisis in transatlantic relations. Others, on the contrary, advanced the argument that common interests, values and norms would keep the allies together. The evidence presented here shows that both arguments are incorrect in assessing the future of the transatlantic alliance. This, however, is not a reflection that I am making in hindsight. The problem that I had noticed, as I began working on this topic a few years ago, was that neither argument, in effect, analyzed the relations in their quintessentially evolving nature. Only by understanding transatlantic relations as a process is it possible to gain an insightful understanding of them. Therefore, it is crucial to investigate the transformation of NATO as a process in which interactions matter, if we want to understand U.S.-European relations and their shortcomings. In our discipline, we are often reminded that, usually, alliances do not survive the disappearance of a common threat. But in 1999, NATO's 50th anniversary was celebrated in Washington, D.C., by dignitaries from all over the world. Why did this happen? Why were they celebrating an alliance that should at a minimum have been struggling to stay alive, given that the Soviet Union was no longer an existential threat? A brief history of NATO's evolution is useful to make palatable the idea that we must analyze transatlantic relations as an ever-evolving process, because even alliances evolve. There is nothing static or fixed in international politics, and maybe this is what is most fascinating about them. In any case, such an analysis will demonstrate how tensions were overcome and how in the process the identity and interests of the allies were redefined, thus inducing further change in the international structure.

As is well known, NATO was founded in 1949, when the USSR was believed to be a major threat to Western Europe. However, even during the Cold War the alliance endured revisions, which for the most part changed its strategic plan. The first formulation of NATO's strategy for security was known as "The Strategic Concept for the Defense of the North Atlantic Area." This document was developed between 1949 and 1950, and it outlined the strategy of the alliance for large-scale operations for territorial defense. However, in the 1950s, the evolving political context set the stage for the reformulation of such a concept and a new strategy, emphasizing deterrence and thus NATO's response to any aggression against its members—including nuclear threats—was developed. This need to revise NATO's policy gave birth to the strategy known as "massive retaliation." But this too was regularly adjusted between the 1950s and the 1960s, until in 1967 "massive retaliation" was replaced with "flexible response." The latest strategy focused on the idea of giving NATO "the advantages of flexibility and of creating uncertainty in the minds of any potential aggressor about NATO's response in the case of a threat to the sovereignty or independence of any single member country."[1] This new strategy was also the result of the changing political context. In effect, the stranglehold that Moscow was exercising on Eastern Europe pushed the West to a response, which emphasized the idea that the aggressor was to perceive any kind of attack as involving unacceptable risks. Moreover, the perception of a dangerous international context, mainly the fear of communist ideology, as well as the supposed military capability of the Soviet Union, had the effect of determining Western security interests. Indeed, from 1949 to the end of the 1980s, NATO maintained more than sufficient military capabilities for the defense of its members in the event of an attack from the USSR.

It should be evident by now that that even during the Cold War, NATO adapted (or adjusted) to the changing East-West relations. Indeed, NATO was flexible, and its member states renovated its strategy in response to the evolving political structure of those times. This evolution and adaptation to the new security context persisted even after the collapse of the Soviet Union. Again, while many expected the dissolution of NATO, the alliance endured. Indeed, the emerging of a new security context changes the perception of who poses a danger to states and how best those states can defend themselves from that danger. In other words, as states perceive new threats they will simultaneously decide both from what danger they need to defend

themselves and what structures they need to have in place in order to ef-
ficiently do so. This process, I contend, will reidentify the state vis-à-vis the
new perceived threat; it will determine the state's interests (i.e., new security
policy) and it will affect its behavior. If we apply this principle to NATO
we can explain how, and why, NATO "survived." So the question becomes
how did the change in the security context lead to the transformation of the
alliance post 1989?

Numerous events have transformed the security environment of Europe
in the last 20 years. At the outset, the tearing down of the Berlin Wall in
1989, beyond its symbolism, boosted the idea of an actually whole and free
Europe where security became conceptualized as indivisible. "The indivisibility of security" in Europe rested on the idea that the security of each
state was/is indissolubly connected to the security of every other nation-
state in the region.[2] This political transformation led to the London Declaration, which included proposals to develop cooperation between Eastern and
Western Europe.[3] Moreover, within the framework of the CSCE Summit
Meeting in Paris in 1990, the 22 NATO members and the Warsaw Treaty
Organization signed a major agreement on Conventional Armed Forces in
Europe (CFE). Additionally, a critical outcome of the new security context
was the Joint Declaration of Non-Aggression, which officially ended adver-
sarial relations and emphasized the goal of the member states to renounce
resorting to the threat of force or to the use of force against the territorial
integrity or political independence of any state, in accordance with the UN
Charter and the Helsinki Final Act.[4]

Once again, NATO proved to be flexible, and, thanks to the resolve of its
members, it responded to the new European security environment by broadening its concept of security "to include dialogue and practical cooperation
with other countries outside the Alliance as the best means of reinforcing
Euro-Atlantic security."[5] At the London Summit in 1990, NATO invited the
six Warsaw Pact nations—Bulgaria, Czechoslovakia, Hungary, Poland, Romania, and the Soviet Union—to initiate regular diplomatic exchanges. The
following year, at the Rome Summit, NATO established a North Atlantic
Cooperation Council (NACC) to oversee the future development of NATO-
Central and the Eastern Europe partnership. In March 1992, participation
in the NACC was extended to incorporate all members of the Commonwealth of Independent States, and by June 1992 Georgia and Albania had
also become members. The construction of the NACC in 1991 emblemized
the challenge to reform and adjust NATO for the new post-Cold War world.
The NACC would have been inconceivable just a few years earlier. But
change in the political context had led to a redefinition of the "self" vis-à-
vis the former enemy, which allowed for the rationale of the NACC. The
NACC was to introduce more consultation and more cooperation among
the members of NATO and the former members of the Warsaw Pact. This
incorporated a wide range of areas, such as civil-military relations, military
doctrines and budgets, defense conversion, and conceptual approaches to

arms control. This progression, enhanced in 1993 with the adoption of the Partnership for Peace program, intended to "expand and intensify political and military cooperation throughout Europe, increase stability, diminish threats to peace, and build strengthened relationships by promoting the spirit of practical cooperation and commitment to democratic principles that underpin the Alliance."[6] The plan was to prime states on the outside for potential membership in the alliance. The security context was dramatically changing.

Another major NATO adjustment, made to adapt to the new security context, was the idea that the alliance would participate in peacekeeping operations, which until then had been the exclusive prerogative of the UN. At the Ministerial Meeting in Oslo on June 4, 1992, NATO reaffirmed its willingness to be of support in peacekeeping operations.[7] It reiterated its readiness "to support, on a case-by-case basis in accordance with (their) own procedures, peacekeeping activities under the responsibility of the CSCE, including making available Alliance resources and expertise."[8] It was not, however, limited to supporting the CSCE, but was determined to support the UN as well. The Final Communiqué of the Ministerial Meeting of the North Atlantic Council in Oslo, on June 4, 1992, also announced that NATO supported "the valuable contribution of the United Nations to conflict settlement and peacekeeping in the Euro-Atlantic region."[9] Thereafter, in 1993, NATO established an Ad Hoc Group on Co-operation in Peacekeeping aimed at (1) developing a common understanding of the political principles; (2) developing the tools for peacekeeping; (3) sharing experience, and thus developing common practical approaches and cooperation in support of peacekeeping under the responsibility of the UN or the CSCE.[10] Again, it is by looking at the process that we can explain why NATO endured and how the context relates to identity, which defines whom we consider a danger and in what way we need to defend ourselves in the face of that danger.

A major moment in the process of the transformation of NATO, which indicated its compliance to change, was its intervention in the Balkans. This was the first time that NATO was employed out of its traditional geostrategic area, and it is an important indicator of how a change in the security context produced a change in the normative context. How was NATO employed? A brief historical account will set the stage for a more in-depth discussion, in the next section, of the normative change that this intervention produced. In 1995, after the EU/UN failure in the Balkans and the consequent abandonment of the Vance-Owen Plan, as well as the Serbs' massacre of thousands of Muslims in two "safe heavens" (Srebrenica and Zepa); and, finally, after the infamous shelling of Sarajevo, NATO launched air attacks on Serb air bases. Thereafter, in August, it launched operation "Deliberate Force" on Bosnian Serb positions.[11] The following December, 60,000 NATO troops arrived in Bosnia. The operation, known as Implementation Force (IFOR), had a one-year mandate, under the Security Council Resolution 1031, to oversee the implementation of the military aspects of the Dayton Peace Agreement.[12] In other words, IFOR's goal was that of guaranteeing the end of hostilities and separating the armed forces of the Federation of Bosnia and Herzegovina from those of the Republika Srpska. The Dayton Accords, however, established that the UN had to turn over to IFOR all peacekeeping operations, giving birth to NATO's first large-scale operational peacekeeping mission. In the following years, NATO missions extended to Kosovo (Operation Allied Forces, March 23–June 10, 1999), Macedonia (Operation Essential Harvest, Amber Fox, 2001–2003), Greece (Distinguished Games, 2004), Pakistan (Earthquake Relief Operation, 2005), Turkey (Operation Display Deterrence, 2003) and the United States (post-9/11 mission).[13] Some of these operations were part of NATO's disaster relief. In fact, in 1998 the alliance also created a Euro-Atlantic Disaster Response Coordination Centre (EADRCC) for coordinating disaster relief efforts for the 46 member countries of the Euro-Atlantic Partnership Council (EAPC) in the case of a natural or technological disaster in the EAPC geographical area.[14]

We will discuss this intervention more at length in the next section. However, in order to further understand NATO's adaptation to the new security environment, it should be recalled that among the operations of the 1990s, the Kosovo mission was the most controversial because it was an aerial bombardment that NATO's governments framed partly as humanitarian intervention and partly as a response to the threat to peace and security in the region. While it is still debatable whether NATO interventions led to a more stable situation in the Balkans, it is clear that NATO's air campaign without a UN mandate created the powerful precedent of external military intervention within the borders of a sovereign state. This is why my analysis of the impact of the interaction between identity, behavior, interests and international norms becomes relevant. This intervention, in response to a shift in the context (i.e., a war in Europe, unconceivable until then) led to change in the normative context (i.e., military intervention within the borders of a sovereign state based on the defense of human rights). Among NATO member states, the central problem in the public debate was, in fact, whether they had the right to intervene militarily in the affairs of a sovereign state. In a critical speech in Chicago on April 22, 1999, Prime Minister Blair implied that the NATO campaign on behalf of the Kosovars had turned the balance between human rights and state sovereignty. He argued, "we cannot turn our backs on conflicts and the violation of human rights within other countries if we want still to be secure."[15] What added fuel to the already incendiary academic debate over the Kosovo mission was the fact that NATO member states justified the intervention as an act for the greater good, and for the defense of individuals whose human rights had been shamefully violated. With this action, NATO demonstrated both its significance in the new security realm, in a post-Cold War world dominated by civil wars and, at the same time, asserted its credibility for the present and for the future. Thus, even though theoretically the end of the Cold War had increased security options for NATO members, in the post-Cold War period, the alliance was strengthened. Indeed, it became more vibrant than ever, and the evidence of its strength was that it initiated missions that during the Cold War would have been unthinkable. Thus, against the expectations of many scholars, mostly realists, not only did NATO not collapse, but on the contrary, grew more assertive and powerful. In the next section, however, we will discuss disagreements among NATO members on whether, and how, to enlarge NATO. The rationale for such an analysis is twofold: first, it indicates that differences were reconciled based on changing interests; and second, it shows that such interests reflected a changing identity, which was resocialized based on the perception (and thus formation) of a new norm: humanitarian intervention.

III. NATO'S ENLARGEMENT: THE AMERICAN WAY, NOT THE EUROPEAN "I-WAY"

Pundits analyzing transatlantic relations at the end of the 1980s may have had reason to be pessimistic about the future of the alliance. Indeed, as a new world order started to take effect, some NATO members showed a high propensity for restructuring the alliance, while others seemed to be much less enthusiastic. This caused a heated debate over the future of the alliance. What happened within NATO vis-à-vis its enlargement, the proposals that were presented to strengthen the role of the Europeans and the settlement ultimately reached, all indicate a process of reidentification that impinged on international norms of behavior, substantially changing the normative structure. In order to understand how this happened, it is important to examine the positions of NATO members as they were assessing its enlargement and transformation.

The most resolute country in favor of the enlargement of NATO was the United States. In 1994, President Clinton announced that the question was "no longer whether NATO will take on new members but when and how."[16] In a speech to the UN General Assembly on September 27, 1994, Clinton argued: "during the Cold War, we sought to contain a threat to the survival of free institutions. Now we seek to enlarge the circle of nations that live under those free institutions."[17] He also emphasized that NATO's enlargement would "advance the security of everyone."[18]

In March 1998, before the Senate's first debate on NATO's enlargement to include Poland, Hungary and the Czech Republic, Clinton wrote a letter to the then-Democratic Senate leader, Senator Tom Daschle, strongly recommending "the Senate to reject any effort to mandate a pause on the process of enlargement." He urged that the mandate was "unnecessary and unwise, for," he continued, "it would reduce our own country's flexibility and leverage, fracture NATO's open door consensus, and draw a new and potentially destabilizing dividing line in Europe."[19]

His pronouncement came as a surprise, since Clinton had won the election in 1993 focusing on the economy, not international politics and certainly not by promising an extension of NATO to defend Europe. In effect, officials in both the legislative and the executive branch of the United States did not think that expanding NATO's membership was a good idea.[20] Even among Europeans, some did not show any particular enthusiasm for NATO's expansion. Moreover, Russia strongly opposed NATO's Eastern enlargement. So, why did the United States move in that direction?

Politics in Washington may explain how NATO enlargement became U.S. foreign policy. According to Goldgeier, Anthony Lake played an important role. He was the "conceptualizer" of NATO's enlargement. Assistant Secretary of State Richard Holbrooke was instead the "enforcer." While President Clinton had initially focused on the U.S. economy, he was apparently persuaded by those two men that NATO's expansion was a good idea. Thus, the officials in the executive, the military and the Pentagon, who had actually opposed NATO's expansion, were outmaneuvered.

It is important to notice that although the United States needed its allies' support to transform NATO, many important decisions were taken in Washington. Indeed, it was the United States that developed the Partnership for Peace, a program of military cooperation. It was decided that the enlargement had to be accomplished through a two-track policy that would allow new members to join in, while establishing a formal agreement with Russia. Moreover, it was the United States that developed the NATO-Russia accord, even though it asked NATO Secretary General Javier Solana to negotiate the accord in order to minimize resentment in Europe and in Russia. Finally, notwithstanding Italian and French interest in the membership of Slovenia and Romania, the United States also decided which countries were going to join in the first round of NATO's enlargement.[21] Thus, in the 1990s, the United States was clearly showing a strong interest in keeping NATO alive. Indeed, the National Security Strategy of 1995 states: "The NATO alliance will remain the anchor of American engagement in Europe and the linchpin of transatlantic security. That is why we must keep it strong, vital and relevant. (. . .) Only NATO has the military forces, the integrated command structure, the broad legitimacy and the habits of cooperation that are essential to draw in new participants and respond to new challenges."[22] Likewise, in a private interview, Dr. Stephen Flanagan, who held multiple senior positions in government between 1989–1999 and who helped to develop U.S. foreign policy strategy for the post-Cold War era, argued that, during the Cold War, having an overarching threat indeed diminished the potential for disputes over other issues, including economics, from becoming too corrosive or too damaging. But he also noted that while many were arguing that we did not need NATO anymore, because there was no Russian/Soviet threat, "suddenly the Balkans came along and we realized that we needed an institution that was capable of conducting military actions to deal with a humanitarian disaster that was causing real security problems along Europe's periphery."[23] Thus, even though the push for keeping NATO alive in the post-Cold War world came from within the Washington circle (although somehow peripheral to the administration's envisaged foreign policy), it finally came through because of the war in the Balkans. That is to say, in the end it was a shift in the security environment that propelled the transformation. Indeed, the fact that NATO showed willingness to adapt its tools, which were designed for very different military problems, to deal with conflict resolution and peace settlement, was remarkable, said Dr. Flanagan. It showed, in his words, "that the alliance was still fundamentally about the security and the defense of the interests of the member states from anyone or any threat that could undermine the security of the members. That was a moment of clarity," he concluded.

The American interest in a thriving alliance for the 20th century was very much welcomed at the NATO headquarter in Brussels, but what was the European reaction? Were the European NATO members pleased with the American plan?

Evidence shows that there was little agreement on how the transformation of NATO was supposed to be carried out. Some European leaders, for example, were preoccupied with Russian reactions to the Eastward expansion. In a 1996 interview, German Chancellor Helmut Kohl stated that it would be wrong to talk about NATO's Eastward expansion with a sense of victory because it would show a lack of consideration for Russia's "understandable security interests."[24] Just a few months later, the German Foreign Minister Klaus Kinkel reiterated the German concern that an Eastward enlargement could challenge Russia.[25] Others, on the contrary, were quite eager to demonstrate their support of a transformed NATO. In a parliamentary debate held in November 1996, Prime Minister of Spain José María Aznar argued: "Spain has now the opportunity to fully participate in a NATO that is more European and more advantageous for our interests."[26] Of course, it should be said that NATO's transformation came at a pivotal moment for Spain, for it coincided with the new government's desire to end the limited relationship with NATO. Spain, which was admitted to NATO in 1982, had experienced limited participation because the communists, in power until 1996, were opposed to Spain's full participation in the alliance.

Between 1996 and 1998, the relationship between NATO members became increasingly tense. There were a few central problems that they had to face if the alliance was to be enlarged. The first problem was that an enlarged NATO could become diluted. That is to say that it could be more extended politically, but the long-standing members could lose power. The second problem was that the Russians did not like the idea of an expanded NATO, and the allies did not want to upset the Russians. The third problem was the question: "if we don't already have an enemy, why are we going to enlarge NATO?"[27]

What is interesting is that, in the new security context, some European members had a vision of the transformation of NATO that exposed an attempt to reidentify themselves within the alliance. It was as if Germany, France and the United Kingdom had constructed themselves within NATO as an "other" (i.e., an alternative with a different identity) with respect to the United States. In 1996, Germany publicly came up with a new political theme for the renovation of NATO, the so-called Europeanization of NATO. Such policy was backed up and carried on by the French and, surprisingly, by the British, who generally tend to side with the United States on security issues. Mr. Volker Ruhe, the Germany defense minister, an Anglophile and committed Atlanticist, began leading the European discussion over the transformation of NATO by arguing that the alliance had to be reformed in a way that would allow Europe to assume more responsibility in crisis management. Even though this proposal was aimed at situations in which Americans did not want to become involved, it was still a significant and potentially strong attempt at changing the relations within NATO. It also constituted a challenge to American leadership.[28] The jargon used to describe this new conceptualization of the security system was an "Atlantic Europe," which included the United States and a "European Europe," without the United States.[29] Mr. Ruhe suggested that NATO's Cold War structures had also to be reformed, so that the expansion could include Central and Eastern Europe without irritating the Russians. The necessity of such a transformation was due, in his words, to the fact that "the Americans want[ed] to be relieved in Europe, and the Europeans want[ed] to have a stronger identity."[30] The British, who usually support American views, shared this position and the British Defense Minister Mr. Portillo also argued for new flexible structures within NATO under European command.[31] "What we are talking about," he said, "is the levels of headquarters, to give the necessary flexibility so that they can be led by Europeans only. The NATO structures now are mirroring very much the past. A lot of the NATO headquarters still mirror the Cold War, and the fixed situation between East and West. We are thinking about radical change. We need to make the Europeans able to deal with a crisis situation that has to be dealt with by Europeans alone."[32] Clearly some Europeans began to conceive themselves as an alternative to the United States as a security provider. However, Prime Minister of Spain José María Aznar has always, on the other hand, defended the idea of an "Atlantic Europe" and so have the Central and Eastern European countries. This was also the moment in which Europeans were discussing the possibility of a European army or a European defense system. José María Aznar, for example, was very skeptical about the idea of creating a European defense separated from NATO. He claimed that "organizing a European security pillar inside NATO as a reaction force in times of crisis was extremely important, but I did not accept the idea of eliminating the interests or the presence of NATO from the European life. I consider it the only security system that really exists." In other words, he said that they could not eliminate NATO or a part of it (i.e., the United States) because that would mean, "substituting one security (NATO) with two insecurities (a partial European defense system and a NATO without the U.S.)."[33]

As some of the Europeans were considering operative changes, so was the United States—but perhaps the changes considered by the United States were not as radical as those considered by Europe. Indeed, over the course of the years since the end of the Cold War, the United States has had quite a consistent policy. As Dr. Flanagan put it: "we want[ed] Europe to be a more capable and more externally engaged partner."[34] This view dates back to 1991–1992, when Secretary of State James Backer III stressed the need for Europe to become a "full" partner. But the United States was concerned at the idea of a European defense, and it was also preoccupied that it could duplicate or, eventually, undermine NATO. The U.S. government in effect, Dr. Flanagan said, saw its interests well protected in NATO, where Americans had "a seat at the table." But the problem for the United States was that they did not have any decision-making power in Brussels. Thus, the concern was "are we going to lose influence?" or "is Europe going to create, with limited resources, European tools that will undermine NATO?"[35]

Accordingly, U.S. Defense Secretary William Perry affirmed that the time had come "to streamline and modernize NATO, recognizing that our challenge is no longer simply to execute a known plan with already designated forces as it was during the Cold War."[36] Yet, at the NATO Berlin Summit in June 1996, the United States accepted the proposal to allow the European allies to conduct operations under the NATO umbrella, even when the United States was not involved.[37]

For some, however, this promise was not enough and, in September, France, which at the beginning of the year had declared its desire to resume an active role in NATO (conditional upon reforms made to the alliance) threatened a boycott of the discussions at the upcoming NATO meeting unless the United States agreed to let France, Spain, and Italy, on a rotating base, have NATO command for the Mediterranean.[38] The American response to French President Chirac on that point has always been a categorical "No!" The justification for his response was twofold: the Mediterranean had to be commanded by an American because of (1) the presence of the U.S. Sixth Fleet; and (2) American strategic interests in the Mediterranean, the Middle East and the Gulf region.[39]

Germany and others in Europe backed the French proposal, to the extent that Mr. Ruhe proclaimed that the question of the AF South command was "not a French demand but a European demand."[40] Nonetheless, when President Clinton finally agreed to support a plan for a new rapid-reaction force to handle crises in the Southern Mediterranean, with France commanding the force, Germany, Italy and Spain withdrew their support and argued instead that the French proposal be considered in five or six years' time.[41] The reaction of Germany, Italy and Spain to France's proposal revealed that disagreements existed not only between the United States and some Europeans, but also among the Europeans themselves.

Another element of contention among NATO allies in those years was the question regarding the so-called flexibility of NATO. In a speech in Berlin in May 1998, President Clinton articulated the American stance on this point. He said, "yesterday's NATO guarded our borders against military invasion, tomorrow's NATO must continue to defend enlarged borders and defend against threats to our security from beyond them—the spread of weapons of mass destruction, ethnic violence and regional conflict."[42] On this question, the French disagreed with the Americans. French Foreign Minister Hubert Vedrine argued that it was already difficult to maintain the cohesion of NATO within the parameters of its traditional mission. His concern was that, because the expansion of the alliance membership was occurring at the same time as the shift in its action and decision-making mechanisms, NATO's energy could be drained.[43]

Some Europeans, notably France, Germany and the UK, disapproved of the American idea that NATO could react to crises anywhere in the world, if these predicaments had "implications for the defense of common interests."[44] At a NATO meeting in Saint-Malo, in December 1998, Secretary of State Madeleine Albright actually suggested that the alliance should be allowed to deal with any global crisis if it had such implications. As a result, British Prime Minister Tony Blair and French President Jacques Chirac made a bilateral declaration in which they stated that "the Union must have the capacity for autonomous action, backed up by credible military forces, the means to decide to use them and a readiness to do so, in order to respond to international crises."[45] To this, Madeleine Albright responded by stressing the need for Europeans to avoid "the three Ds": "decoupling" European decision making from the alliance, "duplication" of NATO structures and planning processes, and "discrimination" against allies (i.e., Turkey) who are not EU members.[46] Additionally, French Foreign Minister Hubert Vedrine and German Foreign Minister Joschka Fischer expressed concerns that the United States was trying to transform NATO into a global policeman. U.S. Secretary of State Madeleine Albright denounced their interpretation as "hogwash," insisting that the United States was not trying to create a "global NATO."[47] France and Germany also feared that the broadening of NATO's role would be used by the United States as a pretext for using military action without the approval of the UN. The idea that the United States could act through NATO without UN support also made Russia uneasy. France and Germany supported Russia's insistence that "any use of force must first be approved by the United Nations Security Council."[48] Finally, a compromise was achieved that each decision of NATO intervention was to be taken on a "case by case" basis.[49] Referring to the Kosovo case, in which NATO had indeed acted without the UN Security Council mandate, a French official said, "We will do it again if necessary, but we have no intention of giving NATO a blank check."[50] A British official added that it was "not good for NATO to arrogate to itself what sound[ed] like a unilateral right—if only because it might give similar ideas to the Russians or the

Chinese about invading some small neighbor of theirs."[51] But in the end, the United States, the United Kingdom, France and Germany all agreed on the premise of NATO's humanitarian war in Kosovo.

Thus, the transformation of NATO was far from being smooth. Some members, mainly the Germans and the French, tried to enhance their position within the alliance by substantially designing a European "way" of transforming NATO. This, however, could indicate the existence of an "alter ego": that is to say, a distinct identity that led to an attempt to reidentify themselves within the alliance. Consequently, they proposed alternatives ideas to the U.S. vision of how to transform NATO. However, this developing separation was interrupted by the more critical issue of the war in the Balkans.

IV. OPERATION ALLIED FORCE AS A WESTERN HUMANITARIAN WAR

The conceptualization of Operation Allied Force as a humanitarian war is critical for assessing how the allies resolved their differences in a moment of transition. In the previous section, I examined how the Europeans and the Americans had different visions for the transformation of NATO. I argued that this was mainly the result of a new perception of the "Self," which was inducing and thus promoting new roles for the Europeans in security matters (inside and outside NATO). In essence, the change in the security context was renewing their identity and thus shaping their interests inside and outside the alliance. But something happened that changed this dynamic and gave way to a new development: the war in the Balkans, a war in the "backyard" of Europe. The reaction to that war has tremendous relevance for understanding transatlantic relations and for making sense of the developing normative context. Indeed, for the first time since the creation of the UN, NATO member states explicitly justified the use of force against another state on humanitarian grounds and without Security Council authorization. This action, that many at the time considered illegal and with ambiguous humanitarian purposes, produced two main results: on the one hand, NATO's air attacks proved its reliability within the new security context of the post-Cold War period.[52] The eagerness of the allies to demonstrate NATO's dependability in situations of crisis showed their determination to not cast further doubt on NATO's future role. On the other hand, in Kosovo, the allies reformed two normative principles: the principle of the nonuse of force, if not in self-defense, and the principle of nonintervention in the internal affairs of other nation-states. By justifying the intervention in Kosovo as a "just war," the transatlantic allies challenged accepted and recognized international norms. In so doing, they reidentified the West as the protector of human rights. NATO became instrumental for such a change. From a political and military alliance, NATO developed into an organization for the diffusion of Western values. In essence, it became the expression of "an alliance of values, universal values."[53] According to José María Aznar, the new strategy for NATO was that of defending such values, which he identifies as freedom, democracy, rule of law, gender equality, equality before the law, pluralism and tolerance. Some are skeptical of the idea that a war can be "humanitarian" in the sense that it can be waged and justified to enforce human rights. What is relevant, however, is that this instance demonstrated a revived sense of Western identity built around values. The West, with the intervention in Kosovo, began to conceive of itself as a group of nation-states that defends and universalizes its values through NATO. This process took place during the 1990s. The new Western identity was socially created by the interactions between countries within the alliance. As a consequence, this reidentification and behavioral change began a process of transformation of the international context and of its normative structure. Military intervention in civil wars thus started to develop into normatively acceptable behaviors. How did this happen?

As tensions in Kosovo escalated, the Clinton administration promptly condemned the forced Serbian expulsion of Kosovars. In March 1998, Madeleine Albright announced that in Kosovo the international community would not stand by and watch ethnic cleansing, as it did in 1991 in Bosnia. She declared, "We don't want that to happen again."[54] The idea of defending human rights in Kosovo, however, could have provoked the Russians, which, given the delicate transitory moment, had to be avoided. The Contact Group thus condemned both the Serbian forces and the Kosovo Liberation Army (UCK, Ushtria Clirimtare e Kosoves) for the violence in Kosovo and asked for a cessation of hostilities.[55] Security Council Resolution 1160 reinforced the Contact Group's position and called upon the Federal Republic of Yugoslavia to take further necessary steps, through dialogue, to achieve a political solution to the situation in Kosovo.[56] Although no country voted against this resolution, Russia and China were quick to point out that the Security Council was interfering in what they considered to be a matter of "domestic jurisdiction." According to international law, because this was a civil war, which by definition takes place within the boundaries of a state, other nations were not supposed to intervene.

In effect, the domestic, or internal, jurisdiction of a state pertains exclusively to the state and interfering in such a matter constitutes a violation of international law, which forbids such an intervention. Thus, from a legal standpoint, Russia and China were correct. This norm, which originates from Roman law, was codified into the United Nations Charter. Art. 2 (7) clearly states that "nothing contained in the present Charter shall authorize the United Nations to intervene in matters which are essentially within the domestic jurisdiction of any state or shall require the Members to submit such matters to settlement under the present Charter."[57] Nonetheless, NATO countries argued that human rights violations in Kosovo constituted a clear threat to peace and security in the Balkans, and it was necessary to put an end to that threat. Some argue that the dreadful sight of Albanian refugees leaving Decani (Kosovo) shocked Tony Blair and his administration, and this was why he embarked on a forceful response.[58]

The British, therefore, gave impulse to the redefinition of the normative context. But while they took the lead in arguing in favor of the use of force, the United States followed closely, actively participating in the evolution of what was considered customary behavior. Defense Secretary William Cohen in effect announced at the September 1998 NATO meeting of defense ministers that if Serbs did not agree to a cease-fire, "we shall act." The "we" Secretary Cohen was referring to were the NATO allies. But among NATO members, not everybody agreed on the use force. Germany, Italy and Greece, for example, were reluctant to agree to such an option. The main question that concerned these latter countries was the issue related to NATO acting without explicit Security Council authorization. The United Kingdom and the United States seemed to be less preoccupied with this perspective and more focused on the discourse of the protection of human rights. Still, in June, Robin Cook called for a UN Security Council mandate. Such a mandate, according to Mr. Cook, had to also address Russian concerns by explaining why it was crucial that the Russians did not "stand in the way."[59] Again, the problem was that in the absence of Security Council authorization, allowing the alliance to use force would have made unlawful any forceful NATO action. But framing the intervention as a humanitarian action was already making it "more acceptable," at least by international law standards. By September 1998, however, it became evident that the Security Council was not going to issue the resolution that Cook and Cohen had hoped for. The Security Council, in fact, was deadlocked with Russia and China, having expressed, in informal consultations, that they would have vetoed any resolution that legitimized the use of force against the Serbs.[60]

The solution, and here is the novelty that instigated renovation in the normative context, was to tie a desirable military action to the concept of "humanitarian intervention" as well as to previous Security Council resolutions. This had the goal of ensuring the lawfulness of NATO's military action. In other words, it would have made the intervention legal by the standards of international law. But the extraordinary consequence of this behavior lies in the fact that it was correspondingly modifying the normative context. Some NATO members, however, were not fully persuaded to pursue this course of action, and among them, Germany was the most concerned. Germany Foreign Minister Klaus Kinkel was particularly worried about justifying NATO's intervention through Resolution 1199.[61] The question for Germany was that NATO air strikes would have targeted the Federal Republic of Yugoslavia and that was worrisome both because it would have taken NATO outside of its region and because Germany had sour memories of WW II in the Balkans.[62] However, despite these concerns, in October, the German Bundestag, after a long political debate on the matter, approved Germany's participation in air strikes.[63] The German Federal

Government recognized the legal flaw of the absence of a Security Council authorization, but argued that the situation was so desperate that it justified the use of force, even without UN authorization.[64] Kinkel emphasized that the decision of NATO (on air strikes against the FRY) was not supposed to set a precedent. Yet this behavior, as I have stated earlier, had already begun modifying the normative structure.

While changes in international norms were already set in motion, in 1998, NATO air strikes against Serbian targets were avoided at the last minute, thanks to the successful talks the Contact Group Special Envoy Richard Holbrooke had with Milosevic, who agreed to the cessation of hostilities (the so-called October Agreement). The October Agreement, however, did not last long, and by the end of the year it became clear that the cutback in fighting had only been transitory. In February 1999, due to the parties' refusal to reach an agreement, negotiations were suspended until March in Paris. But as the Paris talks were collapsing and the Serbs were resuming ethnic cleansing, the alliance members, on March 23, 1999, made their final decision to launch air strikes against the FRY.

The justification that the allies offered for those strikes are indicative of their understanding of the security situation, which in turned shaped their action. Once again, their conception of the security realm affected how they perceived themselves and shaped their intervention. This chain of actions/reactions ultimately led to a redefinition of themselves and to a change in the norms governing the behavior of states vis-à-vis civil wars. The motivations offered were essentially four. First, the allies argued that their actions were intended to stop a humanitarian catastrophe; second, that the credibility of NATO was at risk (that is, NATO could not just threaten to conduct air attacks, it had to really conduct them); third, that the ethnic cleansing in Kosovo posed a long-term threat to European security; and, finally, that NATO's use of force was conforming to Security Council resolutions. In a statement before the House of Commons, Robin Cook justified the allies' decision by emphasizing some of these points. He claimed that the allies were left with "no other way of preventing the present humanitarian crisis from becoming a catastrophe than by taking military action to limit the capacity of Milosevic's army to repress the Kosovar Albanians."[65] He added that the conflict would have spilled over to Europe, which would have inevitably triggered a NATO reaction, but in more difficult conditions.[66] The Clinton administration offered a similar rationale to the American people. In a speech at the American Foundation of State, County and Municipal employees, Clinton argued that the West had a moral responsibility to stop the terrible atrocities that were taking place in Kosovo. For example, he talked about "innocent people being massacred at NATO's doorstep."[67] He stressed that NATO could possibly be discredited, but most important, he argued that Americans had to decide whether the United States had to stand up against ethnic cleansing. He concluded by framing the Kosovo situation as a humanitarian issue and reminding everybody that this was "about our values."[68]

While there have been arguments that the humanitarian and security motivation offered by the West was an excuse to expand its sphere of influence into the Balkans, there is not much evidence to support the argument that Operation Allied Force was induced by *realpolitik*. Instead, this is a case in which an important element of the decision to use force in Kosovo was the belief among policy makers that this was a "just war." Therefore NATO air attacks were rationalized as a "humanitarian war."[69]

However, if we look at the justifications provided with regard to international law, we find that there were in fact two breaches of international law embedded in the provisions of the Kosovo war as "humanitarian": the nonuse of force if not in self-defense and the principle of sovereignty (i.e., the noninterference in a matter of domestic jurisdiction). But what is important for the transformation of the normative context is that by adopting the logic of a humanitarian war, the West initiated a revision of accepted norms of international law, also known as *jus cogens*. These are a group of norms, which, according to the Vienna Convention, art. 53, cannot be modified by norms established by treaties. Hence, they can only be reformed through change in the behavior of states. Two are the elements necessary in order to produce this normative change: (1) states' behavior (*praxis*) and (2) the belief that such behavior is legal and binding (*opinio iuris*). *Ius cogens* norms are accepted and recognized by the international community and can be modified only by subsequent norms with the same character.[70] States can modify them only by acting in a way that they consider legitimate and mandatory. One example of *ius cogens* norms is the principle contained in the United Nations Charter art. 2 (4) that establishes that "[a]ll Members shall refrain in their international relations from the threat or use of force against the territorial integrity or political independence of any state, or in any other manner inconsistent with the Purposes of the United Nations."[71] The exception to the nonuse of force is set up in art. 51 that permits "individual or collective self-defense if an armed attack occurs against a Member of the United Nations."[72] The rationale of Operation Allied Force as humanitarian intervention is relevant for our understanding of transatlantic relations, because it sheds light on the process of the reidentification of the allies through NATO and points to a shifting identity that underpins shared values.

V. CONCLUSION

This chapter has shed light on a few important points with respect to change in the international context vis-à-vis change in the normative context. In essence, in this chapter I have examined the endurance of NATO; the conflicting transatlantic visions of its transformation; and, most important, the reconciliation of those differences. By defining the Kosovo situation as a humanitarian catastrophe, the West reidentified itself based on common values for the post-Cold War period and, by doing so, also modified the norms that regulate the behavior of states in civil wars.

What came out of the Kosovo experience was a reconstituted West. Although there were security concerns (i.e., that the war could have spilled over to Europe), U.S. and European policy makers believed that their action in Kosovo was guided by a moral purpose (the defense of human rights). The agonizing German decision to participate in the NATO air strikes even in the absence of Security Council authorization is also an indication of the morality and value-laden backdrop of the intervention in Kosovo. Ethnic cleansing could have been overlooked, and it would not have been the first time. The West could have decided to interpret the violence in the Balkans as a matter of domestic jurisdiction and therefore not have intervened and, in so doing, would have maintained a legal and customary position. On the contrary, in this case, the intervention was built on the morality of the action despite its breaching of international norms. However, and this is what is significant, by acting in this way, the allies redefined their common security interests. They acted in this way because such action reflected an evolved idea of who they were. During the Kosovo crisis, in effect, they developed a perception of themself as a group of states committed to protecting human rights (even) by force, and again, this led them to modify recognized norms of behavior.

Furthermore, it should be noted that the Clinton administration's determination to expand both NATO's membership and its scope is an indication of the prominence that the alliance had for the United States. The American administration's strong commitment to preserving NATO ultimately minimized the preoccupation among some European countries, mainly France and Germany, about the enlargement as sustained by Washington. On the other hand, the attempts by France, Germany and the UK to gain more influence within NATO suggest that, even though concerned at times as to how to transform the alliance, they also wanted NATO to endure. Thus, while there were disagreements on how to transform NATO, the war in the Balkans helped to reidentify the West as well as to renovate NATO as a political alliance that could protect not just the Western territory, but also its values.

Some scholars and pundits have argued that states are interest driven and that national interests guide their actions. While this seems to be a reasonable claim, the question remains as to how states and governments define their national interests. What are the basic national interests? Energy? Security? Border protection? These are important concerns. But then states have to address the question of how to keep themselves secure. The collective approach to defense has been preferred since the end of World War II. Certainly it made sense, especially from an economic perspective (it was less costly), and this is still very important today. We live in a globalized world that is characterized by a complex security environment and by a substantial economic crisis. Many countries cannot develop counterterrorism and intelligence capabilities that are needed in the post-9/11 world on their own. Yet within NATO, collectively, such capabilities can be achieved, and this is probably why Ukraine asked to join NATO in 2008.

Nonetheless, values are important. Article 2 of the NATO treaty states that NATO members will contribute to peace and friendly relations by "strengthening their free institutions" and also "by bringing about a better understanding of the principles upon which these institutions are founded." Since the 1990s, NATO has been doing this even more vigorously than during the Cold War. It has used force to stop violations of human rights in the Balkans and consequently has contributed to the diffusion of a new normative context that allows for external intervention in these cases. It has, however, also strongly reidentified the West as the champion of the protection of human rights. Likewise, the most recent intervention in Libya was a case of intervention for the protection of human rights. It was not just about oil; rather it was about the West not allowing innocent civilians to be massacred by Queddafi. As Dr. Flanagan put it, Americans and Europeans were asking themselves, "Do we want to send the message that if you kill enough of your people the West won't bother you?"

The case of Libya shows that identity and values do matter in the calculation of national interests. It demonstrates that they do indeed affect the behavior of states and, ultimately, it indicates that identity, interests and behavior affect the normative context in which states operate.

5 The International Criminal Court

Europe Goes on in Spite of American Distress

I. INTRODUCTION

This chapter focuses on another critical aspect of transatlantic relations, namely, international justice, and in it I argue, as I did in the previous chapter, for an understanding of transatlantic relations as a dynamic process. Policy disagreements between the United States and Europe are symptomatic of the evolving nature of such relations. Their practices in the case of the establishment of the International Criminal Court (ICC) show that the transatlantic partners share common principles (i.e., protection of human rights), but disagree on the policies to put in place in order to prevent violations of those rights. While in the security area they appear to have overcome policy divergences through "unifying" practices, which have allowed for a redefinition of Euro-American relations for the post-Cold War era, in the case of international justice, sharing the idea that human rights should be protected did not result in policy conformity. In examining the reasons behind the disagreements on the ICC, I consider how different interpretations of concepts such as justice and sovereignty influenced the U.S. and European practices on preventing human rights violations.

The academic debate on the ICC has focused primarily on the extent to which the court could contribute to bringing to justice perpetrators of the most serious crimes in the international community (i.e., genocide, crimes against humanity and war crimes) and on preventing potential atrocities from occurring.[1] While these questions are certainly important, this chapter approaches the issues inherent in the ICC from a different perspective, the aim here being to investigate identities that may have emerged in the absence of the common threat and which, consequently, may have produced divergent policies, thus providing grounds for the claim that the fabric of the Atlantic community was fraying. The key element that emerges from this case, and can be already mentioned here, is that there is a discrepancy over the meaning of certain central values or norms, such as, for example, justice and sovereignty. This is relevant because some scholars, mainly neoliberals, have argued that the United States and Europe share common values and that because they share such values, along with shared norms, political identity and common institutions, they will continue to cooperate with each other. However, evidence shows that divergent conceptualizations of justice and sovereignty have produced different behaviors and have ultimately led to a transatlantic clash over the ICC.

This chapter will offer a brief history of the ICC and of the idea of an international tribunal. Then, drawing from statements of American policy makers, I will provide an analysis of the official American state policy on the ICC for the years 1998–2002.[2] I will then articulate, based on the statements of American and European Union policy makers, their different interpretations of the concepts of justice and sovereignty. Finally, I will conclude the chapter by offering my considerations on the divergence between the United States and Europe over the ICC.

II. THE INTERNATIONAL CRIMINAL COURT: ORIGINS

The evolution of the ICC in the 20th century can be traced back to four main phases: the emergence of the idea of an international court (1899–1945); the embodiment of such an idea during the Nuremberg international military tribunal (1945); the attempts to establish the international court in the Cold War era (1945–1992); and, finally, the establishment of the two ad hoc tribunals (Yugoslavia and Rwanda), along with the negotiations leading to the adoption of the Court's Statute at the Conference of Rome (1993–1998). Although the entire history of the court can be fascinating, this work deals mainly with the Cold War and the post-Cold War period, hence in this chapter I will focus on those two periods.[3]

Without going too much into the history of the establishment of a permanent court, it is safe to argue that over the course of the years one of the biggest objections to the court has been its supranational power, which could potentially limit the power of the states over their own territory and their own nationals. In fact, many states had been concerned with the idea of losing their sovereignty. States did not want to abdicate the exercise of their sole authority over their own territory, and thus they opposed the idea of an international court that could put on trial and sentence their citizens. In essence, those states made the case that a court with such broad-ranging authority would be incompatible with the notion that international law governs only interstates relations.

Nonetheless, right after WW II, the United Nations reconsidered the idea of establishing a permanent ICC, despite the unsolved question of sovereignty. Many states in fact recognized that ad hoc tribunals had intrinsic problems.[4] Because of the limits of such tribunals, the question of the permanent court was raised once again, this time in connection with the formulation and adoption of the Genocide Convention in 1948. But the efforts to create an international penal court failed once more because the International Law Commission (ILC), which had been appointed by the General

Assembly of the UN to study the possibility of establishing a permanent criminal court, was deeply divided. The division was, again, about the question of sovereignty.[5] In 1951, the ILC produced two separate reports: one supporting the court's establishment and one rejecting it. Given the stalemate, the General Assembly passed the question of the ICC to the Committee on International Criminal Jurisdiction, which had the task of elaborating concrete proposals for the General Assembly to consider.[6] The committee recommended the establishment of a "semi-permanent" court that would hold sessions only when matters before it required consideration.[7] It also proposed that the subject matter of the court's jurisdiction be limited to international crimes "provided in conventions or special agreements among States' parties."[8] Finally, the committee suggested that cases should proceed only if the state or states of the accused national, and the state or states in which the crime was alleged to have been committed, expressly conferred jurisdiction upon the court.

However, because the question of sovereignty was still an unsolved problem, very few member states committed to the statute and, in 1953, the General Assembly requested a second committee to issue a new report with an amended version of the statute. The Commission of 1953 modified the text of the previous statute, although not substantially. The 1951 and 1953 statutes were never implemented for lack of political consensus. Instead, the idea stalled in the UN for more than 35 years.

The legal national and international complexities related to the establishment of the ICC, as well as the deadlock in the UN resulting from the Cold War, rendered the achievement of a draft for an international criminal court nearly impossible.[9] Thus, the question of the creation of the ICC remained on the General Assembly's agenda until the relations between East and West began to normalize, thus allowing the work on the ICC to be resumed. In 1981, the General Assembly requested the ILC to prepare a Draft Code of Crimes. As work began, members of the commission called attention to the need to establish the code's implementation, and constantly asked the General Assembly whether the ILC should prepare an ICC statute. Finally, in 1988 the General Assembly asked the ILC to consider the question of the code's implementation, and in 1989 explicitly demanded that the ILC undertake the question of the creation of an ICC. The ILC provisionally adopted a Draft Code of Crimes in 1991, and in 1992 created a working group to focus on the establishment of an international criminal court. In 1992, the Working Group produced an extensive report delineating the general bases upon which the establishment of the ICC could proceed.

Following the 1992 report, the General Assembly granted a mandate to the ILC to work on a draft statute for the ICC.[10] But the project gained momentum only after the establishment by the Security Council of the International Criminal Tribunal for the Former Yugoslavia (ICTY), to be held in The Hague. The adoption of this specific tribunal suggested that a permanent court was needed and that countries, including the United States, might be willing to support the establishment of the ICC, at least under certain circumstances.[11] The success of both the ICTY and the ICTR[12] demonstrated that serious violations of international humanitarian law could be successfully punished by international criminal prosecutions and thus emphasized the need for a permanent institution.[13]

The ILC's 1994 draft neither defined nor codified crimes under general international law, but the drafters in Rome took the opposite position and defined the crimes within the court's jurisdiction.[14] This involved protracted and difficult negotiations between states that wanted broad definitions of crimes and those that wanted narrow definitions to make the court less effective. The Diplomatic Conference to consider the April draft statute was held in Rome from June 15–July 17, 1998, and, after five weeks of negotiations, a statute that reflected nearly a century of work was finally approved. However, while the European Union applauded the Rome Statute, U.S. officials did not sign it, signaling a discord that seemed to supersede the bonds between the transatlantic partners. Thus, while the prediction of those who envisaged a loosening of the sense of commitment to the Atlantic community seems to be accurate in its end results, a more correct evaluation of their claim requires an appropriate investigation of the causes of the discord within the North Atlantic alliance. A nuanced examination of that discord is what the following sections will address.

III. AMERICAN OFFICIAL STATE POLICY AND THE ICC

In the 1990s, President Clinton issued numerous calls for a permanent war crimes tribunal. Speaking in Rwanda, he called for sharper vigilance against genocide and swifter prosecution of its perpetrators in a new permanent ICC. Clinton acknowledged that the world could have protected the victims of Rwanda's 1994 genocide, but did not. After listening to the stories of several victims, he stated: "we cannot change the past, but nations should learn from it."[15] Later, in his address before the UN General Assembly, President Clinton responded to recent horrors in Sierra Leone, Kosovo, and East Timor by calling for the strengthening of the international community's capacity "to prevent and, whenever possible, to stop outbreaks of mass killing and displacement."[16] However, an analysis of the domestic political process of the United States reveals continuous tensions between improving international norms and limiting the power of states to use force.[17]

The tension within the Clinton administration between the determination to establish a permanent war crimes tribunal and the need to protect the action of American officials is evident in David Scheffer's words. Scheffer, Albright's ambassador-at-large for war crimes issues and head of the U.S. delegation in Rome, became quite emotional when describing a trip that he had taken to Rwanda in 1997, an indication that he deeply cared about the establishment of the ICC.[18] Supposedly, Scheffer grew silent for a moment, gazing out toward the Coliseum, before continuing:

> I have this recurrent dream in which I walk into a small hut. The place is a bloody mess, terrible carnage, victims barely hanging on, and I stagger out, shouting, "Get a doctor! Get a doctor!" and I become more and more enraged because no one's reacting fast enough.[19]

After that, Lawrence Weschler claims, Scheffer made the argument for the importance of establishing a permanent war crimes tribunal. At the same time, however, Scheffer also argued that

> the American armed forces have a unique peacekeeping role, posted to hot spots all around the world. Representing the world's sole remaining superpower, American soldiers on such missions stand to be uniquely subject to frivolous accusations by parties of all sorts. And we simply cannot be expected to expose our people to those sorts of risks. We are dead serious about this. It is an absolute bottom line with us.[20]

Sheffer in this quote raises a real concern that could explain America's reluctance to sign the ICC: angry parties could blame the United States for all kinds of crimes in an effort to dissuade them from participating in foreign actions. However, Europeans do participate in peacekeeping operations, but they did not have similar concerns.[21]

Clinton had to balance the effects of a signature for the ICC both domestically and internationally.[22] Internationally, it would have been a win-win situation. In fact, signing the ICC treaty would have increased the role of U.S. leadership in the international community. On a domestic level, however, between 1998 and 2000, Clinton had to make sure that his international commitment would not hurt the Democratic candidate for the American presidency, his vice president Al Gore. He probably did not want to be perceived as the president who had not pondered the risk that American officers might incur once the ICC, as it was being conceived, was acknowledged by the United States.[23] Furthermore, between 1998 and 2000, Republicans held the majority in Congress. Senator Jesse Helms, the Republican head of the Foreign Relations Committee, had in fact already let it be known that any treaty emerging from Rome that would subject American servicemen and officials to being seized, extradited and prosecuted for war crimes would be "dead on arrival."[24]

Because of congressional opposition, the Clinton administration paid extraordinary attention to the question of the possible foreign jurisdiction over Americans. The United States worked and negotiated on the treaty for at least five years with the dual goal of (1) establishing an appropriate instrument for international justice on a permanent basis, and (2) guaranteeing proper precautions to avoid American personnel being subject to any groundless investigation or prosecution by the court.[25] In essence, the Clinton administration identified the need for the exemption of U.S. nationals from the court's universal jurisdiction. The United States opposed the ICC's power to exercise jurisdiction over the nationals of the non-states parties[26] of the statute without the consent of those states.[27] The fact that such power would be exercised only when the national of the nonparty was suspected, on reasonable grounds, of committing genocide, crimes against humanity, or war crimes on the territory of a state party, and when his/her country was found unable or unwilling to proceed genuinely against the individual, was not considered sufficiently reassuring.[28] Scheffer claimed that this system would endanger Americans.

> Consider the following—he argued—A state not party to the Treaty launches a campaign of terror against a dissident minority inside its territory. Thousands of innocent civilians are killed. International peace and security are imperiled. The United States participates in a coalition to use military force to intervene and to stop the killing. Unfortunately, in so doing, bombs intended for military targets go astray. A hospital is hit. An apartment building is demolished. Some civilians being used as human shields are mistakenly shot by U.S. troops. The state responsible for the atrocities demands that U.S. officials and commanders be prosecuted by the ICC. The demand is supported by a small group of other states. Under the terms of the Rome Treaty, absent a Security Council referral, the Court could not investigate those responsible for killing thousands; yet U.S. senior officials, commanders, and soldiers could face an international investigation and even prosecution.[29]

Both before and during the Rome Conference, the United States aimed at shaping a court that it could control, in order to avoid proceedings that could be used against its nationals. Although it had flaws, the Treaty on the International Criminal Court negotiated in Rome had many provisions that the United States supported. It promoted values that are part of the American fabric, such as justice, due process, and respect for the rule of law.[30] It had been the profound hope of the United States, as reflected in President Clinton's long commitment to establishing an appropriate international criminal court, that in Rome the conference would achieve a consensus on the resolution adopting the treaty.[31]

But the United States was not successful in achieving its aim in Rome, and because of the vehemence of the criticism voiced by the Defense Department and Congress, it voted against the adoption of the statute.[32] However, surprisingly, two years later, on December 31, 2000, the United States signed the 1998 Rome Treaty on the ICC, despite its internal political division. Clinton argued that in doing so the United States wanted to reaffirm its "strong support for international accountability and for bringing to justice perpetrators of genocide, war crimes, and crimes against humanity."[33]

Clinton also made clear that signing such a treaty showed the American pledge "to remain engaged in making the ICC an instrument of impartial and effective justice in the years to come."[34] He further claimed that the United States had a long history of commitment to the principle of accountability. He pointed to America's involvement both in the Nuremberg tribunals, which brought Nazi war criminals to justice; and also in the effort to establish the International Criminal Tribunals for the former Yugoslavia and Rwanda. He declared: "Our action today sustains that tradition of moral leadership." Clinton, however, was well aware that the ICC treaty was going to be "dead on arrival" because of the opposition it would encounter in a Republican-controlled Congress, and he waited until the deadline for signatures, December 31, 2000, was reached before signing it. However, when he signed the treaty, he stated: "I will not, and do not recommend that my successor submit the Treaty to the Senate for advice and consent until our fundamental concerns are satisfied."[35] The question of the ICC and the protection of American servicemen and women was thus an issue that preoccupied Democrats and Republicans equally. In fact, this was not an issue that divided Congress, Democrats too were concerned about the ICC version that the Europeans supported. One U.S. prosecutor who was politically affiliated with the Democrats admitted that even if the Democrats had the majority, the ICC treaty would not have been ratified because they shared many of the concerns voiced by the Republicans.[36]

However, the Bush administration abandoned all efforts to negotiate and to obtain "protections" for American officials. The policy of the Clinton administration was replaced by a policy of active hostility, which led to the dodging of the ICC jurisdiction. The initial stance of the Bush administration, over the early course of 2001, was one of withdrawal from the ICC process, as the administration worked to develop a policy distinct from that of his predecessor. The attacks on September 11, 2001, and U.S. retaliations against Afghanistan suspended this process until the early months of 2002. As it became clear that the ICC was going to become a reality, the United States became more and more concerned, and Washington began to issue negative statements about the ICC.[37] It soon became evident that the Bush administration was planning to denounce the fact that the Clinton administration had signed the treaty. The event that triggered the negative U.S. reaction was the simultaneous ratification of 10 states at a special ceremony held at the UN on April 11, 2002. This event brought the number beyond the 60 needed for ratification. At this point it was clear that the statute would enter into force on July 1, 2002. At the time of the deposit[38] of the Rome Statute's 60th instrument of ratification, states parties included permanent Security Council members, France and the United Kingdom (with Russia as a signatory), as well as the entire EU and all NATO members, with only two exceptions.[39]

In response to the future establishment of the ICC, on May 6, 2002, the United States delivered a letter to UN Secretary General Kofi Annan declaring that the United States did "not intend to become party to the treaty," and that consequently the United States had "no legal obligations arising from its signature on 31st December 2000."[40] Secretary of Defense Donald Rumsfeld asserted that the action "effectively reverse[d] the previous U.S. government decision to become a signatory."[41] This act demonstrated an unprecedented and very controversial U.S. reliance on Article 18 of the Vienna Convention on the Law of Treaties for authority to undo the obligation, incurred with a signature in order to respect the object and purpose of a treaty.[42] Furthermore, Under Secretary for Political Affairs Marc Grossman detailed a series of U.S. policy commitments related to international justice, which attempted to frame the "un-signing" as in line with the U.S. commitment to accountability on international crimes.[43] It claimed that the United States believes in justice and the promotion of the rule of law and stressed that Americans

> believe those who commit the most serious crimes of concern to the international community should be punished. We believe that states, not international institutions are primarily responsible for ensuring justice in the international system. We believe that the best way to combat these serious offenses is to build domestic judicial systems, strengthen political will and promote human freedom. We have concluded that the International Criminal Court does not advance these principles.[44]

The reasons he gave are the following:

> We believe the ICC undermines the role of the United Nations Security Council in maintaining international peace and security. We believe in checks and balances. The Rome Statute creates a prosecutorial system that is an unchecked power. We believe that in order to be bound by a treaty, a state must be party to that treaty. The ICC asserts jurisdiction over citizens of states that have not ratified the treaty. This threatens U.S. sovereignty. We believe that the ICC is built on a flawed foundation. These flaws leave it open for exploitation and politically motivated prosecutions.[45]

To such statements, the European Union replied: "the U.S. unilateral action may have undesirable consequences on multilateral treaty making, and generally on the rule of law in international relations."[46]

Yet, Grossman declared that the United States would "work together with countries to avoid any disruptions caused by the Treaty, particularly those complications in U.S. military cooperation with friends and allies that are parties to the treaty."[47] The State Department seemed to have a similar position. Colin Powell argued that even though the ICC deals with the kinds of war crimes that the United States abhors, and although the United States supported the tribunals for Yugoslavia and for Rwanda, the United States did not believe that the ICC was appropriate for American men and women in the armed forces or American diplomats and political leaders.[48]

According to Powell, the Bush administration was particularly concerned with the fact that the prosecutor of the ICC did not answer to any higher authority, and that the Security Council or any other institution had no power to refrain him. Powell argued that the prosecutor has "the authority to second-guess the United States after we have tried somebody and taken it before the ICC." This, in Powell's view, was not appropriate. Unquestionably, he feared that countries, which had open disputes with the United States, could have used the provisions of the ICC in retaliation. Therefore, reasonably, the United States focused on bilateral immunity agreements, also known as Article 98 agreements, as a way to avoid ICC jurisdiction.[49] These agreements were permitted by the Rome Statute and allowed the United States to remain engaged internationally with their friends and allies while trying to provide American citizens with essential protection from the jurisdiction of the ICC, particularly against politically motivated investigations and prosecutions. However, these agreements did not, in the view of the United States, constitute a sufficient form of protection because they did not ensure that the ICC would not initiate an investigation or issue an indictment against American nationals. Therefore, Article 98 agreements, although fundamental, did not satisfy those American policy makers who sought a total exemption for their nationals.

In order to achieve such an exemption, the United States used its veto power at the UN, announcing that it would veto the resolution for a UN peacekeeping mission in Bosnia-Herzegovina if its demands were not met. After two weeks and the statements of several government objecting to the U.S. initiative, a compromise resolution was agreed upon. Resolution 1244 requested that the ICC refrain from commencing or proceeding with an investigation or prosecution of any case involving current or former officials or personnel from a contributing state that is not party to the Rome Statute, for a period of one year from July 1, 2002. In addition, it also expressed the intention of the council to renew the resolution "for as long as necessary."[50] This measure assured only a temporary and unstable form of exemption because the United States had to keep gathering votes for renewals.

In my personal interview with Marisa Lino, U.S. senior negotiator at the Political Military Affair Bureau during those years and U.S. negotiator for Article 98 agreements, she affirmed that the United States needed such bilateral agreements. Those agreements, she said, established that "we will not turn over to the ICC your people without your permission and we don't want you to turn over anybody from the U.S. to the ICC without our permission."[51] She also added, "at home we had a tremendous amount of pressure to put in those provisions that would protect the U.S. from frivolous or politicized accusations of war crimes against humanity or genocide." Lino also underlined that the administration had problems with the principle of complementarity.[52] She gave an insightful example as to why the United

States did not feel sufficiently protected by such provision. She said, "If tomorrow Donald Rumsfeld retires, already there are cases accusing our high level officials before the ICC. What happens? He is now a private citizen and he goes to Europe. Is he going to be arrested? The U.S. government is not going to put Rumsfeld on trial for crimes against humanity, even though some people in Europe think he is a war criminal because of what has happened in Iraq and Afghanistan."[53] Thus, beyond the public discourse about the protection of the U.S. military, there was another, less spoken-about concern, that of protecting the administration's policy makers. Nonetheless, the Clinton administration was probably more open to working multilaterally to ease domestic concerns, while the Bush administration took the more rigorous position of rejecting the ICC. The Bush administration adopted an openly hostile policy, seeking to undermine the legitimacy of the court through the Article 98 agreements.

In sum, the main objections of the Bush administration to the court were that it seriously threatened sovereignty and allowed states hostile to the United States to misuse the court and turn it against U.S. military personnel in mission. The Europeans, on the other hand, conceptualized the principles of the Rome Statute in line with Europe's fundamental principles and objectives: commitment to freedom based on human rights, democracy and the rule of law.

IV. CRITICAL DIFFERENCES WITHIN THE ICC DEBATE

The relationship between the United States and Europe is not fixed and tends to shift by virtue of their interactions and the mutable social environment. In addition, as for every actor, the actions that they take generate international norms. Thus, the behavior of the United States and Europe vis-à-vis the ICC has both influenced and shaped international law and/or the context within which states function.

The United States aimed at a court with limited power and rejected the idea that an independent prosecutor could decide which cases to pursue. The European countries, together with NGOs (nongovernmental organizations), on the other hand, were determined to have a different kind of court with an independent prosecutor and relative freedom from the UN Security Council.[54] The Europeans also sought considerable autonomy for an "Assembly of States Parties" to oversee the court, allowing it to expand the scope of crimes or add new ones by a two-thirds vote. Inclusion of the crime of aggression, not well defined by customary international law, became a further point of contention between those who favored the court model of the ILC,[55] supported by the United States; and the practitioners of the "new diplomacy,"[56] the EU and Canada. Europeans argued that the principles of the Rome Statute were fully in line with the principles and objectives of the Union.[57] In fact, the European Council stated that from its very beginning,

European integration had been firmly rooted in a shared commitment to freedom based on human rights, democratic institutions and the rule of law, which were the principles included in the Rome Statute.[58] These common values have proved necessary for securing peace and developing prosperity in the European Union.[59] The European countries were unified by common values and goals, by a unique model of society, and by particular economic and legal arrangements.[60] At the international level they tend, when possible, to present a unified foreign policy. The EU Commissioner for External Relations Chris Patten argued that the court "is the most important advance for international law since the establishment of the United Nations."[61] In this context, the U.S. rejection of the ICC was taken as a challenge. "We will allow nobody to water down the commitments contained in the ICC treaty," he warned. Contrast his words with that of Mr. Bolton of the American Enterprise in his testimony before the Committee on Foreign Relations. He asked: "why should we believe that bewigged judges in The Hague will be able to prevent what cold steel has failed to prevent?"[62]

The American policy makers' image of international justice seems to be besieged with questions of use of force, lack of trust and conspiracy theory. Senator Rod Grams (R-Minnesota) claims: "I believe the greatest force for peace on this Earth is not an international court; it is the United States military . . . a treaty which hinders our military is not only bad for America, but it is also bad for the international community."[63] Dr. Jeremy Rabkin, a professor in the Department of Government at Cornell University, in his testimony in the U.S. Senate, is even more explicit on the idea that justice should advantage the strongest. "Opponents," he argued, "insisted it would send an unacceptable signal to provide exemptions for the great powers. But won't it send an even better signal to launch a prosecution against an American official?"[64] The U.S. concept of justice differs somewhat from that of the Europeans. For Washington, the superpower's justice system is flawless; for Europeans it is flawed. Under Secretary for Political Affairs Marc Grossman states that the United States believes "the ICC undermines the role of the United Nations Security Council in maintaining international peace and security."[65] Furthermore, he argues, the United States believes that "states, not international organizations are primarily responsible for ensuring justice in the international system."[66]

What is evident from a reading of the public statements made at the time is that there is/was a great deal of mistrust for the international judicial system in the United States. Mr. Bolton asks, as I mentioned earlier, "why should we believe that bewigged judges in The Hague will be able to prevent what cold steel has failed to prevent?"[67] Mr. Grossman argues that a transitional government has to deal with its collective past and that the state should choose how it does so. He claims that a Democratic government should decide whether or not to prosecute crimes or to reconcile and that the ICC should not take these decisions. The European Union (also supportive of both the Rwanda and Yugoslavia tribunals, but conscious of their limits)[68] did not appear to be threatened by the ICC. "No longer will the international community have to create international criminal tribunals after the fact—after the crimes that we all deplore have already been committed."[69] The European Commission warmly welcomed the inauguration of the International Criminal Court in The Hague. The EU believes it to be a fundamental means to maintain peace. "The Union is convinced that compliance with the rules of international humanitarian law and human rights is necessary for the preservation of peace and consolidation of the rule of law."[70] The ICC "is an essential means of promoting respect for international humanitarian law and human rights, thus contributing to freedom, security, justice and the rule of law as well as contributing to the preservation of peace and the strengthening of international security, in accordance with the purposes and principles of the Charter of the United Nations."[71] In the European context, the court was framed within the human rights discourse, which contributed to the creation of a positive image of the court itself as well as generating a positive image of Europe as the paladin of human rights.

The consolidation of the rule of law, respect for human rights and international humanitarian law, the preservation of peace and the strengthening of international security are among the priorities of the external relations of the EU. The Union is strongly committed to promoting the early establishment of the ICC and its Rome Statute, which represent a key prerequisite for achieving these priorities.[72]

In presenting the Council Common position on the ICC, Chris Patten, stated:

> The inauguration of the International Criminal Court is a historic achievement, perhaps the most significant development in international law since the creation of the United Nations. This landmark has been made possible by the joint efforts of governments, international organizations and civil society worldwide. The Court brings hope for the thousands of victims who have suffered in the past from atrocities over which the Court will have jurisdiction: crimes against humanity, genocide and war crimes. The Court sends a powerful message to any potential perpetrator of such crimes: impunity has ended.[73]

In a personal speech one year earlier he had underlined that

> In the twenty-first century, potential tyrants and mass murderers will know in advance that the international community is prepared to hold them accountable for massive violations of human life and dignity. It is our belief and our hope that this awareness will help reduce the frequency and the severity of such crimes. But when it does not, and the relevant national legal authorities are unwilling or unable to act, the international community will have in place a complementary system of criminal justice that is fair, transparent and effective.[74]

The implications of this speech are as follows: (1) for the Europeans the court constitutes a protection against violations of human rights; (2) international organizations, not states, should deal with gross violations of human rights. The whole discourse revolves around humanitarian questions. While this discourse conveys the European understanding of international relations and regulations of controversies, it also gives the sense of a possible new European identity built around themes and images of *humanitarianism*.

The Europeans built consensus on the ICC over values shared by many other countries and NGOs. Under Secretary of State Marc Grossman, in explaining the American policy toward the ICC, claims that the judicial system established by the ICC does not have "checks and balances," which he says is something the United States strongly believes in. He affirms that the U.S. political system is based on the principle that an unchecked power could be abused notwithstanding the good intentions of those who established it. However, the European nation-states political systems are also based on checks and balances, and EU members ratified the Treaty of Rome instituting the ICC. Furthermore, transferring his reasoning of checks and balances to the international system, it could be argued that the United States is an unchecked power and that its power could be abused notwithstanding the good intentions of the American government.

According to then-Secretary of State Colin Powell, the court would have the authority to "second-guess the United States" after Americans had tried somebody and had taken him/her before the ICC. He argued that this is not a situation the United States believes is appropriate for "our men and women in the armed forces or our diplomats and political leaders."[75] Secretary of Defense Donald Rumsfeld says that "clearly the existence of an International Criminal Court, which attempts to claim jurisdiction over our men and women in uniform stationed around the world, will necessarily complicate U.S. military cooperation with countries that are parties to the ICC treaty."[76] In fact, "those countries may now incur a treaty obligation to hand over U.S. nationals to the court, even over U.S. objections. The United States would consider any such action to be illegitimate . . . any attempt to turn a U.S. national over to the ICC would be regarded as illegitimate by the U.S." and that "we must be ready to defend our people, our interests and our way of life."[77] Secretary of State Powell even commented that the United States is no longer bound in any way to the ICC's purpose and objective.[78] Chris Patten reaffirmed "its determination to encourage the widest possible international support for the ICC through ratification or accession to the Rome Statute and its commitment to support the early establishment of the ICC as a valuable instrument of the World Community to combat impunity for the most serious international crimes."[79]

The American emphasis on the question of jurisdiction leads to another critical issue, which hinders U.S.-European relations: their different conceptualization of sovereignty. Sovereignty, as it is generally known, is the states' right to do whatever they want. The 20th century, however, has inaugurated restrictions to unlimited state action. The Hague Conferences of 1899 and 1907 set up the rules governing the conduct of wars on land and at sea. The Covenant of the League of Nations limited the right to wage war, and the Briand-Kellogg Pact of 1928 condemned war as "the" solution to resolve international controversies as well as its use as a tool of national policy. These treaties were followed by the Charter of the United Nations (Article 2), which established the responsibility of member states to "settle their international disputes by peaceful means in such a manner that international peace and security, and justice, are not endangered" and supplemented it with the injunction that all members "shall refrain in their international relations from the threat or use of force. . ."

Yet the UN Charter specifies as one of the crucial principles of the UN "the principle of sovereign equality of all its Members." Because of such developments, sovereignty is no longer equated with unrestricted power. Those states have accepted a considerable body of law limiting their sovereign right of acting as they please. In essence, those states imposed limits on themselves. However, they cannot impose new rules on a state without its consent.

The degree of international restrictions is intertwined with the degree of national sovereignty. More limits to action in the international scenario restrict domestic decision making. Americans always associate the ICC with loss of sovereignty.[80] Mr. Caspar Weinberger, former secretary of defense, referring to the ICC states that "the whole concept really tests whether the idea of sovereignty exists any longer. And it is a very major step along the road toward wiping out individual national sovereignty."[81] Jeremy Rabkin affirmed: "what we should worry about is not simply a physical threat to our servicemen but a wider threat to our national sovereignty. Other countries may want to share their sovereignty with an international criminal court. We should make it clear in advance that we would regard such action as an extremely hostile act against the sovereign rights of the United States. We should make it clear that we will defend our own sovereignty, whatever other countries may do."[82] For Rabkin, the ICC attempted to undermine the United States, but Ruth Wedgwood, professor of law at Yale, pointed out that "many countries thought it would be more deferential to national sovereignty to have a court be treaty based or not at all."[83] Rabkin, however, reiterated, "I think one of the reasons why so many people want this institution to be established is they want to establish in principle that there is an international authority which rightly sits above sovereign states and judges them. And I say in principle that is wrong."[84] He continued, "There should not be anything higher than the United States . . . I am sure it will have bad consequences, because it promotes a certain way of thinking, which is, to use an old-fashioned term, subversive. It is literally subversive of our constitutional order . . . God is above us, as above all other states. And that is very important. To set up an international authority that is higher than our own Government really is, I think, and surely the Founding generation would have said, that is almost blasphemous. It is putting international authority in the place of God."[85] It should be noted that Rabkin's testimony was applauded by the president of the U.S. Senate Committee for Foreign Relations, Jesse Helms.

V. CONCLUSION

The ICC represents an unusual disagreement. In fact, there is no doubt that the United States and Europe, over the course of the years, have condemned the violation of human rights, the most serious crimes of genocide, crimes against humanity and war crimes. To that extent, in the 1990s, they undertook military interventions (i.e., Bosnia and Kosovo) and established ad hoc tribunals (Rwanda and Yugoslavia). The key, as this chapter has tried to show, is that their support takes a different form because of different conceptualizations of certain values/norms. The disagreement over the ICC thus supersedes the bonds of the Atlantic community. The tension between the transatlantic partners is not consequential to the disappearance of a common enemy. The different interpretation of such values produced different policies, which amplified frictions within transatlantic relations. Furthermore, Europeans came to conceive the promotion of human rights as the ideological foundation of their foreign policy. This has defined, and is defining, their identity and consequently their interests and their policies. The United States instead understands itself as a military superpower that cannot, and should not, be tamed, and as such it has rejected the treaty. These identities, resulting from a redefined understanding of key values, are changing the normative context and the social context and producing tensions.

The ICC case also allows for a consideration of the different experience the United States and European countries have had with international institutions, especially tribunals. Europeans are accustomed to international tribunals. The European Court of Human Rights in Strasburg handles thousands of cases every year, and when it sentences governments to do something, they comply. The United States has not had a similar experience and resents any limitation of its sovereignty. Consequently, Europeans believe that international tribunals are a good form of prevention and enforcement to thwart international violations because of their everyday experience with supranational tribunals. By contrast, the United States has never had to practice diplomacy among equals. When it was a rising power, isolationism protected it from the European powers, and when it broke with its isolationism to intervene in World War II it did so as a superpower, taking over "the leadership of the free world." The U.S. preoccupation with limitations of its sovereignty and the protection of its service members should thus be understood within the larger social context of the events of the post-Cold War era, as of the 20th century as a whole.

6   Debt Relief
Development and Social Values

I. INTRODUCTION

This chapter is devoted to my investigation of another key area of transatlantic relations: economic development. This case study, like the previous ones, aims to analyze the behavior of the United States and Europe in order to determine the nature of the difficulties they encounter in engaging with each other. In addition, again as I did in the previous case studies, I examine the U.S. and European practices and the redefinition of transatlantic relations in the post-Cold War era. While the renovation of NATO would suggest a renewed identity because of the social practice of "humanitarian intervention" that would bring the allies closer, the case of the ICC indicates that on issues of international justice, different concepts of justice and sovereignty resulted in policy divergences. The issue of debt relief, however, points to common Euro-American positions, within the G7,[1] for solving the problem of unsustainable debt burdens. However, even in this situation, the issue revealed differences in the conceptualization of values. I suggest that in order to understand the future of transatlantic relations, we must consider U.S. and European practices and values as elements that always have the potential to influence their ongoing relations and define their identity. In fact, the continually evolving consolidation of these identities determines their contingent policy preferences. The case study in this chapter involves an economic policy question, which encompasses social and cultural values, such as unsustainable debt burden, poverty and social justice. In the case of debt relief, advocacy movements—Jubilee 2000 in particular—believed that the high level of debt in third world countries constituted a wrong that creditor nations had the moral obligation to address. In response to their activism, a policy was drafted in which the value-laden idea that the unpayable debts of the poorest countries ought to be forgiven. That policy became the nucleus of the HIPC Initiative, a comprehensive approach to debt reduction undertaken in a joint effort by the IMF and the World Bank.

In June of 1999, the G7 leaders[2] announced that they had "decided to give a fresh boost to debt relief to developing countries."[3] They explained that even though in recent years the international creditor community had introduced a number of debt relief measures for the poorest countries (i.e., The Heavily Indebted Poor Countries, HIPC), it was clear that further efforts were needed "to achieve a more enduring solution to the problem of unsustainable debt burdens."[4] The communiqué offered new hope to the world's most impoverished countries while at the same time presenting a united image of collaboration between the United States and major European countries to the skeptics who foresaw a disintegration of the Atlantic community in the post-Cold War world, for the simple reason that the explicit message of the communiqué suggested that the G7 were ready, collectively, to undertake measures to solve the question of unpayable debt. What is it about debt relief that has so captured the attention of many Western world leaders? What factors have contributed to the initiative of debt cancellation at the national political level? These are some of the questions I will address in this chapter.

In this chapter, I first look at commonalities within the G7 and specifically at what the United States and Europe agreed to do in order to solve the problem of unsustainable debt burdens. Then I analyze the Cologne Initiative and show how the IMF and the World Bank incorporated those decisions into the HIPC Initiative. I then provide the G7 leaders' arguments to further highlight the widespread Euro-American agreements on this topic. I also discuss the compliance of the G7 countries with their pledges in order to try to determine if indeed they were united on the issue. Finally, I outline how an NGO, Jubilee 2000, a coalition of religious and labor organizations whose goal was to cancel the unpayable debts of the most impoverished countries by the dawn of the new millennium, pressured policy makers both in the United States and in Europe to write off such debt. The different approach the organization adopted is indicative of Euro-American distance in the area of traditional/secular values, in line with the most recent Ronald Inglehart cultural map of the world dated about 2000 (see Appendix).[5] This should suggest a divergence of values, and thus identity, which in the end could impinge on transatlantic harmony.

II. INTERNATIONAL PERSPECTIVE: DEBT RELIEF AND WESTERN COMMUNALITIES

Debt relief is not a new issue on the international agenda. Discussions over the problem of what developed countries, many of whom are IMF and World Bank shareholders, should do about the unpayable debt of the world's poorest countries have filled newspapers and academic journals since the first oil crisis in 1974. What makes the topic significant in this study is the renewed interest in the issue between 1997–2000 and particularly the commitment of the transatlantic allies in 1999 to follow through in resolving it. In this section, I look at the G7, the institution in which the United States, Britain, France, Germany and Italy, along with Japan and

Canada first initiated discussions on this issue. An analysis of G7 documents indicates that these countries all agreed on debt reduction. In essence, the G7 nations committed themselves to forgiving up to 90% of the debt directly owed to them (usually referred to as bilateral debt).[6] In addition, they also pledged to contribute to a Heavily Indebted Poor Countries (HIPC) "trust fund" to help international financial institutions—primarily, regional development banks, such as the African Development Bank and the Inter-American Development Bank—to write off loans to HIPC participants (usually called multilateral debt). Two other institutions, the IMF and the World Bank, played a crucial role, however, for they managed the HIPC program and forgave part of the debt owed to them. The most important document that shows the commonality of intent with regard to debt relief was the G7 Cologne Initiative, which successively led to the World Bank and the IMF's enhancement of the HIPCs.

From its very beginning, the Initiative was seen, both by the United States and Europe, as a means to eliminate a burden that was impoverishing and deteriorating already feeble economies. For example, between 1970–2002, Africa received $540 billion in loans. However, even though in that same period African countries paid back $550 billion, $10 billion more than the original loans, in 2002 they still owed an additional $293 billion.[7] This was due to the external debt, whose interests exceeded what these countries could pay, forcing them to borrow even more.

In reaction to the build-up of foreign debt owed by many poor countries, in the late 1980s, the Paris Club and other bilateral creditors rescheduled some of those debts, but the problem persisted. Many poor countries faced debts whose value had more than doubled by the mid-1990s.[8] To respond to this crisis, in 1996 the World Bank and the IMF launched the HIPC Initiative.[9] The HIPC, as it is generally referred to, was comprehensive and called for "the voluntary provision of debt relief by all creditors, whether multilateral, bilateral, or commercial and aim[ed] to provide a fresh start to countries struggling to cope with foreign debt that plac[es] too great a burden on export earnings or fiscal revenues."[10] The HIPC Initiative was certainly a major departure from previous debt relief efforts. In fact, this was the first time that the debts owed to the World Bank and the IMF were included for write-off under the scheme. As Jubilee 2000 claims, the HIPC was also the first comprehensive attempt to deal with the debts of the poorest countries. Indeed, prior to that, borrower countries negotiated on an individual basis, which added great cost, but HIPC changed that.[11] Even if it constituted the first step in a positive direction, the HIPC was heavily criticized for "providing too little relief, too late." In effect, many critics condemned the so-called structural adjustment (SAPs) conditions attached to the HIPC debt relief.[12] Among the harsher critics in academia were Jeffrey Sachs and Alfred Stieglitz, who over the course of the 1990s opposed the SAPs and criticized both the IMF and the World Bank, accusing them of foul play. Similarly, Macleans Geo-Jaja and Garth Mangum argued that structural adjustment programs and stabilization polices have rarely accomplished anything; what is more, they have often worsened human conditions and further exacerbated already precarious economic situations.[13]

In 1999, the G7 launched what is known as the Cologne Debt Relief Initiative to enable the HIPCs to obtain "faster, deeper and broader debt relief" in return for firm commitments to channel the benefit into "assisting the most vulnerable segments of population."[14] Poverty alleviation, however, also required the intervention of two key institutions: the IMF and the World Bank. The Cologne Initiative called on the IMF and the World Bank "to develop a new framework for linking debt relief with poverty reduction," which had to focus on the "better targeting of budgetary resources for priority social expenditures, for health, child survival, AIDS prevention, education, greater transparency in government budgeting, and much wider consultation with civil society in the development and implementation of economic programs."[15] Thus, in 1999, the World Bank and the IMF enhanced the HIPC Initiative "to provide a deeper, more rapid relief to a wider group of countries, and to increase the Initiative's links with poverty reduction."[16] As a result, currently 29 countries are profiting from HIPC debt relief, 19 of which have reached a so-called completion point.[17] Ten additional countries are benefiting from some debt relief, and another 11 will become eligible as soon as the agreement of macroeconomic reforms and poverty reduction becomes effective.[18]

Few cases in the recent history of U.S.-European relations, particularly after 1991, have shown such a united and determined attempt to pursue a common policy. The shared enthusiasm among creditors to come through on their financial commitments is evident in the speeches of the G7 leaders. For the president of France, Jacques Chirac, the G7 debt reduction measures represented an "intelligent, generous and courageous" move, which allowed "countries to benefit rapidly."[19] Similarly, the German Chancellor Gerhard Schröder said prior to the meeting that "without drastic reduction in their foreign debt the world's poorest countries will never be able to integrate into the world economy."[20] Afterwards, he declared the summit to have been an "extraordinary success,"[21] and Tony Blair, the British prime minister, was no less enthusiastic. He said, "we will be writing off literally billions of dollars' worth of debt," adding: "I believe this summit will mark probably the biggest step forward in debt relief."[22] Finally and most important, President Clinton called the Cologne Initiative a "historic step to help the world's poorest nations achieve sustained growth and independence."[23] In March, prior to the Cologne Summit, Clinton had announced: "our goal is to ensure that no country committed to fundamental reform is left with a debt burden that keeps it from meeting its people's basic human needs and spurring growth. We should provide extraordinary efforts to build working economies." Indeed, the G7 reached a degree of consensus that is relatively unique. The debt relief with its moral basis seems to have appealed to both the United States and Europe, thus giving birth to the Cologne Initiative, but the "morality" of the issue, as I will discuss later, was perceived differently by the two sides. While in the United States the advocacy movement appealed to the policy makers' Christian values, in Europe it was presented as an issue of social justice. Thus, in the European cultural-political context, it was a secular question, whereas in America it was a religious one.

An analysis of the G7 countries on the question of debt relief reinforces what I have argued so far: that the United States and Europe were indeed united on this problem. A compliance study put forward by the G8 Research Group shows compliance from every country except the United States.[24] However, the study was published prior to October 2000, when Congress appropriated the additional $435 million needed for 100% debt cancellation, allowing the United States to fulfill its commitments.

The study also confirms that France made reasonable efforts to comply with the Cologne Initiative. In 2000, the French Minister of Economy, Finance and Industry, Laurent Fabious, insisted that France "would not betray this commitment."[25] In effect, the French government pledged to cancel its entire bilateral development debt as well as all its commercial debt for countries eligible for the Paris Club Treatment. Approximately 8 billion euros were allocated for debt cancellation. Likewise, the German Gerhard Schröder was ready to comply completely with the debt initiative. He even revealed, at the EU-Africa Summit in April 2000, that he would recommend that Germany entirely write off the debt of the poorest countries, a commitment of 700 million deutschmarks.[26] The Italian government respected the terms of the Cologne Initiative and cancelled all commercial and Official Development Assistance (ODA) debt for countries with a per capita income lower than $300.[27] Moreover, it contributed $60 million to the ESAF-HIPC Trust Fund, and another $70 million to the World Bank's HIPC Trust.[28] In the case of Britain, Tony Blair announced at the House of Commons that the debt initiative was the most important achievement of the summit. In addition, Britain has been the first country to propose full cancellation of the bilateral debts of countries eligible for HIPC and remained at the vanguard of international debt relief efforts. The United States also followed through, thanks to the money approved by the Senate.

III. NATIONAL PERSPECTIVE: DEBT RELIEF AND DIVERGING U.S.-EUROPEAN PATHS

As I mentioned at the beginning of this chapter, an advocacy movement, known as Jubilee 2000, initiated a transnational campaign to cancel the unpayable debt of the world's poorest countries. I also suggested that the movement adopted a strategic framing that tapped into the values of the targeted policy makers in order to get their attention and build a broader coalition. However, even though the advocacy movement exploited seemingly common values in the United States and Europe, the persuading strategies adopted still reflect differences in those values.[29] In effect, as Inglehart's cultural map of the world (about the year 2000) shows, there is a remarkable difference in the "value systems" of the transatlantic allies. On the traditional vs. secular dimension, the United States ranks far below the United Kingdom, France and Germany and, indeed, Jubilee 2000 adopted secular arguments in Europe and Christian ones in the United States.

This difference begs the question of how the policy makers were motivated through distinct moral concerns? In the United States, the fault line for foreign aid tends to run along party lines, with center and leftist Democrats tending to support it, while Republicans, especially in the conservative wing, opposing it. However, the tendency in this case seems to have been shifted to allow for an important exception, especially on the Republican side. The religious foundations of the Jubilee 2000 movement, in fact, struck a chord with some members of the Republican Party. Among these, John Kasich of Ohio, the Conservative Republican chairman of the House Budget Committee and Spencer Bachus of Alabama, an ultraconservative who became one of the most passionate supporters of debt relief.[30]

But the transnational organization had an outsider who played a crucial role in helping the cause. In 1997, the Irish rock star Bono was approached by Jamie Drummond, at the time a Jubilee 2000 organizer. Drummond recalls that Bono turned out to be "a very brilliant political lobbyist."[31] In fact, Bono's lobbying efforts helped bring other Republicans into the fold, most notably Republican Senator Orrin Hatch of Utah as well as the chairman of the Senate Foreign Relations Committee, the Republican Senator of North Carolina, Jesse Helms. In late 1999, Bono arranged a meeting with Congressman John Kasich, who was a key player for debt relief, given his position as chairman of the House Budget Committee. Kasich, however, was not an easy candidate to enlist in the campaign, mostly because he was highly critical of foreign aid, which he considered "a joke."[32] The Congressman, however, admitted to having been very impressed by Bono's powerful arguments. Apparently Bono, aiming at Kasich's Christian values, talked of "biblical injunctions to succor the poor and downtrodden" and convinced Kasich to join in.[33] In spring 2000, Bono met with Senator Jesse Helms, another foreign aid skeptic. Once again, Bono understood that his usual arguments in favor of debt relief were not going to make the crusty Republican change his mind. Thus, Bono recalls, "I started talking about Scriptures. I talked about AIDS as the leprosy of our age."[34] He told Jesse Helms that married women and children were dying of AIDS, and governments encumbered by debt could not do anything about it. *The New York Times Magazine* reported that the Senator broke down and wept and then, grabbing his cane, said to Bono: "I want to give you a blessing." Then he hugged the singer and added, "I want to do anything I can to help you." In its almost naïve simplicity, Bono's statement seems to reflect the motivations, but also the limits, of American policy on debt relief, a policy that springs out of a deeply rooted belief in the "Christian way of life" and in the conviction that good Christians help the poor and the underprivileged. Bono's *modus operandi* on this particular issue became a pattern: By talking to the Republicans as Christians, he helped them cross the ideological divide.

Bono's Christian-value arguments proved to be critical. In effect, on Capitol Hill, Clinton's goal for a budget amendment seeking a total of $920 million for bilateral and multilateral debt reduction over the next four years had run into resistance from Republican leaders and, after weeks of struggle, the administration and congressional negotiators reached a very limited compromise. Congress would appropriate $110 million for bilateral debt relief for the year 2000 and would suspend until the following year deliberation over the White House request for funds for both multilateral and bilateral loan forgiveness.[35] In 2000, the administration submitted a new request for debt relief funding. It demanded $210 million in supplemental funds for multilateral debt relief for 2000; $225 million as a combination of bilateral and multilateral debt reduction for 2001; and, finally, $375 million in "advance appropriation" for the same reason. At this point Congress, primarily the members of the House Foreign Operations Subcommittee and their chairman, Sonny Callahan, an Alabama Republican, had to make an important decision for the future of debt relief. In order to get Callahan to rule in favor of debt relief, the rock star "ginned up" the clergy members in his district, and the issue of debt relief became a "speeding train," the Congressman said later to *The New York Times* and added: "we've got the pope and every missionary in the world involved in this thing, and they persuaded just about everyone here that this is the noble thing to do."[36] Callahan subsequently admitted: "priests and pastors sermonizing on debt relief on Sundays, telling their congregations to tell Callahan to take care of this, including my own bishop. Eventually I gave in."[37] Soon after October of that year, Congress appropriated the additional $435 million needed for 100% debt relief. "It's not often we have a chance to do something that economists tell us is a financial imperative and religious leaders say is a moral imperative," said President Clinton, satisfied with the outcome in Capitol Hill.[38]

The approach used in Washington to lobby lawmakers by appealing to their Christian morality indicates that the debt relief was handled as a traditional (religious) issue, not a secular one and that the strategy was to go after policy makers.

By contrast, the spark that provoked European policy makers into forgiving the debt was nonreligious protests triggered by social justice arguments. Jubilee 2000, notwithstanding its religious roots, pressured European lawmakers through the involvement of public opinion. The movement never felt compelled to engage public opinion in the United States: on the contrary, it concentrated its efforts on the pursuit of policy makers. In effect, even though the organization worked its way through churches and used congregations to make the debt relief pass in Congress, the larger public in the United States was mostly unaware of the debt relief question and by and large uninformed of the social justice campaign in Europe. According to Ann Pettifor, at that time the director of Jubilee 2000, in the United States "the campaign never took off because it never left the beltway."[39] She argued that the people working in NGOs in Washington were "completely fixated on Capitol Hill." She also said that in their experience, in the U.K., they learned "to ignore the institutions of power and go to the streets and the churches and the trade unions and community organizations, and you had to teach them about international finance and debt, which takes a lot of hard work. It requires traipsing up and down the country, making speeches, talking to people, educating them really."[40]

David Bryden, the former head of Jubilee 2000 United States, partially disagrees with Pettifor. He believes that the reason why the campaign did not reach the public has to do with the fact that debt relief had no connection to American self-interests, and he claims that Europeans felt more responsibility toward debt relief because they had once colonized those debt-ridden countries. Bryden also claims that organizations like Bread for the World and the Presbyterian and Methodist Churches gathered and triggered thousands of members on the debt relief issue. However, he admits that "[o]ur task in the U.S. was to convince, first and foremost, Congress to go along with the idea because that's the way the system works in the U.S."[41]

The idea of involving public opinion on the question of the debt relief took off with Ann Pettifor's acknowledgment that in the United Kingdom the public was unaware of the problem. When she was hired by a group of aid agencies in the United Kingdom to push the debt relief agenda, they thought that her idea of attracting the public to the cause was ridiculous because the origin of the debt was too arcane.[42] However, she followed through and began working with two elderly advocates, Martin Dent and Bill Peters,[43] who decided to connect the question of debt cancellation to the Old Testament idea of the Jubilee, thus linking an economic issue to Christian values. According to the Old Testament, in fact, every 50 years all debts should be canceled, land should be returned to the dispossessed and all slaves should be set free.[44] Dent and Peters believed that Jubilee 2000 had the potential to become the new abolitionist movement. The reason behind it, as they put it, was that "third world indebtedness was the new form of slavery."[45] Therefore, the founders of Jubilee 2000 began a political campaign that "was part religious crusade, part telecommunications war" and part social crusade.[46] The movement first promoted its ideas through evangelical churches all over the world, where it obtained a major victory for their cause, and then it pulled in other religious groups, human rights groups and third world aid organizations, as well as labor unions and non-profits. What these groups brought into the Jubilee 2000 campaign was a global and social-oriented communication network.[47] All the efforts that Jubilee 2000 made on behalf of debt relief were rewarded at the Birmingham G8 Summit, not so much in terms of actual policy making, but rather in terms of popular participation in the quest for debt cancellation, which in turn triggered policy makers to pay attention to the cause. The rationale for dropping the debt had clear social justice connotations. Jubilee 2000 argued, "we are not against all debt—all countries rely on credit (which becomes debt). But we are calling for an end to unjust, or 'illegitimate' debt, which should not be paid, either because payment is an intolerable burden on poor countries, or because the supposed 'debt' itself is simply unfair."[48]

The world leader who was most passionate about the issue was Tony Blair, who became an advocate for debt relief.[49] However, he had not always been so enthusiastic about it and initially he was not even interested in listening to what the movement had to say, but public opinion changed his mind.

In May 1998, at the G7 Birmingham Summit, Jubilee 2000 organized a chain of 70,000 people with the dual goal of symbolizing the bonds of debt and pushing world leaders to debt forgiveness. Ann Pettifor recalls that after months of preparation and coordination with British authorities, the Summit was moved away from Birmingham. Seemingly Helmut Kohl, Germany's chancellor, had a problem with the protesters because thousands of postcards had been sent to him to remind Germans that their debt had been forgiven in 1953, giving German children a future and asking him whether African children could be given the same hope.[50] She also recollects that the day before the demonstration Britain's International Development Secretary Clare Short called in a small group of Jubilee 2000 leaders to point out that she did not want Tony Blair or any leader of the G7 to be embarrassed by them. But the promise that it would be a peaceful demonstration did not reassure Ms. Short and consequently, in Birmingham there were no world leaders, but 9 kilometers of people demonstrating for debt cancellation.[51] However, as Pettifor writes, there were also 3,000 journalists sent to cover the G7 summit, who were, at that point, without a meeting to cover. To her, this was the most exciting moment because the journalists, not having much to report, turned to covering the demonstrators and after that it did not take long for Tony Blair to fly back to Birmingham to meet with the Jubilee 2000's leaders.[52] When they met, the protesters presented Tony Blair with a petition that contained 1.5 million signatures. He responded to the Jubilee 2000 petition by announcing that he welcomed "the commitment so many of you have shown today to help the poorest countries in the world. Your presence here is a truly impressive testimony to the solidarity of people in our own countries with those in the world's poorest and most indebted. [. . .] I can assure you that [. . .] we are all committed to helping heavily indebted poor countries free themselves from the burden of their unsustainable debts."[53]

This statement represents the first political acknowledgment of the Jubilee 2000 campaign, and it is relevant because it indicates the magnitude of the involvement of public opinion in Europe, which eventually mobilized into a mass movement. In Europe the cause of debt relief was a bottom-up issue, which spread from the streets to the media and finally engaged policy makers. Media coverage was particularly important in Europe in raising awareness of debt relief and engaging politicians. Between 1997 and 2001, many articles in European newspapers addressed the movement surrounding debt relief, as well as the issue itself.[54] The first article to be published was an editorial in *The Guardian*, which argued that "debt is a comparable injustice to the slave trade." In December of 1997, this was the only article, but things changed because of what happened in Birmingham. The campaign saw an opportunity and took advantage of it. It swayed more public opinion toward the cancellation of the debt and claimed that this was a social justice issue. *The Guardian* in the U.K. began to support Jubilee 2000's campaign.[55] To that extent, on January 21, 1999, it published the opinion that foreign debt was "crippling parts of Africa, Asia and Latin America." It backed up that statement with numbers, saying that 21 million children would die because of debt. In addition, *The Guardian* stated that millions more would "grow up unable to read or write as government budgets for health and education are dwarfed by debt repayments to the West. [. . .]" It then concluded that existing provisions were "too little and too slow" adding that "debt cannot be left to the bankers and the economists; it needs a mass campaign. It is time to break the chain. This is not about charity, it is about justice. At the end of the 20th century, it is the New Slavery."[56] Thus, "justice" was the reason offered as a motivation for action. Paul Vallely, writing in *The Independent*, commented "in the early days, a call for unilateral action by individual countries was seen as hopelessly utopian, but thanks to the moral agenda articulated by Jubilee 2000, the ground of the argument has shifted."[57]

The Guardian never stopped reporting on what had to be done to give voice to the campaigners. It also offered information on how the debt should be dealt with through articles and editorials, and by maintaining a website with links to the NGOs involved in the campaign. The message that the newspaper sent was as clear as the title of one among many of its editorials "Cancel Debt Now."[58] Other newspapers and magazines did not immediately endorse the campaign and often criticized it. The *Financial Times* and *The Economist* were quite skeptical and cynical about the idea of any debt being cancelled as well as about the benefits of such a cancellation. However, whenever negative coverage of the issue appeared, Jubilee 2000 responded, and the previously challenging press mutated into advocacy.[59] In December 1999, for example, *The Economist* wrote: "debt campaigners are right that the new century ought to bring a new deal between rich and poor countries, and that the rich can afford to do more for the world's poor. Debt relief is an important way of helping them. But it is not—and cannot be—a magic wand."[60] In the same vein, in 2000 it argued that "[a]bolishing debt would help to create a fresh balance sheet, but for many countries debt-relief would only benefit Ukrainian arms-dealers."[61] However, in 2004, *The Economist* seems to have softened its position, "[w]ith backers that include Bono and the Pope, the campaign for poor-country debt relief has proved a powerful coalition. [. . .] The truth is that poor countries need more resources from the rich. If competition to sound most generous leads rich countries to put more money in the aid pot, then it is worth pursuing."[62] Unquestionably, the campaign was particularly robust in the United Kingdom. But articles and editorials filled the pages of all major newspapers throughout Europe, France, Germany, Italy, etc.[63]

In Europe, other celebrities besides Bono were involved in the debt relief cause, and they too contributed to stirring up public opinion to pressure policy makers. In May1999, Comic Relief's Debt Wish brought people's attention to the problem of the debt, with Ewan McGregor, Lenny Henry and others traveling to Africa. In June 1999, Peruvian songstress Susana Baca performed before thousands of supporters in London. In February 2000, Jubilee 2000 used the stage of San Remo, Italy's biggest music festival, to support debt cancellation. On that occasion, Italian pop star Jovanotti, opera singer Luciano Pavarotti and other artists, including Bono, delivered a fervent plea to a television audience of 17 million people, to raise awareness of the debt crisis and call on political leaders to cancel the debt. After that, then-Italian Prime Minister Massimo D'Alema promised to reconsider his government's approach and "agreed to consider doubling the number of countries eligible for cancellation of all their debts to Italy."[64] In September, the fashion magazine *Marie Claire* ran a special "drop the debt" feature over 40 pages long.

American newspapers, on the other hand, had a narrow political and economic approach to debt relief and did not focus as European newspapers did on the mobilization of people around the world to cancel the debt. *The New York Times, the Los Angeles Times* and the *Wall Street Journal* for the years 1997–2000 shared this approach. In 1997, those newspapers did not publish articles or editorials on the debt relief issue. In March 1998, the *Wall Street Journal* announced: "Africa needs debt relief, roads, environmental protection, health care, education and an end to grinding poverty and malnutrition. But these problems are surmountable. Years ago, few people thought the poverty-stricken nations of Southeast Asia could become self-sufficient. But until the recent crisis, their growth was dazzling. Likewise, once-impoverished Latin America today is growing rapidly and attracting massive investments that fuel further growth."[65] A few days later, the *Los Angeles Times* published a single article about Africa and the debt, reporting Bill Clinton's historic visit to sub-Saharan countries, which, according to the newspaper, highlighted a new U.S. partnership with Africa.[66]

In January 1999, the *Los Angeles Times* reported that Vice President Al Gore had announced that "the administration would propose new funding to relieve the debt smothering the world's developing countries."[67] In 1999, *The New York Times* published two articles on debt relief. One article announced President Bill Clinton's proposal for extensive debt forgiveness for "some [of the] poorest nations" while, at the same time, warning that Congress's approval was required. It also remarked that such an approval would be difficult to obtain because "the fund has traditionally been reluctant to endorse such programs for fear that they breed expectations among borrowing nations that if they wait long enough, they will not have to repay their loans."[68] A second article appeared in November and reported that the House had approved a compromise foreign aid bill by a vote of 316 to 100.[69] In June 1999, within the context of the restructuring of the global financial system, *The Wall Street Journal* mentioned that "religious and social-action groups, organized under the banner of 'Jubilee 2000' have given a big push to debt relief. Thousands of activists have turned up at the G-7 summit here and at last year's summit in Birmingham in Britain to urge a complete write-off of developing nations' debt by the year 2000."[70] Even so, they did not cover the grassroots movement nor did they funnel debt relief into social justice arguments. Thus, between 1997 and 1999, American newspapers seem to have been disengaged from the mass movement and from a grasp of the extent to which debt relief was an issue of social justice as it had been characterized by the European newspapers, and they simply treated the issue of debt cancellation. The issue is in truth a political-economic question, but discussing it merely on those terms would not and did not contribute to mobilizing the American public. In January 2000, the *Los Angeles Times* published another article on debt relief, which explained the critics' concerns, but it did not endorse the social duty of cancelling the debt. The article further informed readers that some had complained that "the stringent structural adjustments required by international lenders could perpetuate the paternalistic north-south dynamic that has shackled the continent throughout its modern history" and added that others had countered that "without such tough guidelines, inept African leaders will squander the money they save."[71] Once again, it was not treated as a social justice issue and, in addition, there was no discussion of "values" or moral implications, which had in fact finally pushed the policy makers in the United States to forgive the debt. Finally, in April 2000, the *Los Angeles Times* published an editorial, which reported on the debt relief movement with an angle similar to the articles that had been published in Europe. This commentary states that "debt relief for the world's poorest countries is supported by a movement known as Jubilee 2000. . . . This worldwide movement," the article continues, "was begun by Christians who believe that the 2,000th anniversary of the coming [of] Christ is a Jubilee year."[72] After explaining the meaning of the Jubilee for Christians the article encourages support for the issue by hinting at Christian values. Waters, the writer of the commentary, argues that "relief from debts is desperately needed by many poor countries throughout Africa and Latin America. Debt relief will give those countries a fresh start and improve their ability to serve their people. Supporters of Jubilee 2000 now include a diverse group of Catholic, Protestant and Jewish religious groups. These activists know that forgiving the debts of the world's most impoverished countries is the right thing to do."[73] Yet there was no major coverage of the mass mobilization in Europe, and one article is clearly not sufficient for initiating a nationwide movement or reaction.

This leads one to conclude that in the United States, debt relief was not a bottom-up issue, but rather a top-down one. Congress passed debt relief legislation because of intensive lobbying in Washington and because of the NGO's and celebrities' skillful ability to exploit the "Christian values" aspect of the issue. In addition, because Jubilee 2000 representatives in the United States had a general sense that in the United States things happen in Washington, not in the streets, they did not try to engage the American media and its public opinion on this issue.[74] U.S. newspapers did not cover mass protests in Europe, thus inhibiting the possible formation of a mass movement in the United States. In Europe, to the contrary, there was a grassroots movement that started in the U.K. and eventually engaged all of Europe. Governments in Europe responded to the mass protests. There are several examples of protests, all of which were covered by the European media. The media thus helped to propel the idea of debt relief. These differences tell us that even when the United States and Europe agree on one issue they deal with it differently. They also tell us that the United States and Europe were responsive to different stimuli at the national level, at least in the case of debt relief.

IV. CONCLUSION

While in the United States, Jubilee 2000 and its most well-known activist, Bono, appealed to Christian values through biblical language and metaphors, in Europe their approach was much more secular and detached from traditional values arguments. This approach reflects the aforementioned Inglehart's cultural map of the world about the year 2000 (see Appendix), and his corresponding argument that the United States has a much more traditional value system than any other European society except for Ireland. Within the transatlantic allies, the United States ranks far below European states, and while there is no doubt that debt relief captivated the attention on both sides of the Atlantic because of moral concerns, the NGOs' strategy indicates that there are still value differences that need to be accounted for if we want to understand where the transatlantic relations are going, as well as the meaning of the West in the post-Cold War world.

The manner in which Jubilee 2000 framed the issue highlights the value distances within the North Atlantic core countries, as laid out in Inglehart's map. This, in turn, seems to partially disprove the neoliberal argument of common values as a unifying factor within the West, while at the same time challenging the realist interest-based argument that the end of the Cold War would bring separation within transatlantic relations. Yet, both in the United States and Europe, there was a moral commitment to the issue of debt relief. The difference rests on how decision makers were motivated to make foreign policy decisions based on moral reasons. Therefore, the end result (i.e., the G7 agreement on debt relief as well as appropriations in the United States, the United Kingdom, France and Germany) leads us to conclude that the neoliberals were accurate in predicting political cooperation.

This chapter also leads to the conclusion that there are instances in which the allies operate in a cohesive fashion even when their social values diverge. This case indicates that both the United States and Europe were committed to debt relief, but it also confirms their cultural-value distance. Such cultural distance does not imply that they cannot cooperate or that they will not cooperate in the future, but we need to be aware of such differences if we are to fully understand the future of transatlantic relations. Arguing that they will cooperate because they share institutions, norms and values seems too vague of a statement if applied to a real case like the one of debt relief. At least in this case, belonging to the same institutions, the G7 along with the IMF and the World Bank, did not necessarily mean sharing norms and values. If we look more carefully at their cultural values, the United States and Europe are not so close. Therefore, having distinct social values, or at least a distinct understanding of them, may not prevent them from adopting common policies. However, such differences are also what causes them at times to behave differently, as, for example, in the case of the ICC.

Part III

Transatlantic Relations from 9/11 to Today

7 The Arab Spring
A Missed Opportunity for a Common Transatlantic Agenda

On December 17, 2010, a young Tunisian vendor, Mohamed Bouazizi, set fire to himself as a protest against the local police who had confiscated the fruit and vegetables he was selling from a street stall in Sid Bouzid. Bouazizi quickly became a martyr and a hero to his fellow citizens. His death on January 4, 2011, led to a popular uprising in Tunisia, which rapidly spread through Northern Africa and the Middle East and became known as the Arab Spring. Tunisians took to the streets to protest against rampant corruption, injustice and high unemployment. This unprecedented turmoil toppled Zine el-Abidine Ben Ali's 23-year dictatorship. On January 14, just 10 days after Bouazizi's death, Ben Ali fled to Saudi Arabia.[1] Nine months later, in October, the country held its first free elections. A clash between Islamists and secularists captured everybody's attention, especially in the West, but in the end the moderate Islamist party Ennahda, which had been banned for many years, won the election. It took 41.47 percent of the vote and 90 of 217 seats in an assembly that would create the new constitution.[2]

The upheaval in Tunisia rippled well beyond its borders, shaking other authoritarian Arab states. Egypt, Yemen, Bahrain and Libya were the first countries to be "contaminated." Galvanized by the events in Tunisia, anti-government protests began across Egypt on January 25, 2011. Thousands of demonstrators poured into the streets of Cairo and especially into Tahrir Square, and citizens in Alexandria and other cities called for Egyptian President Hosni Mubarak's resignation.[3] Mr. Mubarak, who had become president in 1981 after Anwar el-Sadat was slain, governed the country for almost three decades, but lost control of Egypt when he decided to use violence against the demonstrators. After 18 days of large-scale protests, on February 10, 2011, he resigned and turned power over to the military.[4]

While the West hoped for a political transformation that would have preserved Egypt as secular and democratic, the parliamentary elections that ended in January 2012 brought to power the Muslim Brotherhood, which believes that Sharia law should control some aspects of political and everyday life. The ultraconservative Salafis, who hold that Sharia law should be enforced in all aspects of public and private life, gained about 25% of the votes (the Muslim Brotherhood won 40%). Consequently, it is clear that almost two thirds of Egyptians want Islam to play a bigger role in politics and in everyday life. So the first presidential elections held since the ouster of President Hosni Mubarak were won by Mohamed Morsi of the Muslim Brotherhood.[5] Paradoxically, the results of Egypt's first competitive presidential elections have the potential to worsen rather than to improve relations between the West and Egypt, and the Middle East and North Africa in general.

On February 3, 2011, antigovernment protests took place in yet another Middle Eastern center, Sana'a, the capital of Yemen. On the same day, President Ali Adbullah Saleh, who had ruled for more than three decades, pledged not to seek another term in office. Nine months later, however, in November, he was forced to transfer power to his deputy, Abdrabbuh Mansour Hadi, after massive street protests calling for him to step down and after he had spent weeks in a hospital recovering from an attempt to assassinate him with a rocket attack on his palace.[6] President Saleh's resignation was furthermore largely due to the fact that he had alienated his international allies. Saudi Arabia, for example, had become increasingly impatient with Mr. Saleh's incapacity to restore order. The United Nations Security Council in October passed Resolution 2014, urging for an "orderly" process of "political transition" and gave Mr. Saleh 30 days to complete the process.[7] Finally, the Unites States, which in 2010 had given $176 million to Yemen for training and other military assistance, reduced its aid to $30 million after President Saleh authorized armed action against protesters. Most recently, in May 2012, President Obama gave the Treasury Department authority to freeze Yemeni assets in the United States. The order also targets U.S. citizens who may engage in activities to obstruct the political transition.[8] This measure is designed to keep Yemen in line with U.S. national interests: that is, to combat the rise of al-Qaeda affiliates in Yemen.

A few days after President Mubarak stepped down, on February 14, 2011, massive protests spread to Bahrain. Demonstrators gathered in the streets of Manama, the capital of Bahrain, to express dissent against the ruling monarchy and against corruption and unemployment and to demand democratic reforms. Bahrain, where a minority Sunni dynasty rules over a Shia majority, is a valued ally of the Unites States. It hosts the U.S. Fifth Fleet and is close to Saudi Arabia. So close that King Hamad Al Khalifa of Bahrain was able to crack down on the "Pearl Revolution"[9] with the military help of Saudi Arabia. On March 14, more than 100 Saudi tanks entered Bahrain in an effort to suppress the uprising.[10] After the violent repression, Bahraini authorities tried to restore their damaged image. King Hamad created a commission of inquiry to investigate the handling of the uprising. However, constitutional and institutional reforms have not been implemented, and there are regular clashes between Shia citizens and the government. Some activists describe the situation as a state of "apartheid," where Shias are fired from their jobs and substituted by Sunnis.[11]

Protests in Libya erupted at about the same time. On February 15 and 16, 2011, the arrest of Fethi Tarbel, a human rights activist who had worked to free political prisoners, started a riot in Benghazi, and on February 24, anti-government militias took control of Misrata after evicting forces loyal to the Libyan leader Muammar Gaddafi. As the rebels gained momentum, the National Transitional Council (NTC) met in Benghazi and declared itself Libya's sole representative. A few days later, on March 10, France recognized the NTC as the legitimate representative of the Libyan people. Meanwhile, in an interview with Euronews, a France-based TV channel, Gaddafi's son, Saif al-Islam, announced, "Everything will be over in 48 hours."[12]

But the next day, on March 17, the UN Security Council adopted Resolution 1973, which approved a no-fly zone over Libya and authorized member states or regional organizations to take "all necessary measures" to protect civilians in Libya.[13] Six days later, after some arguments between NATO's members about giving command of the no-fly zone to the alliance, NATO responded to the UN call by launching an operation to enforce Resolution 1973. On March 24, it began enforcing the resolution, thus banning all flights, except those for humanitarian and aid purposes, in Libyan airspace. In the following months, while NATO's air strikes intensified, diplomatic efforts increased. At the London Conference on Libya, participants agreed on the creation of a Contact Group to help the democratic transition in Libya and to provide a forum for coordinating the international response to the situation in Libya.[14] Meanwhile, on the ground, in August, rebels entered Tripoli, the capital of Libya, with little resistance. Gaddafi, who never gave in, made two audio addresses over the state television, in which he called on Libyans to fight off the rebel "rats," while at the same time letting the national and international community know that he was in Tripoli and that he would be there until the bitter end.[15] On October 20, 2011, Gaddafi became the first dictator to be killed during the Arab Spring.[16] NATO aircraft attacked a stream of vehicles, one of which was carrying Gaddafi, as it was leaving Sirte. The convoy was hit either by a French plane or a U.S. Predator drone. Gaddafi was wounded and fled to hide in a "big pipe of the sewage system."[17] Apparently, the rebels found Gaddafi and killed him with a shot to his head. But to be fair, the exact circumstances of his death are still ambiguous. A video shows that he was wounded as he was being dragged from a car and pulled to the ground by his hair. Next he is seen on the ground, with rebels still grabbing his hair; blood is pouring down his head as the crowd shouts, "God is great!"

But again, nobody so far has confirmed the events of Gaddafi's death. Libya's interim prime minister, Mahmoud Jibril, could not in fact confirm whether the rebels or his own security brigade had shot the old dictator. Rather, Mr. Jibril spoke of "crossfire." Approximately 10 days after Gaddafi's demise, on October 31, 2011, Anders Fogh Rasmussen, NATO secretary general, announced the end of NATO's military operation against Libya.[18]

While Egypt, Yemen, Bahrain and Libya were crucial for the spread of the Arab Spring, protesters called for reforms also in Morocco and in Syria. In February 2011, thousands of people rallied in Rabat, Morocco, calling for constitutional reforms that would curb the power of King Mohammed VI, and within months Morocco had a new Constitution. A few months later, in November 2011, as in Egypt and in Tunisia, the Islamist party won the parliamentary elections. In March 2011, the Arab Spring spread to Syria, where rebels tried to topple President Bashar al-Assad's regime. The Syrian government responded with a bloody crackdown, which, at the time of press, had led to the death of nearly 19,000 people. The United States and the European Union condemned the use of violence and imposed sanctions on the Syrian government. However, the violence continued, with protesters being shot. Carla del Ponte, a UN human rights investigator, urged the UN Security Council to refer Syria to the International Criminal Court.

I. A TARDY TRANSATLANTIC RESPONSE

As the Arab Spring swept across North Africa and the Middle East, Europe and the United States applauded those extraordinary events. Yet they both struggled with finding consensus on a common foreign policy, which could influence the political outcome of those revolutionary upheavals. Europeans and Americans seemed to have been taken by surprise and, even though it might have been difficult for them to determine the course of events, they appeared to be able only to observe, rather than assist. Protesters were asking for something familiar in the West: freedom, democracy, equality, human rights and the rule of law. European and American foreign policy makers, however, while rhetorically supporting the peoples' right to protest, avoided direct involvement and sidestepped criticism of Presidents Ben Ali and Hosni Mubarak. During the first 10 days of the unrest in Egypt, the leaders of France, Germany, Britain, Italy and Spain, in a joint statement, called for the political transition in Egypt to "start now," adding that they were observing the turmoil in Egypt with the "utmost concern" and denounced "all those who use or encourage violence," which, they reasoned, would "only aggravate the political crisis in Egypt."[19] Likewise, on February 18, 2011, in his address to the group of 20 finance ministers at a meeting in Paris, the president of France, Nicolas Sarkozy, said: "In the shorter term, France will ask you to be ready to join forces to accompany our Tunisian and Egyptian friends on the road to democracy, in making economic and social progress."[20] Similarly, German Foreign Minister Guido Westerwelle called on Egypt to persist on its path toward democracy and, in his second visit to Cairo since the uprisings, said, "Egypt, as the key country, will determine if the Arab spring turns into summer or back into winter."[21] Approval of the masses taking to the streets also came from the other side of the pond: U.S. Secretary of State Hillary Rodham Clinton, in an interview with the *New York Times*, said, "We're facing an Arab awakening that nobody could have imagined and few predicted just a few years ago," adding that it was "sweeping aside a lot of the old preconceptions."[22] She was referring, evidently, to the well-known stereotype that portrays Arabs as not fit for democracy. Then again in Europe, the prime minister of Spain, José Luis Rodríguez Zapatero, at his party convention in Zaragoza, said that he wished for a "pacific transition." He stated moreover: "we want for them what we want for ourselves: democratic reforms, freedom, progress and social justice."[23]

Two additional examples of the Western attitude of great support with no straight commitment come from the UK and Italy. While leaving for a visit to Tunisia, the British foreign minister, William Hague, tweeted that the he was "heading to Tunisia to meet the new interim government and show UK support for the people of Tunisia and their democratic hopes." Questioned about the British position on Egypt, a Foreign Office spokesman later clarified: "It's the wrong time to go to Egypt, given the talks between the government and opposition parties and the importance of not interfering."[24] One last illustration comes from Rome, where Italian Foreign Minister Franco Frattini, who undoubtedly epitomized the hesitant majority position in the West when he argued that a swift change of government in Egypt would lead to chaos in North Africa and in the Middle East, where President Hosni Mubarak had played a key stabilizing role. He added: "Mubarak has to keep governing with wisdom and insight, as he always did." President Mubarak, Frattini said, is "a point of reference for the peace process that cannot be removed."[25] Speaking to the foreign press, Frattini also clarified how the situation in Tunisia and Egypt were "deeply" different. He said, in Egypt: "there are civil liberties. It is not a copy of the European model but we are not colonizers of any country, we must not impose our model."[26] Remarkably, Frattini voiced the predominant sentiment in Europe, that of not interfering in the political transformation of the Middle East and North Africa. In effect, after the ousting of President Mubarak, the French foreign minister, Alain Juppé, made the same argument in Cairo, saying, "Egypt has a long political tradition [. . .] and is resuming that role today [. . .] it's up to Egyptians alone to define the shape of the democratic regime they want."[27] He added, "I am here simply to tell them we will accompany them on this difficult path. The world trusts them to complete the journey towards democracy."[28] Similarly, U.S. President Barack Obama in his remarks on the Middle East and North Africa said, "It's not America that put people into the streets of Tunis or Cairo—it was the people themselves who launched these movements, and it's the people themselves that must ultimately determine their outcome."[29] Hence, it is evident that there was no transatlantic consensus on either a concrete plan or a strategy to deal with the Arab revolution. Politicians looked stranded and had difficulties in coming to terms with the new international political scene. The European Union's foreign policy vice president Catherine Ashton said that a clear mandate was hard to achieve because of Mr. Berlusconi's "saying Mubarak is great, France saying you can't talk of free and fair elections now, and others saying you can't tell Egyptians what to do."[30] As Ms. Ashton said in an interview with the German magazine *Der Spiegel*, "Europe isn't as fast and flexible as you would like it to be;"[31] and indeed the EU's delayed response may have been caused by the number of consultations required among all 27 member states. Furthermore, Europeans seemed to "bide their time." In effect, Ms. Ashton admitted, "Europe will not always be the first to react, but it is better to take your time and be right than first and wrong."[32] The timid reaction was undoubtedly made more timid by multiple overlapping dynamics. For example, all the countries involved had special agreements and relationships with the old ruling elites. Nonetheless, what has curbed European enthusiasm with the antigovernment uprisings is the fear of a growing influx of Arab immigrants seeking refuge in a continent in which far-right parties are consistently gaining electoral success.

Indeed, one of the first problems that Europe had to face during the turmoil of the Arab Spring was the immigration stream from the Middle East and North Africa. Europe is not new to this phenomenon and has been dealing with illegal immigration for a long time. To this extent, the Lisbon Treaty compels the EU to adhere to the "development of a special relationship with neighboring countries aiming to establish an area of prosperity and good neighborliness, founded on the values of the Union and characterized by close and peaceful relations based on cooperation."[33] Accordingly, in 2004, the European Union developed the European Neighborhood Policy (ENP) with the goal of avoiding "the emergence of new dividing lines between the enlarged EU and our neighbors and instead strengthening the prosperity, stability and security of all."[34] Despite those political efforts, however, Europeans, like Americans, tend to perceive immigration as a problem and not as an opportunity. This is what comes out of the 2011 Transatlantic Trend, a project of the German Marshall Fund.[35] When the citizens of France, Germany, Italy, Spain, the United Kingdom and the United States were asked about immigration, 52% of the Europeans and 53% of the U.S. citizens identified immigration as a problem. Only in Germany did a slightly higher percentage of respondents (50%) perceive immigration as more of an opportunity than a problem.[36]

Therefore, while being supported rhetorically, the Arab Spring gave way to fear and doubt in Europe. Being afraid of an increasing flood of Arab migration, some European leaders spoke out against refugees seeking asylum and attempted to temporarily change the Schengen policy. France and Italy, for instance, tried to reinstate internal border controls. On April 27, 2011, an Italian-French summit in Rome called for Schengen's rules to be reviewed, so that national governments could effortlessly reinforce border controls "in case of exceptional difficulties."[37] This concerted Franco-Italian initiative came just a few weeks after Rome and Paris had traded insults over the arrival of 20,000 Tunisian migrants in the Italian island of

Lampedusa.[38] Italy wanted other European Union countries to take some of the immigrants. Italian Interior Minister Roberto Maroni told reporters that Italy was facing a "catastrophic humanitarian emergency" and could not be "left alone." Mr. Maroni received some support from Spain, but other EU states did not want to provide any support. German Interior Minister Thomas de Maizière said that Italy was "strained, but not overstrained."[39] Thus, when EU members refused to "share the burden," Italy issued temporary residence permits to the migrants and gave them free train tickets to the French border.[40] France reacted by rounding up many migrants and sending them back to Italy.[41] In effect, once at the border, the Tunisians could move freely anywhere in the EU. This led many countries to protest against Italy's actions, including the Germans and the Austrians.[42] The Belgians accused Italy of "cheating" on the Schengen policy, and the French did temporarily close some of France's borders with Italy.[43] In the end, however, since the Italian prime minister, Mr. Berlusconi, and the French president, Mr. Sarkozy, both had to deal internally with their uncompromising far-right constituencies, they reconciled their differences and appealed to the European Union for a viable solution. They sent a joint letter to the European Union president, Mr. José Manuel Barroso, and the European Council president, Mr. Herman Van Rompuy, urging new rules and a new system to deal with what they called an "emergency."[44] But even though the EU assured its member states that it was already working on new proposals to make changes to the current system, it nonetheless refused to accept that the arrival of 20,000 Tunisian migrants represented an emergency. According to the present rules, to do so would mean the possibility of a suspension of the border-free zone.

While Europe was dealing with immigration issues, the United States was facing its own domestic problems. At the beginning of January 2011, a Congress hostile to the administration was sworn in, promising a fierce challenge to President Barack Obama.[45] With the House of Representatives firmly in the hands of Republicans, the administration delayed its reaction to the events in the Middle East. Besides, at least in foreign policy, in the previous eight months the administration's attention had been drawn to new promising clues that eventually led to a breakthrough in Osama bin Laden's location. In effect, it was on May 1, 2011, after years of fruitless searching, that bin Laden was killed in a helicopter assault by American military and intelligence operatives, thus concluding one of the longest and most frustrating manhunts in American history.[46] Nonetheless, given the U.S. military presence both in Afghanistan and in Iraq, as well as a rampant economic crisis at home, Republicans, who incidentally had initiated such conflicts, would certainly have denied their consent to wage war, even in the defense of civilians being injured or slaughtered by ruthless dictators. Indeed, this is what happened in March, when President Obama notified Congress that the United States would begin military attacks on Libya, to assist in an international effort authorized by the United Nations Security Council. Congress immediately complained that the U.S. president was waging war without congressional consent.[47]

Hence, given its domestic political gridlock, the United States did not have a concrete policy to stabilize the Arab world, but as was the case with the Europeans, it welcomed changes and promised support, or, more precisely, economic support. In May, in his remarks on the Middle East and North Africa, President Obama said, the United States "support[s] political and economic reform," adding, "our message is simple: If you take the risks that reform entails, you will have the full support of the United States."[48] But there were no concrete actions to promote political reforms or to support a transition to democracy. Countries that are new to democracy need help building political and social institutions. They need support to run free and fair elections. They need help writing constitutions that ensure freedom of speech, freedom of assembly, freedom of religion, equality for men and women. Many argued that the Arab Spring was reminiscent of 1989, when Germany crumbled, taking down the Iron Curtain. The similarity is rather striking, and in effect, then too politicians could not keep up with events. Nonetheless, in the 1990s, they initiated efforts to assist the political transition of Eastern Europe. However, in the aftermath of the Arab uprisings, America's support for democracy was essentially concentrated on advancing economic development. "Drawing from what we've learned around the world," President Obama stated, "we think it's important to focus on trade, not just aid; on investment, not just assistance [. . .] America's support for democracy will therefore be based on ensuring financial stability, promoting reform, and integrating competitive markets with each other and the global economy. And we're going to start with Tunisia and Egypt."[49]

The "economic transition" that the administration envisaged was to be managed similarly to the one implemented in Eastern Europe about 20 years earlier. But economic recovery also needs political stability, and in times of turmoil it helps if the state can manage the economy. Yet this was hardly given consideration. In Egypt, where factories were closed, financial markets shut, and tourist trips were canceled, for policy makers and pundits the solution lay with the World Bank, the International Monetary Fund and the European Bank for Reconstruction and Development (EBRD). The concomitant work of these institutions with policies that would facilitate more trade within the Arab region, as well as the promotion of integration with U.S. and European markets, would, according to President Obama, "create a powerful force for reform in the Middle East and North Africa."[50] Thus, the support for the "legitimate aspirations of ordinary people"[51] was essentially understood as economic aid. In effect, in May 2011, at the G-8 Summit of Deauville, representatives of the wealthiest industrialized countries pledged to send billions of dollars in aid to Egypt and Tunisia, hoping to reduce the threat that economic stagnation could have on the transition to democracy.[52] In a communiqué, the group said that, in the short term, its goal was "to ensure that instability does not undermine the process of political reform."[53]

The exact amount these countries will actually provide is still uncertain, given the economic meltdown of Western economies. The group pledged to work closely with multilateral development banks such as the World Bank, the African Development Bank, the European Investment Bank/FEMIP, the EBRD and the Islamic Development Bank.[54] The group also called upon the International Monetary Fund to ensure that investments were suitable and within microeconomic frameworks. The G-8 countries also promised $20 billion to help stabilize the economies of the two countries that initiated the Arab Spring, Tunisia and Egypt. French President Nicolas Sarkozy later said that the amount could be doubled. He pledged that G-8 members would offer a further $10 billion as bilateral aid; and, in addition, Saudi Arabia, Qatar and Kuwait would give another $10 billon.[55]

Thus, the West dealt with its fear that the quest for democracy in the Arab world could be "hijacked" by Islamic radicals mainly through economic operations. In the end, for Europeans, prosperity in the Mediterranean would create new economic possibilities and as a consequence, stop further unwelcome migration streams.[56] The Americans, for their part, would finally see stability in the region, something Washington had been working on for quite some time.

One should not, however, be impressed with the G-8 members' pledges because in the past the group has made commitments that they did not ultimately fulfill. Besides, according to some experts, the assistance offered to the Arab countries in transition has been "both the wrong sort of help (stressing aid, not trade) and of entirely the wrong scale."[57] Furthermore, pundits argue, the Euro-American assistance plan does not happen to be a comprehensive and coordinated strategy capable of responding effectively to the economic challenges of the region.[58] Since the main problem is the absence of a dynamic private sector, what the region really needs, they reason, are trade agreements that can invigorate such a sector.[59]

II. CONCLUSION

The Arab Spring case clearly indicates that the United States and Europe did not find consensus on a common foreign policy for the popular revolt. The evidence presented indicates that it was a matter of divergent conceptualizations of security. Essentially, the Europeans defined their interests in the region as security from "immigration threats" and the United States as security from a "political/military threat." This is not to say that the Europeans did not rhetorically welcome the possibility of democratization. They did indeed welcome it. But the question is more nuanced and in fact has to do with how the transatlantic partners understood the Arab Spring, their resulting practice (what they did or did not do with regard to the uprisings) and how this behavior redefined European interests vis-à-vis American interests.

The international context has been evolving. The Arab Spring has changed the political context of the Middle East and North Africa. For reasons already discussed, the Europeans did not condemn the dictators but called for a political transition, as did the United States. But it was the fear of migration flows due to the regional unrest that determined Europe's behavior. In essence, the influx of Arab immigrants defined European interests. Thus, as constructivism claims, interests are not fixed or innate, and the behavior of states does not depend necessarily on the distribution of power and geography. It can in effect depend on nonmaterial causes like immigration. The European countries' preoccupation with losing their identity because of the penetration of the Islamic cultural tradition, coupled with the rise of neo-Nazi groups, prompted besieged European policy makers to rethink their interests. The Europeans, accordingly, conceptualized their interests in the region as a matter of what can be called "societal" security. As Barry Buzan argued, it can be difficult to disentangle "societal" threats from political ones because external threats can be constructed as attacks on national identity, and thus could fall within the political realm.[60] Language, religion, and cultural tradition are all elements of the idea of the state, and could need shielding from cultural imports. Therefore, for Europeans, immigration during the Arab Spring constituted a threat to their perception of the state's "Self." Migrants thus constituted a societal threat, which could endanger the very identity of European countries, and so they sought security from unwanted migrant floods. It follows that as the international context (i.e., the Arab uprisings) determined European interests, these interests, in turn, defined their identity, which drove practice or lack thereof: that is, the reluctance to intervene. Perhaps Europeans hoped that the old elites would handle the revolutions themselves and prevent the mass migrations.

A second point is important and needs to be emphasized: that is, social meanings and the redefinition of practices. The United States understood the Arab world-changing context as a matter of democratization and stability of the region. Mostly, it was conceptualized as an issue of political/military security. The United States was preoccupied that the democratic handover would lead to Islamic governments, which could generate military threats. Constructivist theory suggests that the social structures of the international system form the identity and interests of individual states. In the instance of the revolutions in the Arab world, the changing political context generated certain American interests in the region, which the United States did not have earlier: that is, the advancement of economic development. American interests in economic aid underline the relevance of social meanings in determining a state's actions. Interests, identities and practices, as constructivists argue, are socially constructed. U.S.-European relations are to be understood through this lens, or it would be impossible to make sense of transatlantic controversies and acquiescence.

This case indicates that the social meanings of the uprising were different across the Atlantic. The lack of a shared understanding of the changing international context and its challenges created a stalemate in a common transatlantic policy. Granted, there is no clear divergence of behavior, but this case shows that Americans and Europeans are having problems engaging with each other. Furthermore, and most significantly, it indicates that the reasons for difficulties in transatlantic relations are due to the changing international context, a context that influences and redefines states' understanding of what constitutes a security threat, which in turn hinders transatlantic common policy.

This case also supports another claim that I make in this book: that is, if the collective "self" shrinks, so does the willingness to work together toward collective security. The Arab Spring case indicates that identity does underpin interests, but interests simultaneously reshape identity. In the case of a shared identity, as in the case of the Western identity, different interests can alter it: the collective identity can be weakened. This would explain why the United States and Europe did not invest in collective security. Different conceptualizations of external threats led to different conceptualizations of what to protect and thus to different practices. In essence, it led to different interests, which led to different behaviors. This explains why the United States and Europe could not find consensus on a common foreign policy.

8 Libya
What to Do? Finding National Solutions to International Problems

I. INTRODUCTION

Given the long history of transatlantic relations and given their shared values (i.e., democracy and capitalism), one would have expected that at a pivotal moment like the uprising in Libya, Europe and the United States would have found agreement, maybe even unity, on how to deal with the crisis. But this was hardly the case. The showdown that took place between February and October 2011 demonstrates serious problems in transatlantic relations. The United States and Europe encountered great difficulties in finding a common position on Libya and, by so doing, set in motion a redefinition of their relations. Post-Cold War transatlantic relations cannot be easily fixed because they are the consequence of a broad structural change (i.e., the end of the Cold War), which has led to an all-encompassing change in the normative structure, in the identity and the practices of the transatlantic allies.

II. THE LIBYAN CRISIS

Following the Libyan uprising in Benghazi, on February 17, 2011, the UN Security Council passed two resolutions: UNSC Res. 1970 (February 17, 2011) and UNSC Res. 1973 (March 17, 2011). Resolution 1970 established an arms embargo, froze the personal assets of Colonel Muammar el-Qaddafi and imposed a travel ban on relevant regime figures. Resolution 1973 authorized member states or regional organizations to take "all necessary measures" to protect civilians in Libya and, to that extent, established a no-fly zone to prevent air attacks on civilians and civilian-populated areas. Resolution 1973 was adopted by a vote of 10 in favor to none against, with 5 abstentions (Brazil, China, Germany, India, Russian Federation). China and the Russian Federation argued that they would have preferred peaceful means for resolving the conflict. Germany, like the other countries, which abstained, emphasized the need for peaceful resolution of the conflict and warned against the unintended consequences of armed intervention.[1]

Here then is the first rift over Libya. France and Britain led the UN effort to pass a resolution that would enforce a no-fly zone as well as the use of "all necessary measures" to protect civilians. Germany strongly opposed the resolution, and the United States, after an initial timid response, decided to get involved in the military intervention. The fact that Colonel Qaddafi was killing his own people and threatening to eliminate many more seems to have convinced many members of the UN Security Council to vote for Resolution 1973.[2] However, Colonel Qaddafi's erratic and authoritarian rule did not help to speed up the decision to give command of the "no-fly" operation to NATO. Only on March 24, the sixth day of air and missile strikes, did the allies reach an agreement. This, however, happened after days of public quarreling that really exposed the divisions among the alliance's members. From the beginning, President Obama declared that the role of the U.S. military was to be limited, both "in time and scope," said Secretary of State Hillary Rodham Clinton in announcing the plan.[3] The Obama administration did not want to be entangled in another Afghanistan/Iraq type of war. Therefore, it was essential that the U.S. role should be limited. The question is why? Was it because of the unpopularity of those wars in the United States? Was it their high costs in a prolonged economic crisis? Maybe the Obama administration is less interested in transatlantic relations. It is possible that President Obama thought that the United States was militarily strained, and therefore it was not wise to get involved in another war. However, most likely, he thought and hoped, that the time had come for the Europeans to take the lead in NATO operations. But then, what does this imply for the future of NATO? By deciding not to lead NATO's operations in Libya, the Obama administration marked a major change in transatlantic relations. That is, it has made the decision that the Europeans could engage in NATO military operations without the United States. That decision represents a shift in the normative structure, or context, within which the United States and Europe used to operate. This new action/practice is the product of the emergence of new security and economic discourses, and it is transforming the relationship between the United States and Europe. Under the previous normative context, it was impossible for Europe to engage in NATO's military operations on its own. Under the new developing structure, it becomes conceivable.

The other issue, which strained the transatlantic relationship at the end of March 2011, was the conflicting strategic division over how exactly the coalition would bring the operations to an end. Tim Friend, Al Jazeera's correspondent in London, venting a collective feeling, inquired, "The question is how far do you go? If Qaddafi's forces are fighting back, do you then step up the response, and if so, how far do you take it?"[4] On this point there was a lot of ambiguity. "We didn't want to get sucked into an operation with uncertainty at the end," a senior Obama administration official said. "In some ways, how it turns out is not on our shoulders," he added.[5] However, in London, Mrs. Clinton as well as other Western leaders confirmed that the

NATO-led operation would end only with the removal of Colonel Qaddafi, even though that was not specified in the United Nations resolution.[6]

Nonetheless, to overcome a somehow still ambiguous approach and to address an even more pressing issue, whether to arm the rebels, a Libya Contact Group was established, following a conference with representatives of more than 40 countries (plus those of the UN and NATO). The conference was chaired by the British Foreign Minister Mr. William Hague. The conference discussed the situation in Libya and established the implementation of UN Security Council Resolutions 1970 and 1973. It considered the humanitarian needs of the Libyan people and identified ways to support the people of Libya in their aspirations for a better future.[7] The statement issued claimed that the group would "provide leadership and overall political direction to the international effort, in close co-ordination with the UN, AU (African Union), Arab League, OIC (Organisation of the Islamic Conference) and EU (European Union) to support Libya."[8] According to Aljazeera, the group did not discuss arming the rebels, but France had already begun talks to this extent. Mr. Alain Juppé, the French foreign minister, declared: "I remind you it is not part of the UN resolution, which France sticks to, but we are ready to discuss it with our partners."[9] Likewise, the Obama administration was engaged in an intense debate over whether to supply weapons to the rebels in Libya. Some officials expressed fear that providing arms would deepen America's involvement in the Libyan civil war, and they feared that some fighters might have had links to Al Qaeda.[10]

Maybe the most indicative expression of this quarrelsome debate was President Obama's answer to NBC News. He said, "I'm not ruling it out. But I'm also not ruling it in."[11] Meanwhile, although Secretary of State Hillary Rodham Clinton made it clear that the administration had not yet decided whether to actually transfer arms, she said that the United States had a right to do so, despite an arms embargo on Libya, because of the United Nations Security Council's broad resolution authorizing military action to protect civilians."[12] France had been at the forefront of arming the rebels. A European diplomat said France was adamant that the rebels be more heavily armed and was in discussions with the Obama administration about how France would bring this about. "We strongly believe that it should happen," said the diplomat, who spoke on the condition of anonymity.[13]

Also within NATO the difficulties are quite evident. NATO, however, gives the appearance of harmony within the organization on its website. On April 14, 2011, for example, it posted that "NATO Allies and the six operational partners contributing to Operation UNIFIED PROTECTOR[14] demonstrated the strongest unity of purpose and determination in implementing fully their obligations as mandated by the United Nations Security Council Resolutions 1970 and 1973."[15] However, according to the English paper *Telegraph*, at the NATO meeting of foreign ministers in Berlin (April 14–15, 2011) Italy, Spain and the Netherlands refused to allow their combat planes to take part in ground strikes, while besieged Libyan rebels pleaded for an intensification of military operations. The United States, Canada, UK, France, Norway and Italy were carrying out air strikes over Libya.[16] On the same day, Reuters reported that U.S. officials, speaking on the condition of anonymity, dismissed French and British complaints about the pace of air strikes. (Matt and Brunnstrom 2011). Spain, on the other hand, said that it had no plan to join the 7 of the 28 NATO states that had been involved in ground strikes.[17] Italy, the former colonial power in Libya, claimed that it would need to hear convincing arguments for it to do so. The French Foreign Minister Mr. Alain Juppé, after talks with Mrs. Clinton in Berlin, said that the United States was not going to review its military position on Libya despite a request from Paris. A senior U.S. official said that NATO had made no direct request to the United States to provide more aircraft. "We have said all along that we want other allies to step up. We are certainly doing our fair share," the official explained.[18] But after the meeting, Secretary General of NATO Mr. Andre Fogh Rasmussen let it be known that NATO's supreme commander, U.S. Admiral James Stavridis, had asked for "a few more precision ground attack aircraft."[19] France tried to pressure the United States as much as it could. For example, French Defense Minister Mr. Gerard Longuet declared that Qaddafi's attacks could not be stopped without U.S. participation in strikes on his tanks and artillery.[20] It was not just the United States, but also the Europeans who struggled with what to do and it was again France, which pushed for action. When a NATO official claimed that the alliance was short of about 10 aircraft to conduct air strikes, a French official named Italy, Spain, the Netherlands and Sweden as countries that could do more to assist operations. But they were hesitant and even Denmark, which was actively carrying out air strikes, decided that it would not be involved in arming the rebels because such an action was not prescribed by Resolution 1973. The Danish Foreign Minister Ms. Lene Espersen said that the Danish parliament had interpreted Resolution 1973 in this way "but," she added, "if anyone else wants to interpret the U.N. resolution in any other way, that's their decision."[21]

While the situation was still confused on whether to arm the rebels Mr. Sarkozy, Mr. Cameron and President Obama crafted a joint letter in which the three leaders committed their countries to pursue military action until Colonel Qaddafi was removed. President Obama seemed to be reengaged. But according to the British newspaper *The Guardian*, the letter was first drafted by Mr. Cameron and Mr. Sarkozy and then sent to Washington, where President Obama made a few changes to the original text.[22] The letter, published simultaneously in the *New York Times*, the *Times* and *Le Figaro*, on April 14, called for the resignation of Colonel Qaddafi but stressed that he would not be removed by force. The letter also contained the vision for the future for Libya of the three leaders: Mr. Cameron, Mr. Sarkozy, and President Obama:

Our duty and our mandate under U.N. Security Council Resolution 1973 is to protect civilians, and we are doing that. It is not to remove Qaddafi by force. But it is impossible to imagine a future for Libya with Qaddafi in power. The International Criminal Court is rightly investigating the crimes committed against civilians and the grievous violations of international law. It is unthinkable that someone who has tried to massacre his own people can play a part in their future government. The brave citizens of those towns that have held out against forces that have been mercilessly targeting them would face a fearful vengeance if the world accepted such an arrangement. It would be an unconscionable betrayal.[23]

At this point, Germany, after abstaining from voting on Resolution 1973, attempted to reengage in the political dynamics of Libya and promised to commit forces for a humanitarian mission. When, later in June, Chancellor Angela Merkel visited the United States to receive the Medal of Freedom, both Mr. Obama and Ms. Merkel showed that they had good intentions. Ms. Merkel claimed, "Germany is showing, will be showing, that it is responsible and committed to the Libyan cause." Mr. Obama talked about "full and robust German support," albeit Berlin's abstention on UN Security Council Resolution 1973, which authorized the use of military force in Libya. The U.S. president spoke of Germany's involvement once the military operation would be over. "There's going to be a lot of work to do when Gadhafi does step down," Mr. Obama said.[24] This new attitude, however, was met with reluctance in the UK and France. Also, Mr. Rasmussen seemed to be more in favor of a European Union humanitarian effort.[25] Why was there so much indecision among the transatlantic allies on arming the rebels? One possible explanation could be the fear in many NATO countries that the Libyan rebels would commit war crimes.[26] A second possibility could be that the weapons given to them would be sold on the black market and bought by terrorists.[27] A third explanation could be the Western powers' lack of confidence in the Interim National Council. Most Western powers did not seem to have any confidence in the INC's capacity to control the mass uprising and did not trust its stated intention to establish a democratically elected Libyan government.[28]

At the beginning of May 2011, the UK decided to intensify the military action against Libya, a decision based on the ministers' perception that the conflict could have dragged on for several months (Norton-Taylor 2011).[29] But Libya also needed financial aid and thus, on May 5 in Rome, the Contact Group decided to give financial assistance to the rebels. The Transitional National Council had asked for $2 to $3 billion for military salaries, food, medicine and other basic supplies. But the British Foreign Secretary William Hague insisted that the funds should not be spent on weapons. At this point the UK had already given $21.5 million to the rebels, and the United States was trying to free about $30 billion in frozen Libyan assets.[30]

Meanwhile, in the United States, there was a searing debate on the United States' participation in the Libyan mission. Republicans were attacking Barack Obama's decision to take military action in Libya. They claimed that he had made the decision without the formal approval of Congress. Republican leaders were worried about the costly foreign military operations. The Republican leader of the House of Representatives, John Boehner, wrote to Mr. Obama claiming that, under the 1973 War Powers Act, the president was obliged to get congressional approval for the Libyan mission.[31] Despite the highly poisoned political debate and perhaps with the hope of winning Republican consensus, on May 18, Philip H. Gordon, assistant secretary in the Bureau of European and Eurasian Affairs, portrayed transatlantic relations as harmonious and collegial in his statement before the Subcommittee on European Affairs of the Senate Foreign Relations Committee. He argued that in Libya, the United States and its European allies had consulted and cooperated closely in order to pass UNSCRs 1970 and 1973. He carefully avoided explaining how the command of the operation was transferred to NATO, nor did he mention any friction between the United States and some European allies on this point. He merely said that "NATO took over" enforcement of UNSCR 1973 on March 31. He then highlighted the fact that NATO's Operation Unified Protector had over 7,000 personnel, over 200 aircraft and 20 ships. Mr. Gordon also emphasized that NATO's operation (over 6,000 sorties, almost half of them strike sorties) had been "primarily a European operation" since over 60% of the aircraft were European.[32] His highlighting of the role of Europe, however, emphasizes a change in the security discourse vis-à-vis the transatlantic relationship. The Obama administration needed to defend its political stand on Libya, but at the same time it also had to stress its limited role, because neither the Republicans nor the Democrats seemed to share security concerns with Europe any longer. The assumption was, and still is, that Europe is united, free and at peace and perfectly capable of handling security threats on its own. Somebody may suggest that, perhaps, it is possibly time for the allies "to see other people," as the Americans say. Nonetheless, it is true that, on May 22, Catherine Ashton, the European Union high representative for foreign and security policy, arriving in Benghazi to inaugurate a Representation Office of the EU, met with the president of the National Transition Council, Mustafa Abdul Jalil, and announced that the new EU office would offer help to the rebels opposing Muammar Qaddafi and to Libyan civil society in general. She spoke of efforts to sustain security, health and education.[33] Later in June, at the Abu Dhabi Contact Group meeting, the international community officially recognized the Transitional National Council as the legitimate representative of the Libyan people. In addition, the contact group promised a financial contribution that would cover, at least, two months of salaries and the basic needs of the population. Before the meeting, the Temporary Financial Mechanism (TFM) was established to be immediately operative.[34] The Italian Minister of Foreign Affairs Mr. Franco Frattini announced that Italy would give 400 million euros to the Libyan rebels and specified that 150 million would be in refined oil and the rest cash. Meanwhile, the Spanish Foreign Minister Ms. Trinidad Jiménez argued that political pressure was the best instrument that the contact group could use to oust Qaddafi and called for an intensification of contacts and negotiations with the Libyan dictator in order to persuade him to leave.[35] However, France did not seem to regard diplomacy as a possible tool and, in July, started to air drop arms to rebels in the Misurata and the Nafusah Mountains. At this point France was the first NATO country to openly acknowledge arming the insurgency. Russia accused France of violating Resolution 1973, but France replied that arming the rebels did not violate the embargo because the weapons were intended to protect civilians from attack. This, according to France, was allowed under the clause "all necessary measures" to be taken to protect civilians contained in Resolution 1973. The United States agreed with France, and a State Department spokesman, Mark Toner, said that the two resolutions, "read together, neither specified nor precluded providing defense materiel to the Libyan opposition."[36] At the Istanbul meeting, on July 15, the United States announced its diplomatic recognition of the National Transitional Council (NTC) as the legitimate governing authority in Libya. Incidentally, this also meant that the United States would be able to fund the rebels with "some of the more than $30 billion in Gahdafi-regime assets that are frozen in American banks."[37] Shortly afterward, on July 27, Mr. William Hague, the British foreign minister, announced that the UK would recognize the NTC as the legitimate government in Libya. He argued that the British decision was the result of both the NTC commitment to a "more open and democratic Libya [. . .] in stark contrast to Qaddafi, whose brutality against the Libyan people has stripped him of all legitimacy" and the contact group's agreement at the Istanbul meeting to treat the NTC as the legitimate government. He then demanded that all Qaddafi regime diplomats leave the UK. He said, "We no longer recognise them as the representatives of the Libyan government and we are inviting the National Transitional Council to appoint a new Libyan diplomatic envoy to take over the Libyan embassy in London."[38] Once the Western powers had recognized the NTC, they called for another meeting on September 1, the "Friends of Libya Conference." Present at the meeting were present countries and/or international organizations with around 60 high-level representatives and foreign personalities. Mr. Sarkozy and Mr. Cameron, who cochaired the meeting, said that the conference had the goal of signaling their continued action and mobilization within a totally different context. They also reaffirmed that it was the responsibility of the Libyans to decide about their future. In addition, the French and the British leaders reaffirmed their commitment to "the new Libya," to supporting the reconstruction of the country and to helping the Libyans in their democratic process (French Ministry of Foreign Affairs 2011).[39] At the "Friends of Libya Conference," rebel leaders reassured the Italian and French oil and gas companies that they would honor existing agreements. As for future energy deals, they also claimed that they would favor the countries that helped in ousting Colonel Qaddafi. In essence, they promised oil and gas contracts to Britain, France and the United States, rather than Russia, China and Germany. France's Foreign Minister Alain Juppé said that the rebel position was "fair and logical" and welcomed investment opportunities. But he also stressed the political importance of the new Libya. Mr. Juppé told RTL radio that although "this operation in Libya costs a lot, it's also an investment in the future because a democratic Libya is a country that will develop, offering stability, security and development in the region."[40] It is worth noticing that President Sarkozy stressed that "for the first time since 1949 NATO was put at the service of a coalition led by two determined European countries, France and Great Britain." He said that Europe must focus more on its military abilities, adding, "President Obama has presented a new vision of U.S. military engagement that implies that the Europeans must assume more of their responsibilities. . . . If we don't draw the necessary conclusions, Europe will wake up to a difficult reality."[41]

III. CONCLUSIONS

The Libya case suggests at the minimum two important theoretical conclusions. First, it shows the weakening of the identity of the West. The military intervention in Libya was not undertaken to defend the West, but rather, at least in the transatlantic political discourse, to defend Libyan civilians from Qaddafi's arms. If the assumption is that states seek to survive, such interest presupposes an identity to be preserved. But what identity were they trying to preserve in this case? The Libyan case suggests that the United States now considers Europe as a strong and equal partner; it is no longer a feeble ally. To the contrary, it has the political and military capabilities to handle an international crisis. Likewise, the French and British leadership are redefining European interests, and thus the identity of the West is fading and, slowly but surely, dying out. Secondly, still theoretically speaking, the Libya case shows that the ever-changing international context influences the actions and identities of individual states. This, in turn, transforms actions and thus the context. The end of the Cold War has dramatically changed the international structure and, as a consequence, the transatlantic relationship. Many scholars have addressed the immediate concerns of the post-Cold War world, but they have left out how the Western identity, painstakingly constructed through NATO, has been transformed and how it has redefined European and U.S. interests. While this is not the place to address such a complex question, it is appropriate to observe that a weakened Western/NATO identity has allowed France and the UK to lead the operations in Libya with a reduced role for the United States. The United States played a significant role in the initial phase of the intervention, but then it pulled back, leaving the military campaign de facto to the Europeans. These kinds of actions transform the context because they redefine interests. Such interests will no longer be expressed in terms of the interests of the West, but rather in terms of national interests. What states will attempt to preserve is a national "self," not a Western "self." Transatlantic relations are reverting to a national approach, rather than a Western one, and this will result in more national solutions to international and transatlantic problems.

The Libya case also suggests a few policy implications for transatlantic relations. First of all, it is clear that Europe can go-it alone under a strong political leadership, and this is a remarkable consequence of the intervention in Libya. After years of dependence, Europe has grown up and has shown itself and to the world that it is capable of taking care of itself. Europe can and should take more responsibility when it comes to security. There is no reason to doubt that it is perfectly capable of leading another military operation should a need occur. Second, European-led military operations in Libya showed that Europe is not a peaceful Kantian establishment. It can resort to war, when deemed necessary, and it can even win popular support for war. In fact, the people supported military action to protect civilians in Libya. Third, Libya was a success that emphasized the importance of strong national leadership. President Sarkozy of France and Prime Minister Cameron of the United Kingdom played a pivotal role in the success of this operation, and this will likely result in more operations involving "coalitions of the willing." Strictly related to the third point is the fourth. The operation in Libya seems to suggest that NATO's role will be reduced, both as a result of the more active roles of nation-states in dealing with international crises and as a result of the colossal economic crisis that is permeating transatlantic economies. Indeed, the reduced role of the United States in Libya had a significant economic motivation. Furthermore, a decrease in defense spending seems to be the new plan in Washington, and this will inevitably affect NATO's ability to sustain operations. The Pentagon plans cutbacks of at least $450 billion for the next 10 years, and NATO currently needs to resupply armaments and equipment that were used in Afghanistan and Libya. In addition, as the United States is cutting back, so are the Europeans. A fifth point: should the Europeans, even in time of fiscal austerity, choose to invest more in their defense budget, they could strengthen NATO's readiness to intervene, and they could become equal partners in the alliance. They would possibly reengage the United States in multilateral operations, thus preventing the United States from going-it alone.

9   Foreign Assistance for Africa
Europe's Defense of Its Programs. A Vital Element of Identity and National Security

In this chapter I will analyze how the global financial crisis is affecting both Europe's foreign assistance capabilities and its ability to defend itself. On a global scale, the largest international aid donors are the European Union and its member states. European soft-power and leadership are the consequences of Europe's Official Development Assistance (ODA) program. The Organization for Economic Cooperation and Development (OECD) estimated that the 15 European member countries of the OECD secured $67.1 billion in ODA in 2009. This amount increases to $80.5 if we add the $13.4 billion from the various institutions of the EU. For the same period, the United States spent $28.7 billion in ODA. In this chapter I make the argument that the global financial crisis and the resulting recession and sovereign debt crisis are leading to a deeper political crisis in transatlantic relations. The reason for the present transatlantic political crisis is that Europe, given the financial disarray it is currently facing, will invest less in collective security and in promoting global growth. The financial crisis could, therefore, lead to a redefinition of the national security policy of the European member states, with the potential consequence of a further straining of transatlantic relations. Likewise, the United States, also economically stressed and with fewer resources to spend on defense, could be forced to rethink what it needs to defend (or preserve), and thus its interests vis-à-vis the partnership. In this prospective, the changing context would once again prove to be the catalyst for change in identity, interest and behavior.

The New Transatlantic Agenda of 1995, envisioned and completed a few years after the fall of the Berlin Wall, called for economic cooperation between Europe and the United States, but it aimed at a wider goal: sustaining transatlantic security. In effect, the document states, a transatlantic "economic relationship sustains our security and increases our prosperity."[1] The Transatlantic Agenda also emphasizes that the United States and Europe "share the largest two-way trade and investment relationship in the world" and stresses that the partners "bear a special responsibility to lead multilateral efforts towards a more open world system of trade and investment."[2] This special responsibility, the agenda continues, is carried out through two institutions: the G-7, which is supposed to "stimulate global growth" and the OECD.[3] Through the work of these two institutions, the transatlantic partners planned to develop strategies "to overcome structural unemployment and adapt to demographic change."[4] The intertwining of their economic relationship, aimed at stimulating their own prosperity and at fuelling global growth, with the ambition of maintaining security is at the heart of the partnership, as highlighted in the post-Cold War agenda. Thus, anything that threatens transatlantic economic prosperity causes an unavoidable strain in transatlantic affairs.

I. IMPACT OF THE FINANCIAL CRISIS ON FOREIGN ASSISTANCE

According to the OECD, international aid to developing countries fell by nearly 3% in 2011. Angel Gurría, OECD secretary general, warned donors that "the fall of ODA is a source of great concern [. . .] the crisis should not be used as an excuse to reduce development cooperation contributions."[5] The global recession, however, seems to be responsible for breaking a long trend of annual increases. Remarkably, 2010 was a record year, and international aid reached levels never seen before. It was up to $128.7 billion from the $120 billion of 2009. However, there was still a great gap between promises made and funds allocated. Nonetheless, in 2011, the world's largest Official Development Assistance (ODA)[6] donors were still the United States, Germany, the United Kingdom and France, as the OECD chart (Figure 9.1) below shows.

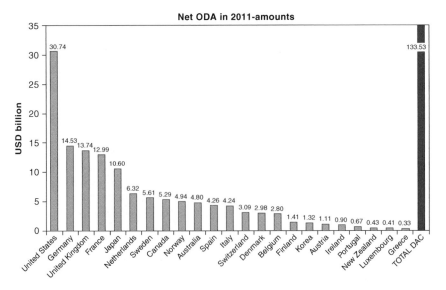

Figure 9.1   Net Official Development Assistance from DAC Members in 2011
Source: OECD, April 4, 2012. http://www.oecd.org/dac/aidstatistics/50060310.pdf

By contrast, ODA fell sharply in Greece (–39.3%), Spain (–32.7%), Austria (–14.3%) and Belgium (–13.3%). The substantial decrease in Greece's contribution was undoubtedly due to the country's severe fiscal crisis. Spain's ODA reduction was also the result of severe cuts in bilateral aid (related to its financial crisis). The drop in aid from Austria and Belgium are slightly different and were mainly due to a decrease in debt forgiveness. However, in real terms, within the transatlantic area, there were also unexpected rises in ODA. This is true for Italy (+33%) and for Sweden (+10.5%).[7] Even in a time of fiscal hurdles, Italy has managed to increase its debt forgiveness grants and has also seen an upsurge in refugee arrivals from North Africa. These two components were factored in the OECD calculation of Italy's performance. As for Sweden, it has continued to allocate 1% of gross national income (GNI)[8] to ODA.

If ODA is ranked in absolute quantity of aid given, then the United States is the outright winner. In contrast, if ODA is analyzed as a percentage of gross national income, then the image is very different (see Table 9.1 below).

Table 9.1 indicates that in 2011 the United States continued to be the largest donor by volume. The net ODA flows amounted to $30.7 billion, but this sum represents a reduction of –0.9% in real terms from 2010. Then if we look at the ODA as a share of GNI, it was 0.20%, a decrease of 1% since 2010. The European donors did much better in comparison. ODA from the 15 EU countries that are members of DAC was $72.3 billion in 2011.[9] This amount represented 54% of the total net ODA from all DAC countries. Also, as a share of GNI, DAC-EU members' ODA was 0.45%, and therefore it was well above the DAC average (0.31%) and more than double that of the United States (0.20%).

The 27 members of the EU are therefore the world's biggest aid donor and, as demonstrated by Table 9.1, they provide more than half of all global aid. Despite the economic crisis in Europe, the DAC-EU members have successfully increased their aid. Three countries (the UK, Germany and France) are ranked among the major global donors. Likewise, four EU members (Denmark, Luxembourg, the Netherlands and Sweden) are among those that have already reached the 0.7% target set in 2005 when EU member states pledged to increase ODA to 0.7% of GNI by 2015.[10] In April 2012, the EU's development commissioner, Andris Piebalgs, complained that the EU needed "a more aggressive approach on the issue . . . because investing in development aid will make the world safer and more prosperous," adding, "solidarity must remain our guiding principle."[11] Hence, the European vision is unmistakably one in which aid must play a major part in the EU response to global challenges. The UK is projected to be the next in line to join the countries that have met or exceeded the 0.7% target. Furthermore, in 2011, Italy and Germany made considerable increases to their aid budget.[12]

The relevance of the data presented is that it indicates how so much of Europe's soft-power leadership originates in its ODA policy. European countries, over the course of the years, have invested in these programs as a

Table 9.1 Net Official Development Assistance from DAC and Other OECD Members in 2011

	Preliminary data for 2011					
	2011		**2010**		**2011**	
					ODA USD million (2)	Percent change 2010 to 2011 (2)
	ODA USD million current	ODA/ GNI %	ODA USD million current	ODA/ GNI %	At 2010 prices and exchange rates	
DAC countries:						
Australia	4 799	0.35	3 826	0.32	4 044	5.7
Austria	1 107	0.27	1 208	0.32	1 036	−14.3
Belgium	2 800	0.53	3 004	0.64	2 605	−13.3
Canada	5 291	0.31	5 209	0.34	4 930	−5.3
Denmark	2 981	0.86	2 871	0.91	2 803	−2.4
Finland	1 409	0.52	1 333	0.55	1 275	−4.3
France	12 994	0.46	12 915	0.50	12 195	−5.6
Germany	14 533	0.40	12 985	0.39	13 746	5.9
Greece	331	0.11	508	0.17	308	−39.3
Ireland	904	0.52	895	0.52	867	−3.1
Italy	4 241	0.19	2 996	0.15	3 987	33.0
Japan	10 604	0.18	11 021	0.20	9 829	−10.8
Korea	1 321	0.12	1 174	0.12	1 242	5.8
Luxembourg	413	0.99	403	1.05	381	−5.4
Netherlands	6 324	0.75	6 357	0.81	5 950	−6.4
New Zealand	429	0.28	342	0.26	379	10.7
Norway	4 936	1.00	4 580	1.10	4 197	−8.3
Portugal	669	0.29	649	0.29	630	−3.0
Spain	4 264	0.29	5 949	0.43	4 007	−32.7
Sweden	5 606	1.02	4 533	0.97	5 008	10.5
Switzerland	3 086	0.46	2 300	0.40	2 604	13.2
United Kingdom	13 739	0.56	13 053	0.57	12 951	−0.8
United States	30 745	0.20	30 353	0.21	30 086	−0.9
TOTAL DAC	133 526	0.31	128 465	0.32	125 060	−2.7
Average Country Effort		0.46		0.49		

	Preliminary data for 2011					
	2011		2010		2011	
					ODA USD million (2)	Percent change 2010 to 2011 (2)
	ODA USD million current	ODA/ GNI %	ODA USD million current	ODA/ GNI %	At 2010 prices and exchange rates	
Memo Items:						
EU Institutions (3)	12 627		12 679		11 870	−6.4
DAC-EU countries	72 315	0.45	69 661	0.46	67 748	−2.7
G7 countries	92 148	0.27	88 533	0.28	87 724	−0.9
Non-G7 countries	41 378	0.46	39 933	0.49	37 336	−6.5
Non-DAC OECD members:						
Czech Republic	256	0.13	228	0.13	237	4.2
Estonia	25	0.12	19	0.10	23	21.1
Hungary	140	0.11	114	0.09	133	16.2
Iceland	26	0.22	29	0.29	24	−18.2
Israel (4)	176	0.07	145	0.07	166	14.9
Poland	417	0.08	378	0.08	399	5.6
Slovak Republic	87	0.09	74	0.09	81	10.1
Slovenia	63	0.13	59	0.13	60	1.7
Turkey	1 320	0.17	967	0.13	1 337	38.2

(1) Chile and Mexico do not yet report their ODA statistics to the DAC.

(2) Taking account of both inflation and exchange rate movements.

(3) Grants only.

(4) The statistical data for Israel are supplied by and under the responsibility of the relevant Israeli authorities. The use of such data by the OECD is without prejudice to the status of the Golan Heights, East Jerusalem and Israeli settlements in the West Bank under the terms of international law.

Note: The data for 2011 are preliminary pending detailed final data to be published in December 2012. The data are standardised on a calendar year basis for all donors, and so may differ from fiscal year data available in countries' budget documents.

Source: OECD, April 4 2012.

core part of their foreign policy. It could even be argued that these programs actually constitute Europe's foreign policy. As Francois Rivasseau, deputy head of the European Union Delegation to the United States, remarked, ODA and culture are the European foreign policy. This policy is what has allowed Europe to be what he called a "smart power."[13]

However, if this is true, ODA does indeed define Europe's role, but it also (and mainly) defines its interests and behavior. It is Europe's identity as a "soft-power" (defined as a "power" whose influence derives from investing in international aid), which shapes its interests and prompts its actions in the international arena. By the same token, if the United States invests half of what the DAC-EU members do in ODA, it means that ODA is less of an identifier, so it must be understood as such. U.S. interests are not shaped by development assistance, and the United States cannot identify itself as a soft-power. Its leadership does not emanate from ODA, but rather from military expenditure. The acknowledgment of this development within the transatlantic realm is the key for understanding the difficulties that the partners are having engaging with each other, as we will see in the next section.

II. U.S. AND EUROPE TRENDS IN MILITARY EXPENDITURE

As we have seen, at a time of heavy budgetary constraints, Europe has managed to increase its development aid. This is remarkable, even if some EU officials may argue that efforts are still required in order to reach the agreed target of 0.7% EU GNI by 2015.[14] Also, frequently in Europe "abstract notions of national security and defense mean little when fundamental issues of social existence are at stake."[15] Therefore, the critical issue becomes the way in which the financial and economic crisis has affected military spending, and thus collective defense spending and how this could lead the transatlantic outlooks to drift further apart.

The data on military expenditure shows a mixed pattern of increases and decreases in 2011 and confirms that there is great variation both within and between regions.[16] The world military expenditure in 2011 is projected to have been $1738 billion, which corresponds to 2.5% of world gross domestic product (GDP) and $249 for each human being in the world.[17] The subregion with the most rapid growth in military expenditure between 2002 and 2011 was North Africa (109%). Other subregions with large increases since 2000 are Eastern Europe (86%), East Asia (69%), Central and South America (62%) and North America (59%). What is interesting in the context of this chapter is that only one subregion has seen a fall in military expenditure: Western and Central Europe. Overall, according to SIPRI data, the military spending of the United States amounted to 41% of the world total in 2011. Following the United States, China's military expenditure accounted for 8.2%, Russia for 4.1% and the UK and France for 3.6% each.[18]

If we look at the most recent trends, since the beginning of the financial and economic crisis in 2008, austerity and deficit-reduction measures have indeed led to cutbacks in military spending, both in the United States and Europe. There is, however, a considerable discrepancy between the percentages of reductions in the United States and in Europe. In the United States, military spending in 2011 was $711 billion, which constitutes a nominal growth from 2010 when it was $69 billion, but in real terms it represents a decrease of 1.2% since 1998.[19]

In Europe, particularly in Western and Central Europe, many governments have imposed austerity packages intended to reduce their budget deficits, which cut the defense sector. The percentages of cuts, even within the subregions, have varied significantly, but since 2008 about two thirds of states have implemented military spending reductions. The governments that have cut their defense spending more deeply have been in Central Europe, with the largest decrease in Latvia (51%). In Western Europe, defense spending decreased most significantly in the countries that faced a severe debt crisis: Greece (26%), Spain (18%), Italy (16%), and Ireland (11%). In the case of other countries such as Poland and Turkey, because the financial crisis did not really have a notable impact on their economies, they increased their military spending (Table 9.2). However, the three European countries that have consistently spent more then the others in military expenditure have also reduced their defense spending. The UK cut its military budget by 0.6%, France by 4% and Germany by 1.6%. Additionally, over the next three years, Germany plans to reduce its defense spending by about 10%, and the UK will slash its defense spending by 7.5%.[20] France's new president, François Hollande, is likely to follow that trend. He has already called for a withdrawal of French troops from Afghanistan by the end of 2012.

At this point, it is important to address the question of the impact that the wave of budget reductions have had on collective security, that is, on NATO. In effect, worries about the impact on future NATO capabilities were quickly expressed at the highest level. In 2010, NATO Secretary-General Andres Fogh Rasmussen warned members of the alliance to avoid deep cuts. He said "there is a point where you are no longer cutting fat; you're cutting into muscle, and then into bone."[21] There was indeed a risk that this would happen, especially considering the earlier remarks by Liam Fox and Harve Morin, the defense ministers of the UK and France. Mr. Morin, in fact, shared Mr. Fox's idea that "the fat" needed "to be trimmed away, because we're not—he said—in NATO as a job creation project."[22] When all is said and done, however, there is no reason to fear the demise of NATO, rather, again, in the aftermath of reductions in military spending, both in the United States and in Europe, what seems to be at stake is its obsolescence. NATO needs to be able to put forces on the field; Europeans should be able to fight alongside Americans and should have the right equipment to do so. Also it would be appropriate for Americans and Europeans to be training

Table 9.2   The 15 Countries with the Highest Military Expenditure in 2010

Spending figures are in US$, at current prices and exchange rates. Countries are ranked according to military spending calculated using market exchange rates (MER). Figures for military spending calculated using purchasing power parity (PPP) exchange rates are also given.

Rank	Country	Spending ($ b., MER)	Change, 2001-10 (%)	Share of GDP (%, estimate)[a]	World share (%)	Spending ($ b., PPP)[b]
1	United States	698	81.3	4.8	43	698
2	China	[119]	189	[2.1]	[7.3]	[210]
3	United Kingdom	59.6	21.9	2.7	3.7	57.6
4	France	59.3	3.3	2.3	3.6	49.8
5	Russia	[58.7]	82.4	[4.0]	[3.6]	[88.2]
Sub-total top 5		995			61	
6	Japan	54.5	−1.7	1.0	3.3	43.6
7	Saudi Arabia[c]	45.2	63.0	10.4	2.8	64.6
8	Germany	[45.2]	−2.7	[1.3]	[2.8]	[40.0]
9	India	41.3	54.3	2.7	2.5	116
10	Italy	[37.0]	−5.8	[1.8]	[2.3]	[32.2]
Sub-total top 10		1 218			75	
11	Brazil	33.5	29.6	1.6	2.1	36.2
12	South Korea	27.6	45.2	2.8	1.7	40.8
13	Australia	24.0	48.9	2.0	1.5	17.3
14	Canada	[22.8]	51.8	[1.5]	[1.4]	[19.4]
15	Turkey	[17.5]	−12.2	[2.4]	[1.1]	[23.9]
Sub-total top 15		1 344			82	
World		1 630	50.3	2.6	100	

[ ] = estimated figure; GDP = gross domestic product.

[a] The figures for national military expenditure as a share of GDP are based on estimates for 2010 GDP from the IMF *World Economic Outlook*, October 2010.

[b] The figures for military expenditure at PPP exchange rates are estimates based on the ratio of PPP to MER-based GDP projections for 2010 implicit in the International Monetary Fund's *World Economic Outlook*. Thus, military expenditure figures at MER rates have been multiplied by the same ratio to obtain the PPP estimates.

[c] The figures for Saudi Arabia include expenditure on public order and safety and might be slight overestimates.

Source: Sam Perlo-Freeman, Olawale Ismail, Noel Kelly, Elisabeth Sköns and Carina Solmirano, Stockholm International Peace Research Institute, "Military expenditure data, 2001–10," *SIPRI Yearbook 2011: Armaments, Disarmament and International Security* (Oxford University Press: Oxford, 2011), Table 4A.1. The 15 countries with the highest military expenditure in 2010, page 183.

together, but spending cuts could jeopardize such an arrangement. Austerity could thus lead to a weakening of the transatlantic military ties, and to Americans complaining even more about their European allies free-riding on U.S. security guarantees.

It is clear that the current financial crisis is inducing Europeans to cut their military budgets, and the impact of those cuts on collective security will further exacerbate transatlantic relations. Ongoing military spending trends are already diminishing the ability of many NATO members to contribute to international security.[23] For example, almost all the European states are postponing the acquisition of some type of equipment. One of the most discussed decisions is that of Denmark putting off buying a replacement fighter for the F-16 fleet until 2014.[24] Other countries are downsizing the amount of equipment they want to buy. Some of these countries are Austria, France, Germany, the Netherlands, Portugal and the United Kingdom.[25] Others, like Germany and Italy, are trying to resell their assets. There is, furthermore, another drawback, which is the allocation of the money spent. Indeed, according to Robert Gates, then-U.S. defense secretary, much of the problem is due to the fact that money spent by Europe on defense is not allocated "wisely and strategically."[26] Even so, in response to the financial crisis, Europeans are cutting their military budgets and are doing so without coordinating those cuts with NATO. This lack of cooperation, along with the military spending cuts, is creating substantial political tensions in the transatlantic alliance.[27]

Table 9.3 and 9.4 will illustrate both Europe's marginal defense expenditure contribution and its decrease since the beginning of the economic crisis (2008).

As such, the financial crisis and the subsequent reduction in defense spending may run the risk of producing a wider gap in the transatlantic alliance. The economic crisis may have a few relevant effects that should be considered. First, the tendency to avoid coordinating defense cuts with NATO could invigorate the propensity of alliance members to pursue defense restructurings on a national base. This may lead to another unwanted consequence: the abandonment of key capabilities. In essence, Europeans cut their military budgets because they tend to count on NATO to provide them with defense. However, if NATO lacks equipment, or has outdated equipment, it cannot fulfill its role. Second, the cost of the operations that NATO ran most recently in Afghanistan and Libya were financed by and large through extra-budgetary funding in most European states. Obviously, in tight fiscal circumstances this is likely to fade. Third, even with a reduced military contribution, until 2008, Europeans gave political support to deployments, even when the operations undertaken might have led to long-term engagements. However, because of the economic crisis, European governments may lose domestic support if NATO operations are not rapid and do not have a clear exit strategy. Fourth, if Europeans decide to decrease their participation in NATO operations, they may lose their already limited

Table 9.3 Defense Expenditures of NATO Countries

Country / Pays (0)	Currency unit / Unite monetaire (million) (-)	1990 (1)	1995 (2)	2000 (3)	2005 (4)	2006 (5)	2007 (6)	2008 (7)	2009 (8)	2010e (9)
		Current prices / Prix courants								
Albania	Leks	//	//	//	//	//	//	//	17356	25038
Belgium (a)	Francs - Euros	155205	131156	139711	3400	3434	3773	4298	4048	3951
Bulgaria (b)	Leva	//	//	//	1051	1116	1415	1553	1273	1230
Croatia	Kunas	//	//	//	//	//	//	//	5356	5057
Czech Republic	Koruny	//	//	44314	52960	54411	51283	52755	59656	50808
Denmark	Kroner	16399	17468	19339	20800	23173	22731	24410	23252	25160
Estonia	Krooni	//	//	//	2568	2945	4246	4595	3978	3922
France (a)(c)	Francs - Euros	231911	238432	240752	42545	44386	45150	45366	39190	39237
Germany (a)	Deutsche Mark - Euros	68376	58986	59758	30600	30365	31090	32824	34166	34032
Greece (a)(d)	Drachmas - Euros	612344	1171377	2017593	15429	5829	5997	6896	7311	6683
Hungary (d)	Forint	//	//	226926	318552	296665	326205	321486	298620	280895
Italy (a)(d)	1000 Lire - Euros	28007	31561	47100	26959	26631	20932	22631	21946	21263
Latvia	Lats	//	//	//	115	176	228	259	160	128
Lithuania	Litai	//	//	//	846	973	1142	1251	998	854
Luxembourg (a)(d)	Francs - Euros	3233	4194	5613	196	197	209	146	145	201
Netherlands (a)	Guilders - Euros	13513	12864	14284	7693	8145	8388	8488	8733	8567
Norway (e)	Kroner	21251	22224	25722	31471	32142	34439	35932	38960	38621

Poland	Zlotys	//	//	13418	17911	19021	21681	20528	23456	26549
Portugal (a)(d)	Escudos - Euros	267299	403478	479663	2527	2514	2418	2536	2691	2777
Romania	New Lei	//	//	//	5757	6324	6358	7558	6785	6784
Slovak Republic (a)	Koruny - Euros	//	//	//	25537	27064	28131	30146	972	828
Slovenia (a)	Tolars - Euros	//	//	//	99084	116400	506	566	575	583
Spain (a)	Pesetas - Euros	922808	1078751	1264299	10497	11506	12219	12756	12196	11568
Turkey (d)(f)	1000 Liras - Liras	13866	302864	6248274	13840	16514	15392	18755	19603	21241
United Kingdom (g)	Pounds	22287	21439	23532	30738	32105	34430	37127	37357	39053
*NATO - Europe**	*US dollars*	*186189*	*184352*	*164349*	*250064*	*261743*	*287761*	*314190*	*282287*	*275348*
Canada	Canadian dollars	13473	12457	12314	16001	17066	19255	21100	21828	24460
United States (g)	US dollars	306170	278856	301697	503353	555950	586106	729544	757466	785831
North America	*US dollars*	*317717*	*287933*	*309989*	*516557*	*570994*	*604032*	*749319*	*776561*	*809566*
*NATO - Total**	*US dollars*	*503906*	*472284*	*474338*	*766621*	*832736*	*891793*	*1063509*	*1058848*	*1084915*

2000 prices / Prix de 2000

Albanie	Leks	//	//	//	//	//	//	//	12969	18137
Belgique (a)	Francs - Euros	189496	141588	139711	3062	3038	3278	3574	3366	3234
Bulgarie (b)	Leva	//	//	//	826	821	953	965	761	713
Croatie	Kunas	//	//	//	//	//	//	//	4017	3749
Republique tcheque	Couronnes	//	44314	46684	47436	43248	43689	48178	41287	
Danemark	Couronnes	21000	19879	19339	18512	20199	19485	20230	19018	20246
Estonie	Krooni	//	//	//	2052	2172	2833	2860	2477	2444

(continued)

Table 9.3 (Continued)

Country / Pays (0)	Currency unit / Unite monetaire (million) (-)	1990 (1)	1995 (2)	2000 (3)	2005 (4)	2006 (5)	2007 (6)	2008 (7)	2009 (8)	2010e (9)
France (a)(c)	Francs - Euros	266045	250494	240752 |	38587 |	39318 |	39025	38223 |	32849	32679
Allemagne (a)	Deutschemark - Euros	80840	59586	59758	28993 |	28655	28810	30113	30913	30550
Grece (a)(d)	Drachmes - Euros	1510759	1504553	2017593 |	4629	4820	4815	5348	5597	4953
Hongrie (d)	Forint	//	//	226926	234875 |	209878	217943	204973	182422	168907
Italie (a)(d)	1000 Lires - Euros	48659	42917	47100 |	20501	18325 |	13404 |	13456	12495	11162
Lettonie	Lats	//	//	//	90	125	134	133	83	66
Lituanie	Litai	//	//	//	835	901	975	973	806	683
Luxembourg (a)(d)	Francs - Euros	4022	4517	5613 |	175 |	170	175 |	117	117	160
Pays-Bas (a)	Florins - Euros	16903	14346	14284 |	6599 |	6884	6956	6868	6961	6745
Norway (e)	Couronnes	26755	24939	25722	27645	27250	28120	28159 |	29187 |	28405
Pologne	Zlotys	//	//	13418	15782	16516	18108	16630	18335	20348
Portugal (a)(d)	Escudos - Euros	452282	475021	479663 |	2174 |	2104	1968	2024	2142	2187
Roumanie	Nouveaux lei	//	//	//	2131	2117	1875	1933	1689	1588
Republique slovaque (a)	Couronnes - Euros	//	//	//	20513	21118	21709	22614 |	738	628
Slovenie (a)	Tolars - Euros	//	//	//	76325	87879 |	367	394	388	392
Espagne (a)	Pesetas - Euros	1412702	1243264	1264299 |	8549	8999	9248	9428	8960	8467

Turquie (d)(f)	1000 livres - Livres	4565927	5052539	6248274	4332	4573	4023	4372	4339	4390
Royaume-Uni (g)	Livres	31578	24172	23532	27078	27444	28577	29927	29699	30054
OTAN - Europe*	Dollars EU	184847	156142	164349	166052	166516	163413	167180	162088	159799
Canada	Dollars canadiens	15998	13515	12314	14217	14768	16147	17008	17974	19600
Etats-Unis (g)	Dollars EU	397652	312398	301697	432665	461873	475792	577450	592793	603169
Amerique du Nord	Dollars EU	408424	321498	309989	442238	471817	486665	588903	604896	616367
OTAN - Total*	Dollars EU	593271	477640	474338	608290	638333	650078	756082	766984	776166

Current prices and exchange rates (million US dollars) / Prix et taux de change courants (million de dollars EU)

Albania	//	//	//	//	//	//	//	183	242
Belgium	4644	4449	3191	4229	4308	5164	6296	5624	5238
Bulgaria (b)	//	//	//	667	716	990	1162	905	832
Canada	11547	9077	8292	13204	15044	17926	19775	19095	23736
Croatia	//	//	//	//	//	//	//	1014	923
Czech Republic	//	//	1148	2211	2408	2527	3090	3129	2672
Denmark	2650	3118	2393	3468	3897	4175	4788	4337	4486
Estonia	//	//	//	204	236	371	430	353	333
France (c)	42589	47768	33815	52909	55682	61796	66454	54446	52017
Germany	42319	41160	28150	38054	38092	42552	48082	47466	45116
Greece (d)	3863	5056	5522	6752	7313	8208	10102	10157	8860
Hungary (d)	//	//	804	1596	1410	1776	1868	1476	1355
Italy (d)	23376	19375	22411	33527	33409	28648	33150	30489	28189
Latvia	//	//	//	204	314	444	539	316	242

(continued)

Table 9.3 (Continued)

Country / Pays (0)	Currency unit / Unite monetaire (million) (-)	1990 (1)	1995 (2)	2000 (3)	2005 (4)	2006 (5)	2007 (6)	2008 (7)	2009 (8)	2010e (9)
Lithuania		//	//	//	305	353	453	531	402	329
Luxembourg (d)		97	142	128	244	247	286 —	214	202	267
Netherlands		7421	8012	5972	9567	10218	11480	12434	12132	11357
Norway (e)		3395	3508	2922	4885	5012	5875	6371 —	6196	6393
Poland		//	//	3087	5536	6130	7833	8521	7518	8836
Portugal (d)		1875	2670	2204	3143 —	3154	3309	3714	3738	3682
Romania		//	//	//	1976	2251	2608	3000	2225	2140
Slovak Republic		//	//	//	823	911	1139	1411	1350	1098
Slovenia		//	//	//	514	609	693	829	799	772
Spain		9053	8651	7001	13054	14434	16724	18685	16944	15335
Turkey (d)		5315	6606	9994	10301 —	11560	11814	14410	12647	14197
United Kingdom (g)		39590	33836	35608	55894 —	59076	68896	68108	58240	60438
United States (g)		306170	278856	301697	503353	555950	586106	729544	757466	785831

* The Czech Republic, Hungary and Poland joined the Alliance in 1999, Bulgaria, Estonia, Latvia, Lithuania, Romania, the Slovak Republic and Slovenia joined in 2004, and Albania and Croatia joined in 2009.

(a) From 2002, data are expressed in Euros (for Slovenia from 2007, and for Slovak Republic from 2009).

(b) Data do not include pensions.

(c) Data include non-deployable elements of Other Forces and from 2006, they are calculated with a new accounting methodology. From 2009, data do not include the Gendarmerie.

(d) Data do not include non-deployable elements of Other Forces; for Greece, Hungary, Portugal and Turkey from 2002, for Italy from 2007 and for Luxembourg from 2008.

(e) From 2009, new methodology used to calculate pensions.

(f) From 2005, data are expressed in new currency.

(g) Data include military pensions, for the United Kingdom from 2005 and for United States from 2006.

* La République tchèque, la Hongrie et la Pologne sont membres de l'Alliance depuis 1999, la Bulgarie, l'Estonie, la Lettonie, la Lituanie, la Roumanie, la Slovaquie et la Slovénie le sont depuis 2004 et l'Albanie et la Croatie le sont depuis 2009.

(a) A partir de 2002, les données sont exprimées en euros (pour la Slovénie à partir de 2007, et pour la République slovaque à partir de 2009).

(b) Les données n'incluent pas les pensions.

(c) Les données incluent des éléments non-déployables des Autres Forces et à partir de 2006, elles sont calculées selon une nomenclature spécifique. A partir de 2009, les données ne comprennent pas la Gendarmerie.

(d) Les données n'incluent pas les éléments non-déployables des Autres Forces; pour la Grèce, la Hongrie, le Portugal et la Turquie à partir de 2002, pour l'Italie à partir de 2007, et pour le Luxembourg à partir de 2008.

(e) A partir de 2009, une nouvelle méthodologie est utilisée pour le calcul des pensions.

(f) A partir de 2005, les données sont exprimées dans une nouvelle monnaie.

(g) Les données incluent les pensions militaires, pour le Royaume Uni à partir de 2005 et pour les Etats-Unis à partir de 2006.

Source: http://www.nato.int/nato_static/assets/pdf/pdf_2011_03/20110309_PR_CP_2011_027.pdf

Table 9.4 Gross Domestic Product and Defense Expenditures Annual Percentage Change (%) (Based on 2000 Prices)

Country / Pays (0)	Average / Moyenne 1990–1994 (1)	Average / Moyenne 1995–1999 (2)	Average / Moyenne 2000–2004 (3)	Average / Moyenne 2005–2009 (4)	2006 (5)	2007 (6)	2008 (7)	2009 (8)	2010 (9)
			Gross domestic product / Produit interieur brut						
Albania	//	//	//	//	//	//	//	3.3	2.6
Belgium	1.3	2.4	1.2	1.8	2.7	2.8	0.8	-2.7	2.1
Bulgaria	//	//	//	//	6.5	6.4	6.2	-4.9	-0.1
Canada	0.4	3.3	2.3	1.6	2.8	2.2	0.5	-2.5	3.0
Croatia	//	//	//	//	//	//	//	-5.8	-1.6
Czech Republic	//	//	2.7	4.6	6.8	6.1	2.5	-4.1	2.5
Denmark	1.6	2.8	0.7	1.2	3.4	1.7	-0.9	-4.7	2.2
Estonia	//	//	//	//	10.6	6.9	-5.1	-13.9	2.4
France	0.9	2.2	1.5	1.4	2.2	2.4	0.2	-2.6	1.5
Germany	6.0	1.5	0.6	1.9	3.6	2.8	0.7	-4.7	3.5
Greece	1.3	3.1	4.3	3.1	4.5	4.3	1.3	-2.3	-3.9
Hungary	//	//	4.0	1.1	3.6	0.8	0.8	-6.7	1.1
Iceland	-0.5	5.1	2.9	3.1	4.6	6.0	1.0	-6.8	-3.6
Italy	0.9	1.4	1.0	0.5	2.0	1.5	-1.3	-5.0	1.0
Latvia	//	//	//	//	12.2	10.0	-4.6	-18.0	-3.5
Lithuania	//	//	//	//	7.8	9.8	2.9	-14.7	0.4
Luxembourg	5.1	4.6	3.0	3.8	5.0	6.6	1.4	-3.7	3.3
Netherlands	2.0	3.9	1.1	2.5	3.4	3.9	1.9	-3.9	1.7
Norway	3.4	4.4	1.8	1.7	2.3	2.7	0.8	-1.4	0.5

Poland	//	//	2.2	5.7	6.2	6.8	5.1	1.7	3.5
Portugal	2.3	4.2	1.0	1.0	1.4	2.4	0.03	−2.6	1.5
Romania	//	//	//	//	7.9	6.3	7.3	−7.1	−1.9
Slovak Republic	//	//	//	//	8.5	10.6	6.2	−4.7	4.1
Slovenia	//	//	//	//	5.9	6.9	3.7	−8.1	0.9
Spain	1.3	3.5	3.2	2.4	4.0	3.6	0.9	−3.7	−0.2
Turkey	3.2	5.3	1.4	3.7	6.8	4.9	0.5	−4.8	8.2
United Kingdom	0.4	3.2	2.5	1.4	2.8	2.7	−0.1	−5.0	1.8
United States	1.9	4.2	1.8	1.4	2.7	1.9	0.0	−2.6	2.7

Defense expenditures / Depenses de defense

Albanie	//	//	//	//	//	//	−22.1	39.8
Belgique	−0.8	−2.7	3.2	−0.8	7.9	9.0	−5.8	−3.9
Bulgarie (a)	//	//	//	−0.6	16.1	1.3	−21.2	−6.3
Canada	−4.4	3.1	6.0	3.9	9.3	5.3	5.7	9.0
Croatie	//	//	//	//	//	//	−11.6	−6.7
Republique tcheque	//	0.9	−0.9	1.6	−8.8	1.0	10.3	−14.3
Danemark	0.2	1.0	2.6	9.1	−3.5	3.8	−6.0	6.5
Estonie	//	//	//	5.9	30.4	1.0	−13.4	−1.3
France (b)	−1.1	1.2	−1.3	1.9	−0.7	−2.1	|−14.1	−0.5
Allemagne	−0.7	−0.8	0.9	−1.2	0.5	4.5	2.7	−1.2
Grece (c)	6.5	−9.8	4.3	4.1	−0.1	11.1	4.7	−11.5
Hongrie (c)	//	2.5	−5.6	−10.6	3.8	−6.0	−11.0	−7.4
Italie (c)	0.7	−1.7	−13.6	−10.6	|−26.9	0.4	−7.1	−10.7

(continued)

Table 9.4 (Continued)

Country / Pays (0)	Average / Moyenne 1990–1994 (1)	Average / Moyenne 1995–1999 (2)	Average / Moyenne 2000–2004 (3)	Average / Moyenne 2005–2009 (4)	2006 (5)	2007 (6)	2008 (7)	2009 (8)	2010 (9)
Lettonie	//	//	//	//	39.1	7.6	-0.9	-37.5	-19.9
Lituanie	//	//	//	//	7.9	8.2	-0.2	-17.2	-15.3
Luxembourg (c)	4.1	5.2	7.3	-7.3	-2.5	2.6	-32.8	-0.4	36.5
Pays–Bas	-2.9	0.6	0.9	1.9	4.3	1.1	-1.3	1.4	-3.1
Norvege (d)	0.3	1.2	5.0	0.8	-1.4	3.2	0.1	3.6	-2.7
Pologne	//	//	2.8	3.9	4.6	9.6	-8.2	10.3	11.0
Portugal (c)	1.2	-1.3	-5.3	-2.1	-3.2	-6.5	2.9	5.9	2.1
Roumanie	//	//	//	//	-0.6	-11.4	3.1	-12.7	-5.9
Republique slovaque	//	//	//	//	2.9	2.8	4.2	-1.7	-14.9
Slovenie	//	//	//	//	15.1	0.02	7.5	-1.6	1.1
Espagne	-3.4	-1.0	4.0	2.8	5.3	2.8	1.9	-5.0	-5.5
Turquie (c)	3.4	5.5	-8.1	-0.05	5.6	-12.0	8.7	-0.7	1.2
Royaume–Uni (e)	-4.2	-1.5	0.9	2.6	1.4	4.1	4.7	-0.8	1.2
Etats–Unis (e)	-5.3	-2.6	7.2	8.0	6.8	3.0	21.4	2.7	1.8

(a) Data do not include pensions.
(b) Data include non-deployable elements of Other Forces and from 2006, they are calculated with a new accounting methodology. From 2009, defence expenditures do not include the Gendarmerie
(c) Data do not include non-deployable elements of Other Forces; for Greece, Hungary, Portugal and Turkey from 2002, for Italy from 2007 and for Luxembourg from 2008.
(d) From 2009, new methodology used to calculate pensions.
(e) Data include military pensions, for the United Kingdom from 2005 and for the United States from 2006.

(a) Les données n'incluent pas les pensions.
(b) Les données incluent des éléments non-déployables des Autres Forces et à partir de 2006, elles sont calculées selon une nomenclature spécifique. A partir de 2009, les dépenses de défense ne comprennent pas la Gendarmerie.
(c) Les données n'incluent pas les éléments non-déployables des Autres Forces; pour la Grèce, la Hongrie, le Portugal et la Turquie à partir de 2002, pour l'Italie à partir de 2007, et pour le Luxembourg à partir de 2008.
(d) A partir de 2009, une nouvelle méthodologie est utilisée pour le calcul des pensions.
(e) Les données incluent les pensions militaires, pour le Royaume Uni à partir de 2005 et pour les Etats-Unis à partir de 2006.

Source: http://www.nato.int/nato_static/assets/pdf/pdf_2011_03/20110309_PR_CP_2011_027.pdf

political clout within the alliance. This, in turn, may cause the transatlantic partners to drift further apart.

III. CONCLUSIONS

In this chapter, I have attempted to illustrate how in Europe the economic crisis and the consequent reduction in military spending (and increase in ODA) may signal a redefinition of identity, interest and, thus, behavior of the allies. I have also made the argument that if in a time of crisis, three major ODA contributors (the UK, Germany and France) increased their ODA in terms of their gross national product it is indicative of ODA's programs being key elements of their foreign policy. They shape the "interests" of these countries. Given the data, however, this logic can be extended to all EU members. ODA programs and cultural programs are foreign policy for European countries and for the EU. That is why even under austerity measures, Europeans keep investing relatively more than the United States on ODA (ODA/GNI). This must be understood within the framework of their influence. They perceive themselves as soft-powers and act accordingly. The perception of who they are is given by their identification as development leaders. They are the ones who spend more on these programs while disinvesting, or investing relatively less, in military spending. What this identification does to the European members is that it shapes their interest (in what to invest, or in what kind of foreign policy to put in place). Likewise, it also shapes their national security policy (how much to invest in national security and in collective security). In essence, the identity of "leader of development" shapes their interests and behavior. Because their interest is that of maintaining their influence as soft-powers, they choose to cut on defense spending while, at the same time, devoting more resources to development assistance. The data presented in this chapter also indicates that, while in absolute quantity of aid given, the United States is the largest ODA donor, when calculating ODA/GNI it still invests less than one third of the Europeans. What this may mean is that the United States has a weaker "development" identity, and development shapes U.S. interests abroad to a lesser extent than it does in Europe. In other words, this identity does exist, otherwise the United States would not participate in ODA programs, but it is not the main interests identifier. Thus, it shapes U.S. foreign policy only marginally.

This discourse is very relevant if one wants to understand transatlantic relations. In effect, there seems to be the development of two identities in the transatlantic partnership. On one side of the pond, the Europeans who identify themselves more and more as development leaders are concerned with maintaining this status and are thus investing, even in a time of crisis, on development assistance. On the other side of the pond, the United States, while devoting a significant amount of money to ODA (almost $31 million in 2011), is spending $711 billion in military expenditure. Military power is thus the identifier for the United States. This identity shapes the interests and behavior of the United States abroad (i.e., military interventions, nation building). Moreover, this identity is valid across the political spectrum and the recent military budget cuts, which Defense Secretary Leon Panetta proposed, will not constitute a deep reduction in military spending over the next 10 years.

These two identities, which at times clash, are weakening transatlantic identity, and thus, solidarity. Then again, given that identity generates interests, the diminishing of transatlantic identity, encouraged by the financial and economic crises and invigorated by dissimilar foreign policies (more ODA vs. more defense spending), can lead to a shrinking relationship on collective security. Such behaviors can seriously threaten the premise of the New Transatlantic Agenda (i.e., the indivisibility of transatlantic security), and they can indeed further strain transatlantic relations.

Part IV
Conclusion

10 Transatlantic Relations as a Process of Redefinition with an Uncertain Outcome

I began this study a few years ago, when experts considered the war in Iraq to be a breaking point in the relations between the United States and Europe. Speculations about a doomed future had just become radicalized, due to Donald Rumsfeld's snide comments comparing a "new" Europe, mainly Eastern Europe along with Italy and Spain, which was ready to embark on military missions and an "old" Europe, primarily France and Germany, which was continuing to count on diplomacy as an effective means to solve international problems. Naturally, some objected to the source of those comments and the evidence or lack thereof linked to the so-called problem. But what is more important is that in 2003, transatlantic relations became less dull for international relations specialists, and they started once again to publish on this subject.[1] They were, however, deeply divided: while neo-realists anticipated a deterioration of Euro-American relations, neoliberals predicted the endurance of transatlantic cooperation, as seen in chapter 3. The debate then shifted and began to address the future role of NATO. It focused on whether a foreign policy common to the whole of the European Union could challenge the harmonious relationship of the allies, and what part, if any, Russia was likely to play within this new context.[2]

In order to assess the validity of the predictions of both the neoliberals and ne-realists, it has, therefore, been crucial to reflect on how the United States and Europe have continued to interact. This book has argued that disagreements between the transatlantic partners are the consequences of changing identities within the Atlantic area. The clash over the Iraq War was not, in fact, a new and defining disagreement, indicating a political rift between the United States and Europe. Rather it was just another crisis that some pundits found alarming. This book has had the aim of demonstrating that disagreements among allies are not really that shocking and that they were certainly not the result of the end of the East/West confrontation, as many have argued. By taking a constructivist stand, I have shown how such disagreements depend on the evolution of the identity of the partners, an evolution that has at its core the question of values. I have revealed how that evolution has influenced and redefined the interests of the partners, and I have shown the impact that this has had on their policies. This redefinition,

I have contended, changes the normative context and, more broadly, the international environment. Thus, contemporary disagreements are to be viewed as a continuation of the evolution, rather than as a breaking point. These reflections also enable us to better understand the West in the post-Cold War era, when defining the West purely by its juxtaposition with the Soviet Union is no longer possible.

I. IDENTITY AND VARIATION

My analysis of Euro-American interactions during the 1990s has shown that a variation in identity and values influences interests and policies. In the security realm, the somewhat elastic use of the term "transatlantic" tends to become more specific, and is generally indicative of Euro-American military cooperation. Notwithstanding the sudden disappearance of the Soviet threat, the transatlantic allies' new security identity has allowed NATO to acquire new tasks and has prolonged the military cooperation between Europe and the United States, despite the fact that differences remain, as shown in the case of Libya. Nonetheless, when we shift from strictly security issues and focus our attention on the realm of international justice, the idea of a compact Western identity seems to be challenged. Such an encompassing identity continues to be appropriate only to the extent that the concept sheds light on common values and corresponding common interests in promoting human rights shared by America and Europe. Yet such interests coexist with different interpretations of justice and a much lesser emphasis on sovereignty—both conceptually and materially. Similarly, in the instance of third world economic development, the transatlantic identity is an effective concept describing American and European common policies, insofar as such descriptions highlight or emphasize common understandings of the cancellation of external debt for third world countries. But such a common identity, in this context, is also limiting, for it obscures the very real distance in sociocultural values between Europe and the United States.

It is only by envisioning and accepting the relations of the United States and Europe as dynamic and evolving that we can begin to comprehend the historical and contemporary significance of such relations and thus make any viable predictions about the future of those relations. Chapter 3 has shown that military cooperation between the United States and Europe has continued within NATO, even though there have been some questions raised about a possible European security *alter ego*. The alliance has survived the disappearance of the external threat that had prompted its creation in the first place, and it has endured as the key security organization for its members. However, subsequent to the disappearance of the Soviet threat, each party has emphasized different means for achieving the newer and evolving goals of the alliance over time. Primarily, the harmony within the alliance was accomplished by redefining the basis of transatlantic relations on humanitarian grounds. The character of this renewed partnership is deeply value laden since the frictions that occurred in the 1990s were reconciled through a re-born identity developed on the protection of human rights as a unifying principle.[3] Thus, even militarily, the unity and self-identification of post-Cold War transatlantic relations is preserved by the common perception that human rights must be defended. This is reinforced, as the Libya case has shown, by current conceptualizations of interventions and rationalizations for their taking place. In Libya, the allies intervened, as we have already seen, in order to protect civilians from attacks by security forces of then-Libyan leader Muammar Gaddafi.

As for issues of international law, in chapter 4 we have seen that for the United States, "justice" should advantage the strongest and with this premise; it is the power of the U.S. military, and not the International Criminal Court, which can ostensibly rectify injustice in the world. Contrary to this approach, in Europe the establishment of the International Criminal Court was conceived within the larger context of promoting respect for human rights. This case has revealed a fundamentally different conceptualization of how to achieve justice, thus it reinforces pessimistic expectations. On this particular issue, the divergence between the transatlantic partners was triggered by different conceptualizations of sovereignty. As Stephen Krasner argued, international law often trumps domestic decision making, and generally states tend to be protective of their own domestic power.[4] Thus, it is within reason to expect some resistance to international law that has the potential to nibble away at sovereignty.

However, while the United States harshly criticized the court as another dangerous attempt to reduce its national sovereignty, Europeans did not engage in this kind of discussion. For them, as chapter 4 shows, the protection of national sovereignty was less relevant than the establishment of a mechanism that could effectively prosecute violators of human rights.[5] The European approach to this question, coupled with the determination to establish a court with extensive jurisdiction, indicates that for Europeans, concerns over specific issues of sovereignty are not of primary importance when human rights violations are at stake. The fact that the protection of sovereignty was not put forward as a rationale for limiting the power of the ICC denotes a lack of concern among European states over limits to domestic power. In short, Europe did not envisage or privilege the protection of sovereignty as being more salient than enforcing international justice, and Europe supported a strong and independent court, while the United States boycotted the International Criminal Court largely on grounds of sovereignty. Thus, in Europe the ICC was framed as an effort to promote human rights and as a means for the preservation of peace and the consolidation of the rule of law.[6] Conversely, in the United States, President Clinton faced much criticism in Congress because of the question of the protection of American officials stationed abroad.[7] In Washington, the ICC was, as Jesse Helms declared in 1998, "dead on arrival."[8]

In the case of third world economic development, the transatlantic partners largely coincide with Northern industrialized countries. This character-
ization has typically positioned the United States and Europe in opposition
to other regions of the world, which are identified by various names such as
third world, less developed, developing or underdeveloped countries. This
case study has shown that even though there was agreement on the cancellation of debt for the poorest regions of the world, the rationale that the
United States and Europe each adopted to reach agreement on what were
ultimately similar policies was significantly different. The difference in rationale, as explained in chapter 5, is due to divergent sociocultural values
and is best described as the more overtly religious inflections of American
society, as opposed to the more secular approach of Europe. Once again,
we should be aware of these differences when we study transatlantic relations and attempt to predict their future, because any conceptualizations
that miss this point are likely the product of an oversimplification of a complex reality.

In essence, the first part of the book, in analyzing NATO's enlargement,
the ICC and Debt Relief, has exposed how different conceptualizations of
certain values/norms lead to different policies. In the case of the ICC, for
example, the United States' conceptualization of itself as a military power
shaped its policy on the establishment of the court. Ultimately, this resulted
in the United States rejecting the ICC treaty. Thus, I have concluded that
changing identities indeed modify the normative and social contexts, and
this can produce tensions. The second part of the book, with more recent
cases, ranging from the Arab Spring, the intervention in Libya and Foreign Assistance in Africa have showed how redefinitions of identity keep
affecting the behavior of the United States and Europe. The case of the
Arab Spring, for example, also suggests the lack of consensus on a common
policy, due once again to divergent conceptualizations, this time of the question of security. This divergence is defining their practices as well as their
behavior and interests.

II. CONSEQUENCES OF CHANGE

My findings have significant policy implications. If an issue is perceived or
constructed as a moral hazard on both sides, the allies will work together
and introduce common polices or norms. This was true in the late 1990s.
Indeed, in Kosovo the transatlantic partners' joint action was conceived as
having a moral purpose, that of the defense of human rights. But since a
similar framing was adopted to justify the intervention in Libya in 2011,
it can be argued that it still holds true. However, American and European
societies are remarkably different culturally, and while Europe tends to be
more secular, religious-bound arguments seem capable of winning much
support in the United States. Activists should thus take divergences in social

values into consideration when strategizing about persuading transatlantic partners to cooperate on certain issues such as the debt relief. Otherwise, different values, or at least different understandings and/or interpretations of values, can produce distinct policies, as the ICC case has indicated. The United States sees itself as a military superpower, and Europe identifies with a more diplomatic, although not entirely pacific, power. This indicates a reconceptualization of the "Self," which in turn redefines interests and policies in a dichotomous way. The fading of a common identity will result in more national approaches rather than transatlantic solutions to international problems. The Libya case, for example, demonstrates that Europe is capable of going-it alone, if and when there is strong political leadership. Furthermore, given U.S. economic constraints, as well as the already budgeted cuts in defense spending, Americans may very well just welcome Europeans taking more responsibility on military security. This, however, does not entail a breaking up of transatlantic relations, but rather a more mature relationship between equal partners.

This study contributes to previous analyses, which focused on identity formation as a result of constant interactions within the international context. It has shown, by way of pre- and post-9/11 case studies and also a comparative framework, that in order to understand, conceptualize and predict transatlantic relations, a constructivist lens, which examines interests, and thus policies, as dynamic, is more suitable than static theories. Previous accounts, neorealist and neoliberal have, in effect, anticipated interests to be fixed, not fluctuating. This has hindered their explanations as well as their projections about the behavior of the transatlantic partners. Neorealists have pessimistically warned that in the post-Cold War world, the United States and Europe would separate. Neoliberals, on the contrary, have been very optimistic. They have predicted an endurance of the relations based on such common values as democracy and a free-market economy. The cases presented, however, show that the behavior of states is dynamic as are their interests. Both are contingent on the changing context and shifting identities. In essence, there is an "adaptation" to new historical realities, but at the same time, through their behavior, the allies contribute to the changing social context in which they live/act, while at the same time they are affected by it. That is why their identity also changes. In this dynamic situation, U.S. and European policies are a consequence and a source of change. In essence, behavior, context, identity and interests are co-constitutive. This dynamic, which explains the endurance of the transatlantic relations despite disagreements and different conceptualizations of values, is invisible if not studied through an approach that is flexible enough to account for change.

This study further suggests that past disagreements were not merely the result of the end of the Cold War, but rather of a complex and dynamic process, which by redefining context and interests caused policies to be revisited. It also suggests that the allies will continue to cooperate, not because of common values, but when and if their interests overlap. Interests, however, as I have frequently stated, do indeed change; and this must be taken into consideration when making any predictions. The cases studied have shown furthermore that a shifting identity does indeed shape policies, but they also confirm my argument that if the common identity shrinks, so does the motivation for cooperation. The cases presented have each shown a degree of reluctance on both sides to working together. Again, this does not signal the end of transatlantic relations, but it rationalizes the difficulties that American and Europeans are having when it comes to collaborating, even when it is a matter of international security and when they have a perceived common enemy.

III. DIFFERENT THEORIES, DIFFERENT EXPLANATIONS

As paradoxical as it may seem for a study such as this that attempts to redefine transatlantic relations as a dynamic process, I do acknowledge that the pessimistic analyses of some neorealist positions on the future of the alliance were in fact well founded.[9] In predicting the probability of a troubled transatlantic relationship they were accurate. Since the 1990s, transatlantic relations have indeed been characterized by internal clashes, and the cases in this book are a few significant examples.[10] The United States and Europe have been at odds on security and international law, and these policy disagreements can justifiably be interpreted as a political split. The flaw within the neorealist view rests, rather, in its inability to predict how certain ongoing redefinitions of identities and interests could contribute to avoiding a more serious split. Furthermore, without an understanding of how some values have influenced their identity, even on security issues, it is impossible to comprehend why those disagreements did not bring about a total split in transatlantic relations. In essence, it is evident that the 1990s and the 2000s were years of change, characterized by disagreements between the transatlantic partners, yet common values, such as the need to protect human rights, partially redefined the partnership beyond the conventional commonalities of being capitalist democracies.

In this book, I have also taken to task the neoliberal approach,[11] with its emphasis on cooperation based on shared values, for not having considered the evolution of transatlantic relations. In this case, an oversimplification has impeded neoliberals from explaining the disagreements of the post-Cold War world. Conversely, this book has drawn attention to conflicted moments in the relations, emphasized by several disagreements, due to the different understanding of some values.[12] This is not inconsistent with my critique of the neorealists' analysis, because, on a broader scale, while it is clear that both the United States and Europe do share, for example, the common value of protecting human rights, there is fundamental disagreement on how to prevent violations of human rights and on how to punish those who violate such rights.

Clearly defined claims, proposed by the neorealists and the neoliberals on the future of transatlantic relations, open the way for a new conceptualization of those relations. This conceptualization must reflect both the agreements and the disagreements within a dynamic process, which should not be conceived as a series of breaks within the transatlantic relations, or as continuous cooperation, but rather as the dynamics of evolving identities that shape interests and policies. Indeed, theories must be proven by empirical evidence, otherwise they are merely intellectual exercises that do not respond to their key purpose, namely, to be able to offer explanations for a given phenomenon and to help us to understand it. In essence, both neorealist and neoliberal theories on the future of transatlantic relations must be confirmed by evidence; otherwise they will be confined to the realm of speculation and will therefore not be useful in predicting the future of those relations.

IV. REFLECTING ON THE FUTURE

Finally, a few reflections are essential on the lessons learned from Euro-American interactions in the 1990s and in the post-9/11 years. On the question of cooperation, a 2005 Pew Survey shows that Americans and Europeans take very different views of the transatlantic alliance, and therefore it seems that those who predicted that a more serious split was coming are to some extent correct. Majorities in every country of Western Europe say that Europe "should take a more independent approach to security and diplomatic affairs than it has in the past."[13] In Great Britain, France and Germany, these percentages rose sharply between 2002 and 2003 and then, by 2005, stabilized. However, the survey also points out, that while in Spain in 2002, 60% of those polled had a preference for looser ties to the United States, in 2005 such a preference declined significantly, to 50%. It is worth noting that, by contrast, Americans increasingly favor a close partnership with Western Europe. Two thirds (66%) feel that the United States and Western Europe should remain as close as in the past.[14] In addition, the survey reveals that there is an even bigger gap between Americans and Europeans over whether the United States should remain the sole global military superpower, or if it would be better if a country or group of countries emerged as a rival to the United States. While Americans reject the idea that another country should challenge America's global military supremacy, in Western Europe, large majorities favor a countervailing military force.[15] In France, Germany, Spain and the Netherlands more than 69% of the public is in favor of such a view. Even most British and Canadians favor a vigorous counterbalance to U.S. dominance. These were all signals that it was indeed possible that the gap would grow in the years to come.

Fearing such a possibility, the U.S. presidential race in 2008 led to endless speculation. The recurring question was this one: will the election of a new president bring the allies closer? The European media were drenched with election coverage and, in general, tended to strongly favor the Democratic candidate, then Senator Barack Obama. Senator Hillary Rodham Clinton's campaign to become the first woman to be president also dominated the headlines in Europe, but public opinion appeared to be infatuated with Mr. Obama.[16] Just to offer a few examples, in Germany, the *Berliner Morgenpost* proclaimed that Obama was "The New Kennedy," and the *Frankfurter Rundschau* compared Obama not only to Kennedy, but also to Presidents Lincoln and Roosevelt.[17] In France, the *Libération* wrote that the new leader of the French Socialist Party should have been someone with Obama's profile.[18] But these "great expectations" generally did not signify snugger relations. The "lead-from-behind" policy in Libya, the lack of leadership in the Arab Spring and disagreements on how to fight the global recession seem to indicate that Mr. Obama was not able to close the transatlantic gap. In effect, the most recent, 2012 Pew survey confirms that Europeans keep feeling an estrangement between the United States and Europe and, most important for this study, that there continues to be a values gap, even on security issues.[19] According to the survey, Europeans reacted to the reelection of President Obama with a "mixture of excitement and relief," an attitude similar to the one they had in 2008. However, Pew pollsters conclude, despite his continued popularity in Europe, Mr. Obama was not able to close "the long-running transatlantic values gap." The survey shows, instead, that on questions such as the use of military force or religion, Americans and Europeans continue to disagree. This distance, as I have been discussing throughout the book, is what ultimately governs the relations between the allies. Values are important because they shape a state's interests and actions in international politics.

The next big challenge for transatlantic solidarity will be on the question of the status of Palestine. The recent vote at the UN, on November 29, 2012, to grant the Palestinians the status of a "non-member observer state," may be just another sign of a fracturing partnership. It could expose the division within NATO allies over policies in the Middle East. In effect, of the transatlantic partners, only the United States and Canada voted with Israel against the Palestinian Authority's request for nonmember observer state status. The Europeans, conversely, were either in favor, as were France, Italy, Spain, Norway, Denmark and Turkey or abstained, as did Germany. The UN General Assembly passed the resolution with 139 votes in favor and 41 abstentions.

Whether this vote will lead to a more serious split in the arena of international politics will depend on the radicalization of the United States and European identities, which explains the use of military force or diplomacy, for example. The United States and Europe have, for now, similar interests in Syria and Iran. They are working to find a possible successor to President Bashar al-Assad, and they both want to contain Iran's nuclear ambitions. However, this solidarity could change. The opposition of the United States and Israel to the status of Palestine as a nonobserver state rose out of the concern that, as a new "entity," Palestine could, like the Holy See, join the International Criminal Court. This would allow the Palestinians to seek criminal charges for war crimes committed by Israel in the occupied territories. It remains unclear what the Palestinians will do, but the motivations behind the vote show, even today, a fundamental moral divide across the Atlantic.

Transatlantic relations are clearly more complex than earlier IR theorists and experts had assumed. Scholars need to see the West not as a monolithic entity but as a heterogeneous set of states, each with a distinct set of values, ideas and identities. In some areas these characteristics combine to produce common policies; in other instances their changing identities pull the partners apart. Further studies of agreements and disagreements among allies would greatly enhance our understanding of the values and policies that are inherent to transatlantic relations. Questions regarding European and American societies and their value system mark another important area for future research. The existing Euro-American value distance, as Pew surveys show, could have important implications for transatlantic relations. Increasing emphasis on traditional values (i.e., a strong sense of national pride and respect for authority) in one society could lead to a growing reliance on the use of military force, while the growing prominence of secular values (i.e., a weaker sense of national pride and weaker respect for authority) could produce more public support for diplomacy.[20]

As Europe and America face future crises that will test their alliance, it is essential that international relations scholars who continue to study the interactions of Europe and America in the 21st century include in their research an acknowledgment and analysis of their continually evolving identity, which determines the continually evolving nature of transatlantic relations. This will allow for a better understanding of those relations.

Appendix

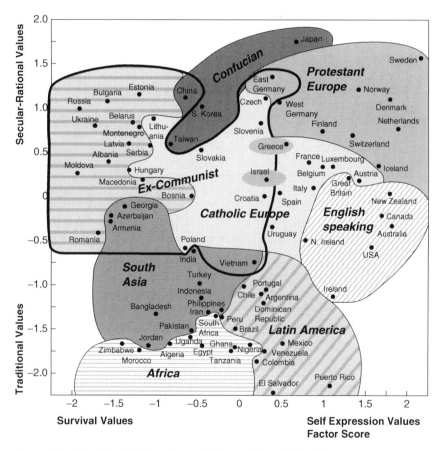

Figure A.1 The World Value Survey Cultural Map 1999–2004
Source: Ronald Inglehart and Christian Welzel, *Modernization, Cultural Change, and Democracy* (Cambridge: Cambridge University Press, 2005). See Figure 2.4 Cultural map of the world about 2000, p. 63.
http://www.worldvaluessurvey.org

Notes

NOTES TO CHAPTER 1

1. "Thatcher's Fight Against German Unity," *BBC*, September 11, 2009, sec. Europe, http://news.bbc.co.uk/2/hi/8251211.stm; "Thatcher and Kohl 'Quarreled Terribly,'" *Spiegel Online*, September 14, 2009, http://www.spie gel.de/international/spiegel/0,1518,648927,00.html.

2. James Blitz, "Mitterrand Feared Emergence of 'Bad' Germans," *Financial Times*, September 9, 2009, http://www.ft.com/cms/s/0/886192ba-9d7d-11de-9f4a-00144feabdc0.html#axzz1wAy4qrGi.

3. Klaus Wiegrefe, "An Inside Look at the Reunification Negotiations," *Spiegel Online*, September 29, 2010, http://www.spiegel.de/international/germany/germany-s-unlikely-diplomatic-triumph-an-inside-look-at-the-reunification-negotiations-a-719848.html.

4. "Upheaval in the East; Gorbachev Voices New Reservations on German Unity" *New York Times*, n.d., http://www.nytimes.com/1990/02/21/world/upheaval-in-the-east-gorbachev-voices-new-reservations-on-german-unity.html?pagewanted=all&src=pm.

5. "Evolution in Europe; The German-NATO Drama: 9 Fateful Months," *New York Times*, n.d., http://www.nytimes.com/1990/07/17/world/evolution-in-europe-the-german-nato-drama-9-fateful-months.html.

6. Iver B. Neumann, *Russia and the Idea of Europe: A Study in Identity and International Relations* (New York: Routledge, 1996); Patricia M. Goff and Kevin C. Dunn, *Identity and Global Politics: Empirical and Theoretical Elaborations* (New York: Palgrave Macmillan, 2004).

7. U.S. Embassy, "New Transatlantic Agenda," October 20, 2011, http://useu.usmission.gov/new_transatlantic_agenda.html; U.S. Embassy, "Transatlantic Declaration of 1990," */1990transatlantic_declaration.html*, October 20, 2011, http://useu.usmission.gov/1990transatlantic_declaration.html.

8. Robert Kagan, *Of Paradise and Power: America and Europe in the New World Order* (New York: Alfred A. Knopf, 2003); Philip Gordon and Jeremy Shapiro. *Allies at War: America, Europe, and the Crisis over Iraq* (New York: McGraw-Hill, 2004); Charles Kupchan, *The End of the American Era: U.S. Foreign Policy and the Geopolitics of the Twenty-First Century* (New York: Knopf, 2002); John Leech, *Whole and Free: NATO, EU Enlargement and Transatlantic Relations* (London: Federal Trust 23 for Education & Research, 2002); Hall Gardner, *NATO and the European Union: New World, New Europe, New Threats* (Burlington, VT: Ashgate Publishing, 2004); Daniel Hamilton and Daniel Sheldon, *Conflict and Cooperation in Transatlantic Relations* (Baltimore, MD: Johns Hopkins University Press,

2004); Elizabeth Pond, *Friendly Fire: The Near-Death of the Transatlantic Alliance* (Pittsburgh, PA: European Union Studies Association, 2004); Werner Weidenfeld, *From Alliance to Coalitions: The Future of Transatlantic Relations* (Gütersloh, Germany: Bertelsmann Foundation Publishers, 2004); Ivo Daalder, *Crescent of Crisis: U.S.-European Strategy for the Greater Middle East* (Washington, DC: Brookings Institution Press, 2006); Matthew Evangelista, *Partners or Rivals?: European-American Relations after Iraq* (Milan, Italy: V&P Publishing, 2005).

9. Ian Hurd, "Constructivism," in *The Oxford Handbook of International Relations* (Oxford Handbooks Online, 2008), 303.
10. Ibid.
11. On falsifiable theories, in Karl Popper's view there is an asymmetry between confirming a theory (verification) and disconfirming it (falsification). Verification is rather irrelevant, but falsification is the key to scientific knowledge. In essence, for Popper and for positivists, empirical tests can be conducted only on a finite number of hypotheses. This means that theories are not "verifiable," but only falsifiable, since it is impossible to test all observable implications of a theory. Gary King, Robert Owen Keohane, and Sidney Verba, *Designing Social Inquiry: Scientific Inference in Qualitative Research* (Princeton, NJ: Princeton University Press, 1994); Karl Raimund Popper and Sir Karl Raimund Popper, *The Logic of Scientific Discovery* (London: Hutchinson, 1968).
12. Alexander Wendt, *Social Theory of International Politics* (Cambridge: Cambridge University Press, 1999); Alexander Wendt, "On the Media: A Response to the Critics," *Review of International Studies* 26 (2000): 165–180; Martha Finnemore, *The Purpose of Intervention: Changing Beliefs About the Use of Force* (Ithaca, NY: Cornell University Press, 2003); Michael Barnett, "Social Constructivism," in *Introduction to Global Politics* (Oxford: Oxford University Press, 2010), 252–270.
13. Hurd, "Constructivism,"307.
14. Richard Devetak, "Postmodernism," in *Theories of International Relations* (New York: Macmillan, 2009), 197.
15. Nicholas Greenwood Onuf, *World of Our Making: Rules and Rule in Social Theory and International Relations* (Columbia: University of South Carolina Press, 1989); Peter J. Katzenstein, *The Culture of National Security: Norms and Identity in World Politics* (New York: Columbia University Press, 1996); Yosef Lapid, *The Return of Culture and Identity in IR Theory* (Boulder, CO: Lynne Rienner Publishers, 1996); Steve C. Ropp and Kathryn Sikkink, *The Power of Human Rights: International Norms and Domestic Change* (Cambridge: Cambridge University Press, 1999); Finnemore, *The Purpose of Intervention*.
16. Martha Finnemore, *National Interests in International Society* (Ithaca, NY: Cornell University Press, 1996), 1.
17. Kenneth Neal Waltz, *Theory of International Politics* (New York: Random House, 1979); John J. Mearsheimer, *The Tragedy of Great Power Politics* (New York: W.W. Norton & Company, 2003); R.L. Schweller, "Neorealism's Status-Quo Bias: What Security Dilemma?," *Security Studies* 5, no. 3: 90–121; Fareed Zakaria, *From Wealth to Power: The Unusual Origins of America's World Role* (Princeton, NJ: Princeton University Press, 1999); Joseph Grieco, "Anarchy and the Limits of Cooperation: A Realist Critique of the Newest Liberal Institutionalism," in *Neorealism and Neoliberalism: The Contemporary Debate*, ed. D. Baldwin (New York: Columbia University Press, 1993); Stephen D. Krasner, *Sovereignty: Organized Hypocrisy* (Princeton, NJ: Princeton University Press, 1999); Robert O. Keohane and

Joseph S. Nye, *Power and Interdependence* (New York: Longman, 2011); Edward D. Mansfield and Brian Pollins, *Economic Interdependence and International Conflict: New Perspectives on an Enduring Debate* (Ann Arbor: University of Michigan Press, 2003); David Allen Baldwin, *Neorealism and Neoliberalism: The Contemporary Debate*; Kenneth A. Oye, *Cooperation Under Anarchy* (Princeton, NJ: Princeton University Press, 1986); Robert O. Keohane and Lisa Martin, "The Promise of Institutionalist Theory," *International Security* 20, no. 1 (1995): 39–51; Robert O. Keohane, "Reciprocity in International Relations," *International Organization* 40, no. 1 (1986): 1–27; Immanuel Maurice Wallerstein, *World-Systems Analysis: An Introduction* (Durham, NC: Duke University Press, 2004); Immanuel Maurice Wallerstein, *The Capitalist World-Economy: Essays* (Cambridge: Cambridge University Press, 1979).

18. Waltz, *Theory of International Politics*; Mearsheimer, *The Tragedy of Great Power Politics*; Stephen M. Walt, *The Origins of Alliances* (Ithaca, NY: Cornell University Press, 1987).

19. Audie Klotz and Cecelia Lynch, *Strategies for Research in Constructivist International Relations* (Armonk: NY: M. E. Sharpe, 2007).

20. Jeffrey Legro, *Rethinking the World: Great Power Strategies and International Order* (Ithaca, NY: Cornell University Press, 2005); Ted Hopf, *Social Construction of International Politics: Identities & Foreign Policies, Moscow, 1955 and 1999* (Ithaca, NY: Cornell University Press, 2002); Katzenstein, *The Culture of National Security*; Rodney Bruce Hall, *National Collective Identity: Social Constructs and International Systems* (New York: Columbia University Press, 1999); Christian Reus-Smit, *The Moral Purpose of the State: Culture, Social Identity, and Institutional Rationality in International Relations* (Princeton, NJ: Princeton University Press, 2009); Jeffrey T. Checkel, "Why Comply? Social Learning and European Identity Change," *International Organization* 55, no. 03 (2001): 553–588; Margaret E. Keck and Kathryn Sikkink, *Activists Beyond Borders: Advocacy Networks in International Politics* (Ithaca, NY: Cornell University Press, 1998); Finnemore, *National Interests in International Society*; Audie Klotz, *Norms in International Relations: The Struggle Against Apartheid* (Ithaca, NY: Cornell University Press, 1999); Jeffrey T. Checkel, *International Institutions and Socialization in Europe* (Cambridge: Cambridge University Press, 2007).

21. Alexander Wendt, "Anarchy Is What States Make of It: The Social Construction of Power Politics," *International Organization* 46, no. 2 (Spring 1992): 391–425.

22. Waltz, *Theory of International Politics*.

23. Wendt uses Giddens's concept of "structuration" according to which the international normative structure produces the identities and interests of the states, and states' practices and exchanges reshape such structure. Anthony Giddens, *The Consequences of Modernity* (Palo Alto, CA: Stanford University Press, 1990).

24. Depending on the context, some identities may be more stable or more inclusive than others, but I agree with Klotz and Lynch that "research should focus on the processes of identity construction that lead to [. . .] variability, rather than staking out on an epistemological position that relies on inflexible assumptions of *either* stasis *or* fluidity." Klotz and Lynch, *Strategies for Research in Constructivist International Relations*, 70.

25. Stephen J. Flanagan and Guy Ben-Ari, *A Diminishing Transatlantic Partnership? The Impact of the Financial Crisis on European Defense and Foreign Assistance Capabilities* (Washington, DC: Center for Strategic & International Studies, 2011).

NOTES TO CHAPTER 2

1. "George Bush, Meet Woodrow Wilson," *New York Times*, n.d., http://www.nytimes.com/1990/11/20/opinion/george-bush-meet-woodrow-wilson.html?pagewanted=all&src=pm.
2. For more on an alternative security approach to NATO, see http://www.osce.org/what.
3. Bruce W. Nelan, "Men of the Year 1990," *Time*, n.d., http://www.time.com/time/specials/packages/article/0,28804,2030812_2030809_2030719,00.html.
4. "Evolution in Europe; The German-NATO Drama: 9 Fateful Months," *New York Times*, n.d., http://www.nytimes.com/1990/07/17/world/evolution-in-europe-the-german-nato-drama-9-fateful-months.html.
5. "Thatcher's Fight Against German Unity," *BBC*, September 11, 2009, sec. Europe, http://news.bbc.co.uk/2/hi/8251211.stm; "Thatcher and Kohl 'Quarreled Terribly,'" *Spiegel Online*, September 14, 2009, http://www.spiegel.de/international/spiegel/0,1518,648927,00.html.
6. James Blitz in London, "Mitterrand Feared Emergence of 'Bad' Germans," *Financial Times*, September 9, 2009, http://www.ft.com/cms/s/0/886192ba-9d7d-11de-9f4a-00144feabdc0.html#axzz1wAy4qrGi.
7. Klaus Wiegrefe, "An Inside Look at the Reunification Negotiations," *Spiegel Online*, September 29, 2010, http://www.spiegel.de/international/germany/germany-s-unlikely-diplomatic-triumph-an-inside-look-at-the-reunification-negotiations-a-719848.html; "Upheaval in the East; Gorbachev Voices New Reservations on German Unity,"—*New York Times*, n.d., http://www.nytimes.com/1990/02/21/world/upheaval-in-the-east-gorbachev-voices-new-reservations-on-german-unity.html?pagewanted=all&src=pm.
8. "George Bush, Meet Woodrow Wilson," *New York Times*.
9. "Clinton Urges NATO Expansion in 1999," *New York Times*, n.d., http://www.nytimes.com/1996/10/23/us/clinton-urges-nato-expansion-in-1999.html.
10. Klaus Wiegrefe, "The Birth of Two Plus Four: An Inside Look at the Reunification Negotiations," *Spiegel Online*, September 29, 2010, http://www.spiegel.de/international/germany/germany-s-unlikely-diplomatic-triumph-an-inside-look-at-the-reunification-negotiations-a-719848–6.html.
11. There is not a uniform quotation of Lord Isamy's famous phrase. In Michael Cox's article is "to keep the Russians out, Germans down, and the Americans in"; see Cox, "Martians and Venutians," pp. 523–532. In Joseph Nye's article is "to keep the Russians out, the American in, and the Germans down"; see Joseph Nye, "The US and Europe: Continental Drift?" *International Affairs*, vol. 76, n.1 (2000), p.53.
12. "Iraq Army Invades Capital of Kuwait in Fierce Fighting," *New York Times*, n.d., http://www.nytimes.com/1990/08/02/world/iraq-army-invades-capital-of-kuwait-in-fierce-fighting.html; "Confrontation in the Gulf; The Oilfield Lying Below the Iraq-Kuwait Dispute," *New York Times*, n.d., http://www.nytimes.com/1990/09/03/world/confrontation-in-the-gulf-the-oilfield-lying-below-the-iraq-kuwait-dispute.html.
13. On August 1990, when Iraq invaded Kuwait, the Security Council adopted Resolution 660, which condemned the invasion and demanded the immediate withdrawal of Iraqi troops from Kuwaiti territory, and thereafter it adopted several more resolutions that dealt with many different aspects: arms and economic, for example. For more on the UN SC resolutions, see: http://www.un.org/en/sc/documents/resolutions/index.shtml.

14. Andrew Rosenthal, "U.S. and Allies Open Air War on Iraq; Bomb Baghdad and Kuwaiti Targets; 'No Choice' but Force, Bush Declares," *The New York Times*, n.d., http://www.nytimes.com/learning/general/onthisday/big/0116.html#article.
15. "Yugoslav Republic Of Croatia Declares Independent Nation," *New York Times*, n.d., http://www.nytimes.com/1991/05/30/world/yugoslav-republic-of-croatia-declares-independent-nation.html. "Serb-Led Presidency Drafts Plan For New and Smaller Yugoslavia," *New York Times*, n.d., http://www.nytimes.com/1991/12/27/world/serb-led-presidency-drafts-plan-for-new-and-smaller-yugoslavia.html.
16. "U.S. Recognizes 3 Yugoslav Republics as Independent," *New York Times*, n.d., http://www.nytimes.com/1992/04/08/world/us-recognizes-3-yugoslav-republics-as-independent.html.
17. "Three Factions in Bosnia Begin Talks in London," *New York Times*, n.d., http://www.nytimes.com/1992/07/28/world/three-factions-in-bosnia-begin-talks-in-london.html.
18. For more on the number of victims, see: http://www.hrw.org.
19. "U.N. Details Its Failure to Stop '95 Bosnia Massacre," *New York Times*, n.d., http://www.nytimes.com/1999/11/16/world/un-details-its-failure-to-stop-95-bosnia-massacre.html.
20. David Owen, *Bosnia and Herzegovina—The Vance Owen Peace Plan* (Liverpool: Liverpool University Press, 2012).
21. Tim Judah, *Kosovo: War and Revenge; Second Edition* (New Haven, CT: Yale University Press, 2002).
22. Joseph Fitchett, "Albright Takes Some Heat For Rambouillet 'Success,'" *The New York Times*, March 5, 1999, sec. News, http://www.nytimes.com/1999/03/05/news/05iht-yugo.2.t_0.html.
23. Albrecht Schnabel and Ramesh Chandra Thakur, *Kosovo and the Challenge of Humanitarian Intervention: Selective Indignation, Collective Action, and International Citizenship* (New York: United Nations University Press, 2000).
24. "Kohl and Mitterrand Renew Pact," *The Independent*, n.d., http://www.independent.co.uk/news/world/europe/kohl-and-mitterrand-renew-pact-1479953.html.
25. "Treaty of Maastricht on European Union," n.d., http://europa.eu/legislation_summaries/institutional_affairs/treaties/treaties_maastricht_en.htm.
26. Geir Lundestad, *The United States and Western Europe Since 1945:From "Empire" by Invitation to Transatlantic Drift: From "Empire" by Invitation to Transatlantic Drift* (Oxford: Oxford University Press, 2005), p. 244.

NOTES TO CHAPTER 3

1. See, for example, David Hastings Dunn, "European Security and Defence Policy in the American Policy Debate: Counterbalancing America or Rebalancing NATO," *Defence Studies*, vol. 1, no. 1, Spring 2001, pp. 146–155, p. 146.
2. On the question of conflicting attitudes toward security and military issues in the United States and Western Europe, it is useful to remember that, as the PEW Research Center has estimated, "Americans are more likely than Western Europeans to believe in the necessity of sometimes using force to deal with global threats." Conversely, "Americans are much more comfortable with the idea of military preemption—the use of force against potentially threatening countries who have not attacked—than are Western Europeans," Andrew Kohut, *Anti-Americanism: Causes and Characteristics*, http://pewglobal.org/.

3. The exercise of power by states toward each other is called "power politics" or "realpolitik." For Mearsheimer, a Germany not checked by American power could become aggressive again and lead to war in Europe. John Mearsheimer, "Back to the Future: Instability in Europe After the Cold War," *International Security*, vol. 15, no. 1 (Summer 1990).

4. Jeffrey Anderson, G. John Ikenberry, and Thomas Risse, *The End of The West? Crisis and Change in the Atlantic Order* (Ithaca, NY: Cornell University Press, 2008).

5. The disagreement over Iraq prompted consensus on the hypothesis that, with the end of the Cold War, the basis for transatlantic relations was eroding. Perhaps the most famous argument that the United States and Europe were growing apart was made by Robert Kagan in his 2002 article, "Paradise and Power," *Policy Review* (June and July 2002), an argument that was later expanded into a book, *Of Paradise and Power: America and Europe in the New World Order* (New York: Alfred A. Knopf, 2003); Robert Kagan, "One Year After: A Grand Strategy for the West?," *Survival*, vol. 44, no. 4 (Winter 2002–03), pp. 135–156.

   See also Francis Fukuyama, "The West May Be Cracking," *International Herald Tribune*, August 9, 2002, p. 4 in which he talks about profound differences between the United States and Europe; Charles Krauthammer, "Reimagining NATO," *Washington Post*, May 24, 2002, argues that NATO is dead; Josef Joffe, "The Alliance is Dead. Long Live the New Alliance," *New York Times*, September 29, 2002. Joffe asserts that the anti-Soviet alliance is dead and has been replaced by one "that allows the United States to pick and choose." Following the Iraq crisis, others envisaged such a crisis as the cause of transatlantic political differences. Tony Judt, for example, argued that "we are witnessing the dissolution of an international system." See Tony Judt, "The Way We Live Now," *New York Review of Books*, March 27, 2003, vol. 50, no. 5, p. 6. Former Secretary of State Henry Kissinger wrote that "if the existing trend in transatlantic relations continues, the international system will be fundamentally altered," quoted in Philip Gordon and Jeremy Shapiro. *Allies at War: America, Europe, and the Crisis Over Iraq* (New York: McGraw-Hill, 2004) p. 4. See also Charles Kupchan who stated that the United States and Europe headed toward "geopolitical rivalry." He makes this argument in *The End of the American Era: U.S. Foreign Policy and the Geopolitics of the Twenty-First Century* (New York: Knopf, 2002) and in "The Alliance Lies in the Rubble," *Financial Times*, April 10, 2003.

6. For more current references on U.S. and European relations, see Francis Fukuyama, "The West May be Cracking Europe and America," *International Herald Tribune*, August 9, 2002, pp. 4–10; John Leech, *Whole and Free: NATO, EU Enlargement and Transatlantic Relations* (London: Federal Trust for Education & Research, 2002); Philip H. Gordon, "*Bridging the Atlantic Divide*," *Foreign Affairs* (January/February 2003), vol. 82, no. 1, p. 70; James B. Steinberg, "An Elective Partnership: Salvaging Transatlantic Relations," *Survival* (June 2003), vol. 45, no. 2, p. 113; Christopher Layne and Thomas Jefferson, "America as European Hegemon," *The National Interest* (Summer 2003), vol. 13, no. 72, pp. 17–30; Ivo H. Daalder, "The End of Atlanticism," *Survival* (June, 2003), vol. 45, no. 2, p. 147; Hall Gardner, *NATO and the European Union: New World, New Europe, New Threats* (Burlington, VT: Ashgate Publishing, 2004); Gordon and Shapiro, *Allies at War*; Jaap de Hoop Scheffer, "New Trans-Atlantic Unity," *NATO's Nations and Partners for Peace*, 2004, pp. 20–24; William Wallace, "Broken Bridges," *The World Today* (December 2004), vol. 60, no. 12; pp. 13–16.

Daniel Hamilton and Daniel Sheldon, *Conflict and Cooperation in Trans-atlantic Relations* (Baltimore, MD: Johns Hopkins University Press, 2004); Tod Lindberg, "We. A Community in Agreement on Fundamentals," *Policy Review* (December 2004/January 2005), no. 128, pp. 3–19; Elizabeth Pond, *Friendly Fire: The Near-Death of the Transatlantic Alliance* (Pittsburgh, PA: European Union Studies Association, 2004); Werner Weidenfeld, *From Alliance to Coalitions: The Future of Transatlantic Relations* (Gütersloh, Germany: Bertelsmann Foundation Publishers, 2004); E. A. Turpen, "Free World: America, Europe, and the Surprising Future of the West," *Choice* (June 2005), vol. 42, no. 10; p. 1895; Ivo Daalder, *Crescent of Crisis: U.S.-European Strategy for the Greater Middle East* (Washington, DC: Brook-ings Institution Press, 2006); Matthew Evangelista, *Partners or Rivals?: European-American Relations after Iraq* (Milan, Italy: V&P Publishing, 2005); Vittorio Emanuele Parsi, *The Inevitable Alliance: Europe and the United States beyond Iraq* (New York: Palgrave Macmillan, 2006). Massimo D'Alema, "Diplomacy Al Dente," *Wall Street Journal*, Jun 14, 2006, p.14; Pierangelo Isernia, Philip P. Everts, "European Public Opinion on Security Issues," *European Security*, Dec 2006, vol. 15, no. 4, p. 451. Thomas Ilgen, *Hard Power, Soft Power, and the Future of Transatlantic Relations* (Burling-ton, VT: Ashgate, 2006). Jeremy Poulter, "NATO as a Security Organiza-tion: Implications for the Future Role and Survival of the Alliance," *RUSI Journal*, 2006. vol. 151, no. 3, pp. 58–62. Andrew A. Michta, "Transatlantic Troubles," *The National Interest* (November/December 2006), pp. 62–67; Ryan C. Hendrickson, "The Miscalculation of NATO's Death," *Parameters* (Spring 2007), vol. 37, no. 1, pp. 98–115; Daniel Dombey, "Transatlantic Climate shift," *Financial Times*, June 4, 2007, p. 2; Richard Haass, "The Atlantic Becomes a Little Wider," *Financial Times*, December 19, 2007, p. 2; Lance Smith, "Is the Transatlantic Relationship Still Important?," *Vital Speeches of the Day* (June 2007), vol. 73, no. 6; pp. 249–252.

7. See Chris Brown, *Understanding International Relations* (Basingstoke: Pal-grave, 2nd ed. 2001).

8. For a balance-of-power explanation of international relations, see the ca-nonical neorealist work of Kenneth Waltz, *Theory of International Poli-tics* (Redding, MA: Addison-Wesley, 1979); see also Stephen Walt, *The Origins of Alliances* (Ithaca, NY: Cornell University Press, 1987) and John Mearsheimer, *The Tragedy of Great Power Politics* (New York: Norton, 2001). It is worth noticing the distinction between neorealists and "classi-cal" realists. While the former stress that the international system is made of great powers, each seeking to survive, the latter, such as Hans Morgenthau, emphasize that states, like human beings have an innate longing to control others, which lead them to conflicts. See Hans Morgenthau, *Politics Among Nations: The Struggle for Power and Peace* (New York: McGraw Hill, 1993. For neoliberals who emphasize the role of international institutions through which concerted action can be achieved, see Robert Keohane, *After Hege-mony: Cooperation and Discord in the World Political Economy* (Princeton, NJ: Princeton University Press, 1984) and Robert Kehoane and Lisa Martin, "The Promise of Institutionalist Theory," *International Security*, vol. 20, no. 1 (Summer 1995), pp. 39–51. On regimes as set of principles, norms, rules and decision making procedures that regulate states' behavior, see Robert Kehoane and Joseph Nye, *Power and Interdependence*, 3rd ed. (New York: Longman, 2001). This book was published in its first edition in 1977. On regimes, see also Hedley Bull who argues that institutions help states' ad-herence to rules. Hedley Bull, *The Anarchical Society: A Study of Order*

150   *Notes*

in World Politics (New York: Columbia University Press, 1977). It is also
important to mention that there is a debate in the study of international relations in the United States between neorealism and liberal institutionalism.
Such debate is presented in David A. Baldwin, ed., *Neorealism and Neoliberalism* (New York: Columbia University Press, 1993). It is important to note
that constructivists, with a focus on the role of norms, identity and culture
in world politics, challenge the dominance of neorealism and neoliberalism
in the field of international relations by offering alternative understandings
of key topics such as the prospects for change in world politics, the relationship between identity and interest, the meaning of balance of power and
of anarchy. See Nicholas Onuf, *World of Our Making: Rules and Rule in
Social Theory and International Relations* (Columbia: University of South
Carolina Press, 1989); Peter J. Katzenstein, ed., *The Culture of National
Security: Norms and Identity in World Politics* (New York: Columbia Uni-
versity Press, 1996) and Yosef Lapid and Friedrich V. Kratochwil, eds., *The
Return of Culture and Identity in IR Theory* (Boulder, CO: Lynne Rienner,
1996); Alexander Wendt, "Anarchy Is What States Make of It: The Social
Construction of Power Politics," *International Organization*, vol. 46, no. 2
(Spring 2002), pp. 391–425.

9. Mearsheimer, "Back to the Future," p. 52; Harries, "The Collapse of 'The
West,'" p.42; Kupchan, "Reviving the West," p. 3; Walt, "The Ties that
Fray," *The National Interest* (Winter 1998–1999), p. 4.
10. See John Mearsheimer, "The False Promise of International Institutions,"
International Security, vol. 19, no. 3, pp. 5–58 and Waltz, *Theory of International Politics*.
11. See Waltz, *Theory of International Politics* and Mearsheimer, *The Tragedy
of Great Power Politics*.
12. Stephen Walt, "The Precarious Partnership: America and Europe in a New
Era." In *Atlantic Security: Contending Visions*, edited by Charles Kupchan
(New York: Council on Foreign Relations, 1998) p. 8.
13. This theory claims that states will seek to balance the power of threatening
states. The most rigorous account of balance of power theory can be found
in Waltz, *Theory of International Politics*. Walt refined such argument by
focusing on the role of threats, rather than power alone, in stimulating balancing behavior. See Walt, *The Origins of Alliances*.
14. Kenneth Waltz, *Theory of International Politics* and Walt, *The Origins of
Alliances*.
15. Joseph Grieco, "Anarchy and the Limits of Cooperation: A Realist Critique
of the Newest Liberal Institutionalism. *International Organization*, vol. 42,
no. 3, pp. 485–507.
16. A more detailed account of these arguments is offered in the following pages.
Here I have prepared a graphic synthesis (Figure 3.1) of their understanding
of what kept the United States and Europe together during the Cold War. My
synthesis was inductively constructed thorough their arguments addressing the
future of transatlantic relations. Giving quotations in the text would just constitute redundancy, thus sensible to parsimony I will provide the sources for which
the arguments were extrapolated, and the graph will illustrate the arguments.
17. A bipolar system has two great rival states or alliance blocs. The "polarity"
of an international power distribution is the number of independent centers
of power in the system. The Cold War period was characterized by two great
rivals: the United States and USSR or NATO and the Warsaw Pact. The U.S.-
Soviet competition seemed to provide stability in the system. Some however
argue that peace is best preserved by multipolarity (i.e., five or six centers of
power, where states are not grouped into alliances).
18. John Mearsheimer, "Back to the Future," p. 52.

19. Mearsheimer, "Back to the Future," p. 5.

20. Mearsheimer, "Back to the Future," p. 52.

21. Mearsheimer, "Back to the Future," p. 18.

22. Mearsheimer, "The Future of the American Pacifier," *Foreign Affairs*, Volume 80, num. 5, (September/October 2001), pp. 46–61.

23. Walt, "The Ties that Fray," p. 4.

24. The argument Walt makes is that the United States needed Europe to be economically strong so it could contribute to the U.S. economic prosperity and that strengthened the transatlantic alliance. See Walt, "The Ties that Fray," p. 6.

25. For neorealists, trade should serve power. Because power is relative, trade is desirable only when the distribution of benefits favors one's own state over rivals. See Joseph Grieco, *Cooperation among Nations: Europe, American and Non-Tariff Barriers to Trade.* (Ithaca, NY: Cornell University Press, 1990). Joanne Gowa, *Allies Adversaries, and International Trade* (Princeton, NJ: Princeton University Press, 1993).

26. Walt, "The Ties That Fray," p. 6.

27. In "The Ties that Fray," after rejecting the argument that cultural and ethnic ties brought Europe and America together, Walt argues that to the extent that such ties reinforced American interests in Europe their success is diminishing in the post-Cold War because, he states that, figures like Dean Acheson, Dwight Eisenhower, Paul Nitze and John Foster Dulles are no longer making foreign policy decisions, and they have been succeeded by a new generation with "different memories." He contends that "watching 'Saving Private Ryan' is no substitute for having lived through the real thing." The lack of a direct experience with WW II is, in Walt's opinion, reason to be pessimistic about the future of the transatlantic alliance. He concludes by saying that even if the new generations might recognize the importance of transatlantic cooperation "it will never kindle the reflexive emotional response that it did for their parents and grandparents." What is significant about such an argument is that while he makes a neorealist argument in the article, with the classical assumptions about power balancing and threat, in the last part, when discussing "generational change, he does not look at the international system or at the state, but rather at the socio-cultural level." Walt, "The Ties That Fray," p. 8.

28. Walt, "The Ties That Fray," p. 8.

29. Among many, see Kagan and Nye cited.

30. Kagan, cited.

31. In order to increase their influence, states can use power capabilities in different ways. Joseph Nye makes a significant distinction between "hard power" and "soft power." "Hard power" is the direct method of exercising power thorough coercion and reward. "Soft power" is influence through attraction and ideology that shape states' preferences. Joseph S. Nye, *Soft Power: The Means to Success in World Politics* (New York: Public Affairs, 2004).

32. Kagan, "America's Crisis of Legitimacy," *Foreign Affairs*, vol. 83 no. 2, 2004, p.71.

33. This is power as *capability*.

34. Ronald D. Asmus, Kenneth M. Pollack, "The New Transatlantic Project," *Policy Review*, Oct/Nov 2002 vol. 115, p. 5.

35. Ivo H. Daalder, "The End of Atlanticism," pp. 42, in Lindberg, Tod. ed., *Beyond Paradise and Power: Europe, America, and the Future of a Troubled Partnership* (New York: Routledge, 2005).

36. For the neoliberals approach to the post-Cold War transatlantic relations, see James Elles, "Towards a New Transatlantic Relationship," *European*

Business Journal, vol. 5, no. 3, pp. 34–41; John Duffield, "NATO's Functions after the Cold War," *Political Science Quarterly*, vol. 109, no. 5, pp. 763–787; Robert Blackwill, *The Future of Transatlantic Relations* (Washington, DC: Council for Foreign Relations Press, 1999); Daniel Deudney and John Ikenberry, "The Logic of the West," *World Policy Journal*, vol. 10, no. 4 (Winter 1993), pp. 17–25; Nye, "The US and Europe"; Robert McCalla, "NATO's Persistence after the Cold War," *International Organization*, Summer 1996, pp. 445–475; Anthony Blinken, "The False Crisis Over the Atlantic," *Foreign Affairs* (May/June 2001), pp. 35–48; Ivo Daalder, "Europe: Rebalancing the U.S.-European Relationship," *The Brookings Institution* (Summer 1999), pp. 22–25.

37. Elles, "Towards a New Transatlantic Relationship," p. 36. Elles claims that "the US has learned that its resources are finite and that the defense of its own legitimate interest, as in the Gulf war, has to be conducted in partnership with others." In this sense Europe is America's "natural" partner because of its economic and military capacity. The logic behind his argument is that they are partners because the United States and Europe are committed to democratic institutions and market economy. Elles, "Towards a New Transatlantic Relationship," p. 36.

38. Duffield, "NATO's Functions after the Cold War", p. 766.

39. Blackwill, *The Future of Transatlantic Relations*, p. 10.

40. Nye, "The US and Europe," p. 54.

41. Deutsch, Karl W. et al., *Political Community and North Atlantic Area: International Organization in the Light of Historical Experience* (Princeton, NJ: Princeton University Press, 1968).

42. Elles, "Towards a New Transatlantic Relationship," p. 36.

43. Deudney and Ikenberry, "The Logic of the West," p. 18.

44. Deudney and Ikenberry, "The Logic of the West," p. 18.

45. Nye, "The US and Europe," pp. 54–55.

46. Nye, "The US and Europe," p. 55.

47. Anthony J. Blinken, "The False Crisis Over the Atlantic," *Foreign Affairs* (May/Jun 2001), vol. 80, no. 3. p. 36.

48. Mark Landler and David E. Sanger, "World Leaders Pledge $1.1.Trillion for Crisis," *The New York Times*, April 2, 2009, p. A1.

49. Deudney and Ikenberry, "The Logic of the West," p. 19.

50. International regimes are set of norms, rules, institutions and decision-making procedures that govern actors' behavior in an issue area. See Robert O. Keohane and Joseph S. Nye, *Power and Interdependence: World Politics in Transition*, 3rd ed. (New York: Addison-Wesley Longman, 2001) and Stephen D. Krasner, ed., *International Regimes* (Ithaca, NY: Cornell University Press, 1983).

51. Elles, "Towards a New Transatlantic Relationship," p. 41.

52. Elles, "Towards a New Transatlantic Relationship," p. 35.

53. Charles Kupchan, "Rethinking Europe," *The National Interest* (Summer 1999), 56, p. 78.

54. Nye, "The US and Europe," p. 55.

55. Blinken, "The False Crisis Over the Atlantic," p. 3.

56. Blinken, "The False Crisis Over the Atlantic," p. 3.

57. Tod Lindberg, "We. A Community in Agreement on Fundamentals," *Policy Review* (December 2004/January 2005), no. 128, pp. 3–19; and Tod Lindberg, "The Atlanticist Community," pp. 215–235, in Tod Lindberg, ed., *Beyond Paradise and Power: Europe, America, and the Future of a Troubled Partnership* (New York: Routledge, 2005).

58. On the justification of the use of force against another state on humanitarian grounds without explicit Security Council authorization and as well as on the question whether violence can serve humanitarian purposes, see Nicholas J. Wheeler, *Saving Strangers* (Oxford: Oxford University Press, 2000).

59. The term "norm" and "value" here are used interchangeably as a set of rules to which states adhere intentionally or unintentionally and that define their identity.

60. Elles, "Towards a New Transatlantic Relationship"; Duffield, "NATO's Functions after the Cold War"; Robert Blackwill, *The Future of Transatlantic Relations*; Deudney and Ikenberry, "The Logic of the West"; Nye, "The US and Europe"; McCalla, "NATO's Persistence after the Cold War"; Anthony Blinken, "The False Crisis Over the Atlantic."

61. In this sense the ICC case shows cultural and identity variation.

62. Ted Hopf, "The Promise of Constructivism in International Relations Theory," *International Security*, vol. 23, no. 1 (Summer 1998), p. 172.

63. Ted Hopf, "The Promise of Constructivism in International Relations Theory," *International Security*, vol. 23, no. 1 (Summer 1998), p. 173.

64. Ted Hopf, "The Promise of Constructivism in International Relations Theory," *International Security*, vol. 23, no. 1 (Summer 1998), p. 173. See also Ronald L. Jepperson, Alexander Wendt, and Peter J. Katzenstein, "Norms, Identity and Culture in National Security," in Katzenstein, *The Culture of National Security*.

65. By "constitutive practices," I mean the practices or praxis that constitute the actor and that determine the actor's politics as understood by constructivists. See Hopf, "The Promise of Constructivism in International Relations Theory," p. 176. See also Katzenstein, *The Culture of National Security*.

66. The term "intersubjective" is used by Hopf in "The Promise of Constructivism in International Relations Theory," p. 173.

67. Ted Hopf, "The Promise of Constructivism in International Relations Theory," *International Security*, vol. 23, no. 1 (Summer 1998), pp. 175–176. There are many constructivist works that have shown how identities set policy preferences. Many of these works can be found in Katzenstein, *The Culture of National Security*. Some examples from Katzenstein are Martha Finnemore, "Constructing Norms of Humanitarian Intervention," pp. 153–185; Robert Herman, "Identity, Norms and National Security: The Soviet Foreign Policy Revolution and the End of the Cold War," pp. 271–316; and Thomas Berger, "Norms, Identity, and National Security in Germany and Japan," pp. 317–356.

68. This term of Greek origin means *action*. In Marxist terminology, it refers both to the relationships between production and labor that constitute the social structure and to the transforming action that the revolution is supposed to exercise on those relationships. Marx and Engels argued that we need to explain the formation of ideas through the "material praxis." See Karl Marx and Friedrich Engels, *The German Ideology* (1845). In customary international law, the norms that regulate the behavior of *all* states are praxis based. The term "praxis" refers to the behavior of the states. States, by believing that their behavior is norm based, repeat such behavior (praxis) and in so doing they establish new norms that are not written but that are nonetheless believed to be legitimate and therefore to be obeyed by all. See Karol Wolfke, *Custom in Present International Law*, 2nd rev. ed. (Dordrecht: Martinus Nijhoff Publishers, 1994) and Benedetto Conforti, *Diritto Internazionale* (Napoli: Editoriale Scientifica, 1997). In International Relations, Martha Finnemore seems to be the closest to this understanding of the

meaning of praxis when she analyzes change in the normative context that shapes states' behavior. See Finnemore, "Constructing Norms of Humanitarian Intervention," pp. 153–185. In a common parlance, praxis means practice as opposed to theory. My conceptualization of praxis follows in the steps of constructivist theorists, such as Hopf, for whom "meaningful behavior, or action, is possible only within an intersubjective social context." As he further explains, "Actors develop their relations with, and understandings of, others through the media of norms and practices." See Hopf, "The Promise of Constructivism in International Relations Theory," p. 173. In the present study, the term *praxis*, most simply defined, means reciprocal interaction of actors in the social context of world politics and it is conceived as a causative force determining politics.

69. For an analysis of the distinction between action and behavior, see Charles Taylor, "Interpretation and the Sciences of Man," in Paul Rabinow and William M. Sullivan, eds., *Interpretative Social Science: A Second Look* (Berkeley: University of California Press, 1987), pp. 33–81.

NOTES TO CHAPTER 4

1. NATO handbook, p.43. Available online at: http://www.nato.int/docu/handbook/2001/.
2. Perrin de Brichambaut, "The Indivisibility of Euro-Atlantic Security."
3. It was also meant to bring the confrontation between East and West to an end. With that in mind the heads of State and government within NATO also offered the Soviet Union and Eastern European Countries the opportunity to establish diplomatic relations with NATO and to work together for a new relationship based on cooperation.
4. The Helsinki Final Act deals with a set of political, economic and social questions that, in the context of the Cold War, were supposed to secure peace and stability within Europe and beyond. Thirty-five heads of state or government from Europe, the United States and Canada signed the document in 1975; among them the leaders of the United States and of the USSR (Gerald Ford and Leonid Brezhnev) and the leaders of the two Germanys (Helmut Schmidt and Erich Honecker).
5. See "NATO Transformed," p.5, available online at: http://www.nato.int/docu/nato-trans/nato-trans-eng.pdf.
6. Carl C. Hodge, ed., *Redefining European Security* (London: Garland Science, 1999), p 19.
7. See http://www.nato.int/docu/comm/49-95/c930610a.htm.
8. See http://www.nato.int/docu/comm/49-95/c920604a.htm.
9. See http://www.nato.int/docu/comm/49-95/c930610a.htm.
10. The Ad Hoc Group was established in accordance with the decision taken at the North Atlantic Co-operation Council meeting on December 18, 1992, http://www.nato.int/docu/comm/49-95/c930611b.htm.
11. September 3, 1992, the United Nations and the European Community began peace negotiations to stop the war in Bosnia-Herzegovina. The two negotiators were Lord David Owen for the EC and Cyrus Vance for the UN, hence the Vance-Owen Plan. Their plan established that Bosnia was to be divided into 10 provinces, but it was rejected by the Bosnian-Serbs.
12. The Dayton Agreement established a cease-fire, the end of the siege of Sarajevo and the partition of Bosnia into two entities, the Serb republic—Republika Srpska and the Muslim-Croat Federation—the Republic of Bosnia Herzegovina.

13. "For the first time in NATO's history, Alliance assets have been deployed in support of Article 5 operations. NATO is sending five Airborne Warning and Control Systems aircraft (AWACS) to the United States and is also deploying its Standing Naval Force Mediterranean (STANAVFORMED) to the Eastern Mediterranean." http://www.nato.int/terrorism/deployment.htm. These are only the past missions; there are many peacekeeping missions still active. They are Mediterranean Active Endeavor, Kosovo (KFOR), Iraq (NTM-I), Macedonia (Allied Harmony), Darfur, Bosnia (Sarajevo HQ), Afghanistan.

14. For more on this topic, see http://www.nato.int/eadrcc/home.htm.

15. Tony Blair, "Speech to the Economic Club of Chicago, April 22, 1999." http://www.pbs.org/newshour/bb/international/jan-june99/blair_doctrine4-23.html.

16. William Clinton. The President's News Conference With Visegrad Leaders in Prague, January 12, 1994.

17. William Clinton, "Reforming the UN," *Vital Speeches of the Day*, vol. 60 (October 15, 1993), p. 10.

18. http://www.nytimes.com/1996/10/23/us/clinton-urges-nato-expansion-in-1999.html.

19. "Clinton Letter to Senator Daschle on NATO Enlargement," March 14, 1998. The text of the letter urging the Senate to ratify NATO's enlargement is available online: http://www.fas.org/man/nato/news/1998/98031602_wpo.html.

20. In December 1997, for example National Security Adviser Samuel Berger sent a memo to Clinton asking for his personal commitment to NATO enlargement. James M. Goldgeier, *Not Whether But When: The U.S. Decision to Enlarge NATO*. (Washington, DC: Brookings Institution Press, 1999), p. 144.

21. Goldgeier, *Not Whether But When: The U.S. Decision to Enlarge NATO*. Washington, DC: Brookings Institution Press), 1999, p. 5.

22. 1995 NNS p. 26.

23. Dr. Stephen Flanagan, Private interview, May 19th, 2011.

24. "Kohl Cautions NATO about Eastward Expansion." Xinhua News Agency, February 3, 1996.

25. "NATO Holds 16 + 1 talks with Russia in Berlin." Deutsche Presse-Agentur, May 29, 1996.

26. Rodrigo, "Spain and NATO's Enlargement."

27. José María Aznar expressed these thoughts on NATO's expansion in a private interview, March 3, 2011.

28. "The Aging Alliance." *The Economist*, October 23, 1999.

29. José María Aznar. Private interview, March 3, 2011.

30. Quentin Peel, "Ruhe's mission to Europeanise NATO: German defence minister is recruiting support for reduced US role in alliance." *The Financial Times*. February 23, 1996, p. 2.

31. At this time, Washington seemed to embrace a stronger European defense identity. See Peel, "Ruhe's mission to Europeanise NATO," p. 2.

32. Peel, "Ruhe's mission to Europeanise NATO," p. 2.

33. José María Aznar. Private interview, March 3, 2011.

34. Dr. Stephen Flanagan, Private interview, May 19, 2011.

35. Dr. Stephen Flanagan, Private interview, May 19, 2011.

36. CNN News, "European Security Check—NATO's Future Role," March 19, 1996.

37. Agence France Presse, "NATO begins talks on Bosnia, reform of the Alliance." Brussels. June 13, 1996.

38. June 1997, NATO meeting. Agence France Presse, "Chirac threatens pull-back from NATO over southern command: Report." Bonn. September 28, 1996.

39. Agence France Presse, "Chirac threatens pull-back from NATO." Jim Mannion, Agence France Presse, "US-France dispute clouds NATO defense ministers meeting." December 16, 1996. Agence France Presse, "Sticks to its guns over NATO southern command." December 17, 1996. Associated Press, "French Defense Minister Visits Pentagon," Washington. March 25, 1997. Deutsche Press Agentur, "Bonn throws weight behind France in NATO dispute on fleet." Paris. July 3, 1997.

40. Agence France Presse, "Sticks to its guns over NATO."

41. On this occasion Mr. Ruhe took a personal position not supported by the Kohl government, which, to the contrary, has always been very supportive of France. See International Herald Tribune, "Clinton offers Paris compromise on NATO; US to endorse a new French-led force." Paris. March 14, 1997. Associated Press, "French Defense Minister Visits Pentagon." In July, in an interview German Foreign Minister Klaus Kinkel said that Germany "unconditionally" supported France on its demand that NATO Southern Command be headed by a European, but the question was already over. See Deutsche Press Agentur, "Bonn throws weight behind France in NATO dispute on fleet." Paris. July 3, 1997.

42. Jeffrey Ulbrich, Associated Press, "Atlantic Alliance expanding its horizons." June 22, 1998.

43. Ulbrich, "Atlantic Alliance expanding its horizons."

44. The UK position must be understood within the context of attempting to build a European Security Defense.

45. Blair and Chirac, "Franco-British Summit. Joint Declaration on European Defense."

46. Madeleine Albright, "The Right Balance Will Secure NATO's Future." *Financial Times,* Dec. 7, 1998.

47. Angus Mackinnon, Agence France Presse, "US clashes with European allies over future NATO strategy." December 8, 1998.

48. See Russian Foreign Minister Igor Ivanov, in Agence France Presse, "Albright told that NATO and Europe's defense are complementary." December 10, 1998.

49. France Presse, "Albright told that NATO and Europe's defense are complementary." December 10, 1998.

50. Joseph Fitchett, "A more united Europe worries about globalizing NATO," *International Herald Tribune*, December 31, 1998.

51. Fitchett, "A more united Europe worries about globalizing NATO."

52. As Walt argues, "because alliances are formed primarily to increase their members' security, anything that casts doubt on their ability to contribute to this goal will encourage the members to re-evaluate their position." Hence, proving that NATO had credibility was crucial to avoid its dissolution.

53. José María Aznar. Private interview, March 3, 2011.

54. She argued "one of the reasons that we believe it is very important to deal with the Kosovo situation is because of its potential impact on the neighbors. We believe that in 1991 the international community stood by and watched ethnic cleansing and the dismemberment, and really watched how the people of Bosnia were attacked. While the international community watched, we don't want that to happen again this time, and we are concerned about refugees and a variety of ways that a disruption of Kosovo might affect the neighboring countries." The full remark can be found in

the Transcript: Albright, Dini Press Briefing in Rome March 24, 1998. On-line at: http://www.usembassy-israel.org.il/publish/press/state/archive/1998/march/sd3326.htm.

55. The Contact Group was created in April 1994 as the Contact Group on Bosnia and Herzegovina and consisted of the Foreign Ministers of France, Germany, the Russian Federation, the United Kingdom and the United States. In May 1996, it was expanded to include Italy. In the fall of 1997, the Contact Group became the main coordinator for handling the Kosovo war.

56. United Nations Resolution 1160, March 31, 1998. Available online at: http://www.un.org/peace/kosovo/98sc1160.htm.

57. http://www.un.org/aboutun/charter/.

58. In the case of Kosovo, Prime Minister Tony Blair and Foreign Minister Robin Cook argued that the only way to stop the Serbs was the use of military force and that Britain and NATO had to prepare to take such actions. Wheeler, *Saving Strangers. Humanitarian Intervention in International Society*, p. 259.

59. Wheeler, *Saving Strangers. Humanitarian Intervention in International Society*.

60. In September 1998, the Security Council adopted Resolution 1199 by 14 votes, with China abstaining. The resolution was passed under Chapter VII, with the Security Council affirming "that the deterioration of the situation in Kosovo, Federal Republic of Yugoslavia, constitutes a threat to peace and security in the region." http://www.un.org/peace/kosovo/98sc1199.htm.

61. Catherine Guicherd, "International Law and the War in Kosovo," *Survival*, 41/2 (1999), pp. 26–27.

62. Wheeler, *Saving Strangers. Humanitarian Intervention in International Society*, p. 262.

63. The Bundestag is the National Parliament of the Federal Republic of Germany. The debate on Germany's participation in air strikes is discussed in Simma, "NATO, the UN and the Use of Force: Legal Aspects," p. 12.

64. Simma, 'NATO, the UN and the Use of Force: Legal Aspects," p. 12.

65. Statement by the Foreign Secretary, Robin Cook, in the House of Commons, March 25, 1999, quoted in Wheeler, *Saving Strangers. Humanitarian Intervention in International Society*, p. 266.

66. Statement by the Foreign Secretary, Robin Cook, in the House of Commons, March 25, 1999, quoted in Wheeler, *Saving Strangers. Humanitarian Intervention in International Society*, p. 266.

67. http://www.presidency.ucsb.edu/ws/index.php?pid=57294&st=&st1=.

68. http://www.presidency.ucsb.edu/ws/index.php?pid=57294&st=&st1=.

69. In discussing ethnic cleansing against the Kosovars, Madeleine Albright said that "opposing ethnic cleansing is central to our values . . . We are reaffirming NATO's core purpose as a defender of democracy, stability and human decency on European soil." Quoted in Walter Isaacson, "Madeleine's War," *Time Magazine*, May 9, 1999. Online at: http://www.time.com/time/magazine/article/0,9171,24446,00.html. See also Foreign Secretary Robin Cook's speech to the Labour Party Conference September 28, 1999. He stated: "In Kosovo Europe witnessed the greatest persecution of a whole people since the days of Hitler or Stalin. We acted because the age of mass deportation and ethnic cleansing belongs to Europe's past. We are not going to let it come back." The document is online at: http://news.bbc.co.uk/1/hi/uk_politics/459926.stm.

70. Art. 53 "A treaty is void if, at the time of its conclusion, it conflicts with a peremptory norm of general international law. For the purposes of the present Convention, a peremptory norm of general international law is a norm accepted and recognized by the international community of States as

a whole as a norm from which no derogation is permitted and which can be modified only by a subsequent norm of general international law having the same character." http://untreaty.un.org/ilc/texts/instruments/english/conventions/1_1_1969.pdf.
71. http://www.un.org/aboutun/charter/.
72. http://www.un.org/aboutun/charter/.

NOTES TO CHAPTER 5

1. Antonio Cassese, "The Statute of the International Criminal Court: Some Preliminary Reflections," *Journal of International Law*, vol. 10, no.1 (1991), pp. 144–171; Tom J. Farer, "Restraining the Barbarians: Can International Criminal Law Help?," *Human Rights Quarterly*, vol. 22, no.1 (2000), pp. 90–117; Giulio Gallarotti and Arik Y. Preis, "Toward Universal Human Rights and the Rule of Law: The Permanent International Criminal Court," *Australian Journal of International Affairs*, vol. 53, no.1 (1999), pp. 95–111; John B. Griffin, "A Predictive Framework for the Effectiveness of International Criminal Tribunals," *Vanderbilt Journal of Transnational Law*, vol. 34, no.2 (2001), pp. 406–455; Henry A Kissinger, "The Pitfalls of Universal Jurisdiction," *Foreign Affairs*, vol. 80, no. 4 (2001), pp. 86–96; Jelena Pejic, "Creating a Permanent International Criminal Court: The Obstacles to Independence and Effectiveness," *Columbia Human Rights Law Review*, vol. 29 (1998), pp. 291–354; Popovski, Vesslin "International Criminal Court: A Necessary Step Towards Global Justice," *Security Dialogue*, vol. 31, no.4 (2000), pp. 405–419; Rudolph, Christopher, "Constructing an Atrocities Regime: The Politics of War Crimes Tribunals," *International Organization*, vol. 55, no.3 (2001), pp. 655–691; Michael L. Smidt, "The International Criminal Court: An Effective Means of Deterrence?," *Military Law Review*, vol. 167 (2001), pp. 156–240; Thomas W. Smith, "Moral Hazard and Humanitarian Law: The International Criminal Court and the Limits of Legalism," *International Politics*, vol. 39 (2002), pp. 175–192; Teitelbaum, Alejandro "Statute of the International Criminal Court: A Critique," *Social Justice* vol. 26, no.4 (1999), pp. 107–114.
2. My sources are public statements made by policy makers, Senate hearings, newspaper articles, academic articles and personal interviews with the policy makers who were so kind as to respond and to talk to me when I contacted them. The analysis in this chapter covers the last three years of Clinton's presidency (1998–2000) and the first two years of the Bush administration (2001–2002). Even though the year 2002 is outside the framework of my debates, I have decided to include it because this is a salient year both for North Atlantic relations in the context of the ICC and for the ICC and its future per se.
3. For a thorough history of the court, see Leila Nadya Sadat, *The International Criminal Court and the Transformation of International Law: Justice for the New Millennium*, (Ardsley, NY: Transnational Publishers, Inc., 2002).
4. Ad hoc tribunals are those established exclusively to deal with a specific situation. They are not permanent, and they are established *post bellum*. In general, no matter how fair the actual trial proceedings are, ad hoc tribunals give the impression of arbitrary and selective prosecution. This charge was actually raised at both Nuremberg and Tokyo. Furthermore, there is the problem of delay. Ad hoc tribunals usually take time to be established and during that time evidence can be destroyed and additional lives lost. Finally, ad hoc tribunals often fail to build the kinds of institutional memory and competence that are the characteristics of permanent courts. Prosecutors who have experience

in international law must be found each time, and other personnel have to be gathered and instructed. These problems can undermine the ability of the court to conduct a fair trial. Examples are the International Military Tribunals at Nuremberg and Tokyo and, more recently, the International Criminal Tribunals for the Former Yugoslavia and for Rwanda. For more on the subject, see John R. Jones and Steven Powles, *International Criminal Practice* (Herndon, VA: Transnational Publishers, 2003).

5. The first report, by Ricardo Alfaro, concluded that an ICC was both "desirable" and "possible." See Ricardo J. Alfaro, *Question of International Criminal Jurisdiction*, UN Doc. no. A/CN.4/15 (1950). The second report, signed by Emil Sandström concluded the creation of an ICC was both possible and desirable. See Emil Sandström, *Question of International Criminal Jurisdiction*, UN Doc. no. A/CN.4/15 (1950).

6. *Report of the Committee on International Criminal Jurisdiction on its Session Held from 1 to 31 August 1951*, U.N. GAOR, 7th Sess., Supp. (no.11), U.N. Doc. A/2136 (1952) art 2, par. 11.

7. *Report of the Committee on International Criminal Jurisdiction on its Session Held from 1 to 31 August 1951*, U.N. GAOR, 7th Sess., Supp. (no.11), U.N. Doc. A/2136 (1952), art. 3.

8. *Report of the Committee on International Criminal Jurisdiction.*

9. As I have underlined earlier, the court was supposed to have the power to try heads of state or other state officials, which resulted in a highly sensitive and political problem. Furthermore, the court's successful operation would ultimately require some concessions of national criminal jurisdiction, as well as extensive cooperation by national authorities. William A. Schabas, *An Introduction to the International Criminal Court* (Cambridge: Cambridge University Press, 2007).

10. Comments and Observations on the Draft Code of Crimes Against the Peace and Security of Mankind Adopted on First Reading by the International Law Commission at its Forty-Third Session, U.N. Doc. A/CN.4/448 and Add.1 (1993).

11. The images of genocide and ethnic cleansing committed in the Former Yugoslavia resulted in a strong awareness of the need to both prevent and punish violators of human rights. Leila Nadya Sadat, *The International Criminal Court and the Transformation of International Law: Justice for the New Millennium* (Ardsley, NY: Transnational Publishers, Inc., 2002), p. 40.

12. ICTR stands for International Criminal Tribunal for Rwanda.

13. William A. Schabas, *The UN International Criminal Tribunals: The Former Yugoslavia, Rwanda and Sierra Leone* (Cambridge: Cambridge University Press, 2006).

14. Leila Nadya Sadat, *The International Criminal Court and the Transformation of International Law: Justice for the New Millennium*, pp. 40–41.

15. James Bennet, "Clinton in Africa: Clinton Declares U.S. with World, Failed Rwandans," *New York Times*, March 26, 1998, p. A 2.

16. M. Shane Smith, "How to Combat Mass Killing," *The Boston Globe*, September 26, 1999, p. E7.

17. Sarah B. Sewall, Carl Kaysen, and Michael P. Scharf in Sarah B. Sewall and Carl Kaysen, eds., *The United States and the International Criminal Court* (Lanham, MA: Rowman & Littlefield Publishers, 2000), pp. 2–3.

18. Lawrence Weschler in Sewall and Kaysen, *The United States and the International Criminal Court*, p. 91.

19. Quoted in Sewall and Kaysen, *The United States and the International Criminal Court*, p. 91.

20. Sheffer quoted by Weschler in Sewall and Carl Kaysen, *The United States and the International Criminal Court*, pp. 91–92.

21. Europe and peacekeeping, see Julian Lindley-French, *Terms of Engagement*, Challiot Papers no.52, May 2002. http://aei.pitt.edu/514/01/chai52e.pdf.
22. On the concept of the two-level games (domestic and international effects), see. Robert Putnam, "Diplomacy and Domestic Politics: The Logic of the Two-Level Games." *International Organization*, vol.42 (1988), pp. 427–469.
23. Most likely if people were concerned for their soldiers and felt that the current administration didn't do enough to protect them, Al Gore could have lost the presidential elections, which he eventually did lose, but not for those reasons.
24. Barbara Crossette, "Helms Vows to Make War on U.N. Court."*New York Times*. March 27, 1998. p. A9.
25. Barbara Crossette, "Clinton Weighing Options On World Criminal Court." *New York Times*. Dec. 11, 2000. p. A5.
26. The expression "non State Party" is international law terminology that refers to states that are not part of a treaty.
27. Through ratification, States accept the jurisdiction of the Court over the crimes in the Statute (Article 12 (1). However, the Court will not exercise its jurisdiction over a crime unless at least one of the state is a party to the Statute art. 12, par. 2 or has consented ad hoc to the Court's jurisdiction article 12, par. 3. See Bruce Broomhall, *International Justice and International Criminal Court: Between Sovereignty and the Rule of Law* (New York: Oxford University Press, 2003), p. 80.
28. Broomhall, *International Justice and International Criminal Court*, p. 164.
29. David J. Sheffer in Sarah B. Sewall and Carl Kaysen, *The United States and the International Criminal Court*, pp. 116–117.
30. David J. Sheffer in Sarah B. Sewall and Carl Kaysen, *The United States and the International Criminal Court*, p. 116.
31. David J. Sheffer in Sarah B. Sewall and Carl Kaysen, *The United States and the International Criminal Court*, p. 116.
32. Broomhall, *International Justice and International Criminal Court*, p. 167.
33. Clinton Announces U.S. Is Signing International Criminal Court Treaty. Statement by the President: Signature of the International Criminal Court Treaty. The White House. Office of the Press Secretary. December 31, 2000. Online at http://usembassy.state.gov/posts/pk1/wwwh01010302.html.
34. Statement by the president: Signature of the International Criminal Court Treaty.
35. Statement by the president: Signature of the International Criminal Court Treaty.
36. Personal interview with Richard Ben-Veniste, who served as one of 10 commissioners on the bipartisan 9/11 Commission.
37. The ICC Statute had reached the number of ratifications that made it active.
38. A good definition of the term deposit can be found in the UNICEF website. "After a treaty has been concluded, the written instruments which provide formal evidence of a State's consent to be bound are placed in the custody of a depository. The texts of the Convention on the Rights of the Child and its Optional Protocols designated the Secretary-General of the United Nations as their depository. The depository must accept all notifications and documents related to the treaty, examine whether all formal requirements are met, deposit them, register the treaty and notify all relevant acts to the parties concerned." http://www.unicef.org/crc/files/Definitions.pdf.
39. Exceptions in NATO are Turkey, which did not sign; and Greece, which signed but had not yet ratified. By December 31, 2000, the deadline for signatures set down in art. 125 of the Statute, 139 states had signed the Rome

Statute, while 27 had ratified. According to its terms, the Statute "shall enter into force on the first day of the month after the 60th instrument of ratification, acceptance, approval or accession with the Secretary General of the United Nations," art. 126 par. 1. With the simultaneous deposit of the 10 instruments of ratification at the UN on April 11, 2002, the number of ratifications rose to 66, triggering the entry into force of the Rome Statute on July 1, 2002. See Broomhall, *International Justice and International Criminal Court*, p. 76.

40. Undersecretary of state for Arms Control and International Security, John R. Bolton, *International Criminal Court: Letter to the UN Secretary General Kofi Annan* (May 6, 2002). http://www.state.gov/r/pa/prs/ps/2002/9968.htm.

41. *Secretary Rumsfeld Statement on the ICC Treaty*, United States Department of Defense News Release no. 233–02 (May 6, 2002), online at http://www.defenselink.mil/news/May2002/b05062002_bt233-02.html.

42. "A State is obliged to refrain from acts which would defeat the object and purpose of a treaty when . . . (a) it has signed the treaty or has exchanged instruments constituting the treaty subject to ratification, acceptance or approval, until it shall have made its intention clear not to become a party to the treaty. . ." *Vienna Convention on the Law of Treaties*, (1969) 1155 U.N.T.S. 331, art.18.

43. Under Secretary of State for Political Affairs Marc Grossman, *American Foreign Policy and the International Criminal Court*, Remarks to the Center for Strategic and International Studies (May 6, 2002) online at http://www.state.gov/p/9949.htm.

44. Grossman, *American Foreign Policy*.

45. Grossman, *American Foreign Policy*.

46. *Declaration by the EU on the Position of the US Toward the International Criminal Court* (May 13, 2002), online at http://www.ue2002.es/principal.asp?idioma-ingles.

47. *Declaration by the EU on the Position of the US*.

48. Colin Powell, secretary of state, May 6, 2002. ABC News Program "This Week."

49. "The international agreements mentioned in Article 98(2) of the Rome Statute are referred to by several terms, including Article 98 agreements, bilateral immunity agreements (BIAs), impunity agreements, and bilateral non-surrender agreements. The United States began negotiating these agreements with individual countries in 2002, and has concluded at least one hundred such agreements. Countries which sign these agreements with the United States agree not to surrender Americans to the jurisdiction of the International Criminal Court." http://www.ll.georgetown.edu/intl/guides/article_98.cfm (last accessed 08/07/07).

50. Security Council Resolution 1422 (July 12, 2002). See Judy Dempsey, "Little Applause on Criminal Court Deal," *Financial Times* (July 15, 2002).

51. Private Interview with Marisa Lino. Florence, Italy, 2004.

52. The principle of complementarity is a provision adopted in the Rome Statute according to which if a case is being considered by a country with jurisdiction over it, then the ICC cannot act unless the country is unwilling or genuinely unable to investigate or prosecute. http://www.icc-cpi.int/about/ataglance/faq.html.

53. Private Interview with Marisa Lino. Florence, Italy, 2004.

54. Those that favored a strong and independent court were also known as the "like minded group" (LMG). This group was composed of middle powers and developing countries (i.e., Canada and some African states).

55. The International Law Commission (ILC) had been appointed by the General Assembly of the UN to study the possibility of establishing a permanent criminal court. The court was envisaged by the Committee as a "semi-permanent" institution that would hold sessions only when matters before it required consideration. The proposed court's subject matter jurisdiction was limited to international crimes "provided in conventions or special agreements among States parties" to the Statute. Finally, cases could proceed only if the State or States of the accused national, and the State or States, in which the crime was alleged to have been committed, expressly conferred jurisdiction upon the court.

56. The phrase is used by David Davenport, "The New Diplomacy," *Policy Review*, Washington, Dec. 2002/Jan 2003, no. 116, p. 17. In Ottawa, to pass the text of the treaty banning anti-personnel land mines, small and medium sized powers, he argues, used "new diplomacy," whose characteristics were innovative technology and amazing speed.

57. European Council Common Position on the International Criminal Court, June 11, 2001 (2001/443/CFSP). Official Journal of the European Communities 12.6.2001. L. 155/19 http://europa.eu.int/geninfo/query/engine/search/query.pl.

58. Giuseppe Mammarella and Paolo Cacace, *Storia e Politica dell'Unione Europea* (Bari: Editori Laterza, 2000)

59. Mammarella and Cacace, *Storia e Politica dell'Unione Europea*.

60. Ruth Wodak and Gilbert Weiss, "European Union Discourses," in Wodak, ed., *New Agenda in (Critical Discourse Analysis: Theory, Methodology and Interdisciplinary* (Philadelphia, PA: John Benjamins Publishing Company, 2005).

61. Statement of Commissioner for External Relations, Chris Patten, on the International Criminal Court and the mandate for the UN Mission in Bosnia-Herzegovina, made at a press conference with Federal Minister of Foreign Affairs Mr. Goran Svilanovic in Belgrade, on July 3, 2002, http://europa.eu.int/comm/external_relations/see/news/ip02_991.htm.

62. John Bolton. U.S. Congress, Senate. Committee on Foreign Relations, *The International Criminal Court: Protecting American Servicemen and Officials from the Threat of International Prosecution*: Hearing before Committee on Foreign Relations. 106th Cong., 1st sess. June 14th, 2000.

63. Senator Rod Grams, Hearing before Committee on Foreign Relations. 106th Cong., 1st sess. June 14th, 2000.

64. Dr. Jeremy Rabkin, U.S. Congress, House. Committee on Foreign Relations, *The International Criminal Court*. Hearing before Committee on Foreign Relations. 106th Cong., 2st sess., July 25 and 26, 2000.

65. Marc Grossman, *American Foreign Policy*.

66. Marc Grossman, *American Foreign Policy*.

67. Bolton, Hearing before Committee on Foreign Relations. 106th Cong., 1st sess. June 14, 2000.

68. Many of the indicted are still on the loose, and this badly reflects on the two courts' image.

69. Council Common Position of June 2001 on the International Criminal Court (2001/443/CFSP). Official Journal of Europe and Communities 12.6.2001. L. 155/19.

70. Council Common Position of June 2001.

71. Council Common Position of June 2001.

72. Council Common Position on the International Criminal Court 2003/444/CFSP Official Journal L. 150 18.06.2003.

73. Council Common Position 2003/444/CFSP
74. Chris Patten, Speech. Plenary Session European Parliament—Strasbourg, September 25, 2002—SPEECH/02/431.
75. Powell. "This Week."
76. Rumsfeld. Statement. May 6, 2002.
77. Rumsfeld. Statement. May 6, 2002.
78. Powell. "This Week."
79. Chris Patten, Prague, December 7/8, 2001. Message of support to the No Peace without Justice Conference on the International Criminal Court.
80. Both Democrats and Republicans had this problem.
81. Caspar Weinberger, U.S. Senate, Committee on Foreign Relations, Hearing, June 14, 2000.
82. Rabkin, United States. Senate. Committee on Foreign Relations, Hearing, June 14, 2000.
83. Wedgwood, United States. Senate. Committee on Foreign Relations, Hearing, June 14, 2000.
84. Rabkin, United States. Senate. Committee on Foreign Relations, Hearing, June 14, 2000.
85. Rabkin, United States. Senate. Committee on Foreign Relations, Hearing, June 14, 2000.

NOTES TO CHAPTER 6

1. The G7 turned into the G8 with the 1998 Birmingham Summit, when Russia first became formally involved in the Summit process. The G7 Group of Finance Ministers and Central Bank Governors continues to exist as an entity that is distinct from the G8 and which excludes Russia. My focus in this chapter is the G7; thus Russia's role is not analyzed. Without intending any offense to Japan and Canada, in order to make this work manageable and for reasons of consistency with the rest of the book, I will analyze only the actions of the United States and the European states members of the G7.
2. The G8 leaders who signed the Final Communiqué in Cologne were Prime Minister Jean Chrétien for Canada, President Jacques Chirac for France, Chancellor Gerhard Schröder for Germany, Prime Minister Massimo D'Alema for Italy, Prime Minister Keizo Obuchi for Japan, President Boris Yeltsin for the Russian Federation, Prime Minister Tony Blair for the United Kingdom, President William J. Clinton for the United States. The Acting President for the European Union Jacques Santer also signed the Communiqué.
3. G8 Final Communiqué Köln. June 20, 1999. http://www.g8.utoronto.ca/finance/fm061899.htm.
4. G8 Final Communiqué Köln. June 20th, 1999.
5. Ronald Inglehart and Christian Welzel, *Modernization, Cultural Change, and Democracy* (Cambridge: Cambridge University Press, 2005). See Figure 2.4 Cultural map of the world about 2000, p. 63.
Inglehart's cultural map of the world about 2000 shows the location of 80 societies surveyed on two main dimensions of cross-cultural variation. The vertical axis reflects the polarization between traditional authority and secular rational authority linked with the process of industrialization. The horizontal axis reflects the polarization between survival values and self-expression values linked with the rise of a postindustrial society. Although his global cultural map is based on a factor analysis that uses less than half as many variables as he used in his 1989–91 Values Survey, and is based on almost

twice as many countries, he concludes that the locations of the respective societies on the cultural map of the world about 2000 are strikingly similar to those on the cultural maps produced earlier. It becomes evident from this map, as Inglehart argues, that the United States has a much more traditional value system than any other post-industrial society except for Ireland. On the traditional/secular dimension, the United States ranks far below other rich societies, with levels of religiosity and national pride comparable with those found in some developing societies.

6. Report of G7 Finance Ministers on the Kolon Debt Initiative to the Kolon Economic Summit. Cologne, June 18–20, 1999. "To achieve debt sustainability, we would be prepared to forgive up to 90 percent and more in individual cases if needed, in particular for the very poorest among these countries." http://www.g8.utoronto.ca/finance/fm061899.htm.

7. http://www.data.org/whyafrica/issuedebt.php.

8. http://web.worldbank.org.

9. For the World Bank it was the International Development Association (IDA), which is the Bank concessional lending arm for poor countries to initiate the process. I contacted the media office as well as the public affairs office at the IMF, but they have not been able to tell me what countries proposed the HIPC Initiative. http://web.worldbank.org.

10. http://web.worldbank.org.

11. http://www.jubileedebtcampaign.org.uk (accessed 10/9/06). The World Bank and the IMF do not give any credit to the Jubilee 2000 campaign for their decision to launch the HIPC Initiative. The World Bank's websites states "Starting in the late 1980s, the Paris Club and other bilateral creditors rescheduled and forgave many of these debts. But by the mid 1990s, with an increasing share of debt owed to multilateral lenders such as the World Bank, the IMF, and regional development banks, a new debt relief initiative was called for, involving these creditors, to address the concern that poor countries' debts were stifling poverty reduction efforts. In response, in 1996 the International Development Association (IDA, the World Bank's concessional lending arm for poor countries) and the IMF launched the HIPC Initiative." Further research should be done to understand the impact of transnational social movements on the debt relief issue. http://web.worldbank.org.

12. SAPs is the acronym for Structural Adjustment Programs. Examples of structural adjustment conditions are privatizations of state industries, local currency devaluation and cuts to social services. According to Fantu Cheru, an economist from Ethiopia, who teaches at the American University in Washington, and who wrote a book entitled *The Silent Revolution in Africa: Debt, Development and Democracy* (London: Zed Press, 1989) "Structural adjustment programs have been particularly divisive, setting farmers against civil servants, civil servants against labor unions. Mass mobilizations for democratic alternatives become almost impossible. Everybody is so poor that survival takes priority over long-term solutions that can build solidarity among urban and rural people". Fantu Cheru, "Please Don't Develop Us Any More," *Middle East Report*, September–October 1990. p. 27.

13. Geo-Jaja Macleans and Garth Mangum, "Structural Adjustment as an Inadvertent Enemy of Human Development in Africa," *Journal of Black Studies*, vol. 32, no. 1 (Sept., 2001), pp. 30–31.

14. Report of G7 Finance Ministers on the Kolon Debt Initiative to the Kolon Economic Summit. Cologne, June 18–20, 1999. http://www.g8.utoronto.ca/finance/fm061899.htm.

15. http://clinton2.nara.gov/.

16. http://web.worldbank.org.

17. "In order to receive the full and irrevocable reduction in debt available under the HIPC Initiative, the country must: (i) establish a further track record of good performance under IMF- and IDA-supported programs; (ii) implement satisfactorily key reforms agreed at the decision point, and (iii) adopt and implement the PRSP for at least one year. Once a country has met these criteria, it can reach its 'completion point,' at which time lenders are expected to provide the full debt relief committed at decision point." http://www.imf.org/external/np/exr/facts/hipc.htm.

18. http://web.worldbank.org. It is also worth noting that in 2006, following the G8 Gleneagles Summit, "the World Bank joined the IMF and the African Development Bank in implementing the Multilateral Debt Relief Initiative (MDRI), forgiving 100 percent of eligible outstanding debt owed to these three institutions by all countries reaching the completion point of the HIPC Initiative. The MDRI will effectively double the volume of debt relief already expected from the enhanced HIPC Initiative."

19. Deutsche Presse Agentur, "Rich Nations Agree Debt Relief for Poorest." June 18, 1999.

20. City briefing, *The Guardian* (London), June 15, 1999, p. 22.

21. Press Release. Cologne. June 21, 1999. http://www.g7.utoronto.ca/summit/1999koln/pr_june21.html

22. Deutsche Presse Agentur, "France Cancelling Poorest Africans' Debt," June 18, 1999.

23. *Washington Street Journal*, June 21, 1999.

24. The study is entitled "Compliance with G8 Commitments: From Koln 1999 to Okinawa 2000. Compliance Studies by Issue Area: Köln Debt Initiative." I will keep referring to the G7 and not the G8 because it was the G7 that committed to the Debt Initiative, not the G8. The document can be found online on G8 Information Center website: http://www.g7.utoronto.ca/evaluations/2000okinawa/compliance/debt.htm.

25. http://www.g7.utoronto.ca/evaluations/2000okinawa/compliance/debt.htm.

26. http://www.g7.utoronto.ca/evaluations/2000okinawa/compliance/debt.htm.

27. ODA are "net disbursements of loans or grants made on concessional terms by official agencies of member countries of the Organization for Economic Cooperation and Development (OECD)." The definition can be found in the glossary of Michael P. Todaro and Stephen C. Smith, *Economic Development*, (Boston: Addison Wesley, 2003), p. 804.

28. "Following extensive discussions on financing of the Heavily Indebted Poor Country Initiative (HIPC) and Enhanced Structural Adjustment Facility (ESAF) initiatives, agreement has been reached on the main elements of a financing package that will enable the IMF to make its contribution to the HIPC Initiative and to continue concessional lending for sustainable growth and poverty reduction in its low income member countries. [. . .] Bilateral pledges amount to about SDR 1.5 billion "as needed" and come from a wide cross-section of the IMF's membership, demonstrating the broad support for the HIPC and ESAF initiatives. Industrial countries as well as a large number of developing countries—including some low-income countries that have had ESAF-supported programs in the past—have made pledges to the ESAF-HIPC Trust." http://www.imf.org/external/np/sec/nb/1999/nb9962.htm.

29. Ronals Inglehart and Christian Welzel, *Modernization, Cultural Change, and Democracy* (Cambridge: Cambridge University Press, 2005). See Cultural map of the world about 2000, p. 63.

30. Esther Scoot. Kennedy School of Government Case Program. "Debt Relief for Poor Nations: The Battle in Congress" (C15–01–1613.0).

31. Tamara Straus, *Jubilee 2000: The Movement America Missed.* Alternet, March 6, 2001, p. 3 http://www.alternet.org/story/10568/.

32. James Traub, "The Statesman," *The New York Times Magazine*, September 18, 2005, p. 86.

33. James Traub, "The Statesman," *The New York Times Magazine*, September 18, 2005, p. 86.

34. James Traub, "The Statesman," *The New York Times Magazine*, September 18, 2005, p. 86.

35. Esther Scoot. Kennedy School of Government Case Program. "Debt Relief for Poor Nations: The Battle in Congress." (C15–01–1613.0).

36. Joseph Kahn, "Leaders in Congress Agree to Debt Relief for Poor Nations," *The New York Times*, October 18th, 2000, p. A12.

37. James Traub, "The Statesman," *The New York Times Magazine*, September 18, 2005, p. 86.

38. Kahn, "Leaders in Congress."

39. Tamara Straus, *Jubilee 2000: The Movement America Missed*, Alternet, March 6, 2001, p. 3, http://www.alternet.org/story/10568/.

40. Straus, *Jubilee 2000*.

41. Straus, *Jubilee 2000*.

42. Straus, *Jubilee 2000*.

43. Martin Dent is a retired professor, and Bill Peters is a retired British ambassador. They had worked on a relief project in Africa and were involved in the 1980s debt reform movement.

44. Third Book of Moses, Leviticus, Chapter 25: "Each seventh year to be kept as a sabbath year—Each fiftieth year to be one of jubilee, in which liberty is proclaimed throughout the land—Laws revealed for sale and redemption of lands, houses, and servants—The land is the Lord's, as are the servants—Usury forbidden." http://scriptures.lds.org/en/lev/25.

45. Straus, *Jubilee 2000*.

46. Straus, *Jubilee 2000: The Movement America Missed*, Alternet, March 6, 2001, p. 2, http://www.alternet.org/story/10568/.

47. Members were connected via email and Jubilee 2000 took advantage of fast communication and organization both in the North and the South. As a result, between 1995 and 1998, Jubilee 2000 opened offices in Ghana, Peru, West Africa, Germany, India, Italy and the United States.

48. http://www.jubileedebtcampaign.org.uk/?lid=2675.

49. In 1999 British Chancellor Gordon Brown (currently British prime minister) and Clare Short, British secretary of state for International Development, put forward a plan to help the world's poorest countries. The plan had four goals: cut debt, boost aid, give a billion and sell the gold. For more on the plan: http://www.hm-treasury.gov.uk/newsroom_and_speeches/press/1999/press_42_99.cfm.

In 2004, Tony Blair launched a commission for Africa. "In early 2004, the British Prime Minister, Tony Blair, established the Commission for Africa. The 17 members of the Commission, 9 from Africa and all working in their individual and personal capacities, published their report "Our Common Interest" on March 11, 2005. The Commission's report is addressed to the leaders of the G8 and to the wider international community. It is also addressed to the people of Africa and the world as a whole. The measures proposed by the Commission constitute a coherent package to achieve the Commission's goal of a strong and prosperous Africa." http://www.commissionforafrica.org/en glish/home/newsstories.html.

50. Ann Pettifor, "A personal view of the Jubilee 2000 'human chain' demonstration on 16th May 1998, during the G8 summit in Birmingham," http://www.jubileedebtcampaign.org.uk/?lid=280.

51. The G8 was moved from the city and held on an estate in the village of Weston-under-Lizard, approximately 20 miles outside Birmingham.

52. Pettifor, "A personal view of the Jubilee 2000 'human chain' demonstration on 16th May 1998, during the G8 summit in Birmingham," http://www.jubileedebtcampaign.org.uk/?lid=280.

53. Response by the Presidency on Behalf of the G8 to the Jubilee 2000 Petition. Online: http://www.g7.utoronto.ca/summit/1998birmingham/2000.htm.

54. My analysis of U.S. newspapers indicates to the contrary that American articles and editorials had a strictly economic, almost technical approach and did not address the protests to cancel the debt. In sum, they seem to confirm the opinion of Pettifor when she argued that the reason for the lack of public opinion involvement in the United States was that there was no attempt to create public opinion on debt relief. My argument about U.S. newspapers is based on an analysis of the *New York Times*, the *Los Angeles Times* and the *Wall Street Journal* for the years 1997–2000, so that it would be a fair comparison to the European newspapers that I analyzed for the same period.

55. Details of the *Guardian*'s campaign for the debt relief can be found at www.newsunlimited.co.uk/debt.

56. http://www.guardian.co.uk/debt/Story/0,,208935,00.html.

57. In his article Vallely discussed then UK Chancellor, Gordon Brown's announcement that Britain would write off 100% of the debts of at least 26 countries. See Paul Vallely, "A Billion People Go to Bed Hungry Each Night," *The Independent*, December 18, 1999.

58. http://www.guardian.co.uk/.

59. *Pettifor, Jubilee Research Analysis, The World Will Never Be the Same.* http://www.jubileeresearch.org/analysis/reports/world_never_same_again/intro.htm.

60. "Do You Believe in Fairies?," *The Economist*, December 31, 1999, p. 3

61. "Special: Africa: The Heart of the Matter." *The Economist*, May 13, 2000, p. 22.

62. "Finance and Economics: Clean Slate; Debt Relief." *The Economist*, October 2, 2004, p. 85.

63. I am addressing only these countries because these are the European North Atlantic countries of my study, except for Italy. Furthermore, they all have a seat at the G8. For France, among many others see "L'Afrique découvre sa compétitivité; Principal handicap pour les économies locales: le poids excessif de la dette," *Le Monde*, February 10, 1998. "Sur fond de litige entre Air Afrique et ses créanciers, la France souhaite une 'prise de responsabilité africaine sur le problème de la dette de la compagnie.–Le tribunal de commerce de Paris saisi du sort d'Air Afrique," *Les Echo*, February 19, 1999, p. 17. "La dette impayable et le jubilé 2000; Christine von Garnier, sociologue et secrétaire du Réseau Europe-Afrique, estime que ce serait une bonne et juste politique à long terme que d'effacer la dette des pays les plus pauvres," *Le Temps*, June17, 1999. "L'Afrique réclame une annulation importante de sa dette." *La Croix*, August 31, 1999, p. 2. "Les Européens veulent aider l'Afrique à s'adapter à la mondialisation; La question de la dette était au centre du sommet du Caire. Pour le président de la Commission européenne, Romano Prodi, un nouveau modèle de partenariat doit permettre

au continent africain de s'adapter à la nouvelle économie mondiale." *Le Monde.* April 5, 2000.

64. http://www.jubileeresearch.org/jubilee2000/news/italy230200.html.

65. Vernon Jordan Jr., "Africa's Promise," *Wall Street Journal*, March 26, 1998.

66. Adonis Hoffman, "The Historic Trip That Could Seal a Partnership," *Los Angeles Times*, March 29, 1998

67. James Flanigan, "Gore Reveals Debt-Relief Plan for Poor Nations," *Los Angeles Times*, January 30, 1999.

68. David E. Sanger, "Clinton to Offer Debt Relief Plan for Poor Nations," *New York Times*, March 16, 1999.

69. Eric Schmitt, "House Passes Compromise Bill for $13.5 Billion in Foreign Aid," *New York Times*, November 6, 1999.

70. Bob Davis, "G 7 Moves to Revamp Financial Systems—West Proposes Reducing Debt of Poor Nations, Steps to Avert Crises," *The Wall Street Journal*, June 21, 1999, p. A23.

71. Dean E. Murphy, "In Africa, Debt Relief Has 2 Sides," *Los Angeles Times*, January 27, 2000.

72. Maxine Waters, "Commentary; Third World Debt Relief Is the Right Thing to Do; Foreign Policy: Poor Nations Are Being Forced to Cut Health and Education Services to Pay Back Debts," *Los Angeles Times*, April 14, 2000, p. 9.

73. Maxine Waters, "Commentary; Third World Debt Relief Is the Right Thing to Do."

74. As I said previously in this chapter, my analysis of U.S. newspapers indicates that articles and editorials had a strictly economic, almost technical approach and did not address the protests to cancel the debt. Once again, my argument about U.S. newspapers is based on the analysis of the *New York Times*, the *Los Angeles Times* and the *Wall Street Journal* for the years 1997–2000.

NOTES TO CHAPTER 7

1. Kareem Fahim, "Slap to a Man's Pride Set Off Tumult in Tunisia," *The New York Times*, January 21, 2011, sec. World / Africa, http://www.nytimes.com/2011/01/22/world/africa/22sidi.html.

2. "Tunisia Elections 2011: Ennahda Islamist Party Official Winner," *Huffington Post*, October 27, 2011, http://www.huffingtonpost.com/2011/10/27/tunisia-elections-2011-ennahda_n_1062709.html.

3. "Protest in Egypt: Another Arab Regime Under Threat," *The Economist*, January 27, 2011, http://www.economist.com/node/18013760; "Egypt Braced for 'Day of Revolution' Protests," *The Guardian*, January 24, 2011, http://www.guardian.co.uk/world/2011/jan/24/egypt-day-revolution-protests.

4. Craig Whitlock, "Mubarak Steps down, Prompting Jubilation in Cairo Streets," *The Washington Post*, February 12, 2011, sec. World, http://www.washingtonpost.com/wp-dyn/content/article/2011/02/11/AR2011021102386.html.

5. David D. Kirkpatrick, "Mohamed Morsi of Muslim Brotherhood Declared as Egypt's President," *The New York Times*, June 24, 2012, sec. World /Middle East, http://www.nytimes.com/2012/06/25/world/middleeast/mohamed-morsi-of-muslim-brotherhood-declared-as-egypts-president.html. Ernesto Londoño and Karin Brulliard, "Islamist Mohamed Morsi Is Sworn in as President of Egypt," *The Washington Post*, July 1, 2012, sec. World, http://www.washingtonpost.com/world/middle_east/islamist-morsi-is-sworn-in-as-president-of-egypt/2012/06/30/gJQA84vZDW_story.html.

6. "Yemen President Saleh Steps Down," *BBC*, February 27, 2012, sec. Middle East, http://www.bbc.co.uk/news/world-middle-east-17177720. "Yemen's Ali Abdullah Saleh Resigns—But It Changes Little," *The Guardian*, November 24, 2011. http://www.guardian.co.uk/commentisfree/2011/nov/24/yemen-ali-abdullah-saleh-resigns; David Blair, Chief Foreign Correspondent, "Yemen's President Steps Down After 33 Years," *Telegraph.co.uk*, November 23, 2011, sec. worldnews, http://www.telegraph.co.uk/news/worldnews/middleeast/yemen/8910946/Yemens-president-steps-down-after-33-years.html.
7. United Nations Security Council, "UN Resolution 2014 Security Council Condemns Human Rights Violations by Yemeni Authorities, Abuses by 'Other Actors', After Months of Political Strife," October 21, 2011, http://www.un.org/News/Press/docs/2011/sc10418.doc.htm.
8. Karen DeYoung, "President Obama Executive Order Gives Treasury Authority to Freeze Yemeni Assets in U.S.," *The Washington Post*, May 17, 2012, sec. World, http://www.washingtonpost.com/world/national-security/president-obama-executive-order-will-give-treasury-authority-to-freeze-us-based-assets-in-yemen/2012/05/15/gIQALWPUSU_story.html.
9. The Bahraini uprising is also known as the "Pearl Revolution," from the name of the traffic circle, Pearl Square, in the capital of Manama, where many protesters rallied.
10. Karen Leigh, "Bahrain: Caught Between Saudi Arabia and Iran," *Time*, March 15, 2011, http://www.time.com/time/world/article/0,8599,2058992,00.html.
11. "Bahrain: A Special Case Among the Arab Spring Uprisings," *The Guardian*, June 19, 2012, http://www.guardian.co.uk/world/2012/jun/19/bahrain-special-case-arab-spring.
12. "Libyan Army Calls for Benghazi to Surrender as Saif Gaddafi Says Town Will Fall Within 48 Hours," *Telegraph.co.uk*, March 16, 2011, sec. worldnews, http://www.telegraph.co.uk/news/worldnews/africaandindianocean/libya/8385250/Libyan-army-calls-for-Benghazi-to-surrender-as-Saif-Gaddafi-says-town-will-fall-within-48-hours.html. The Security Council had also passed Resolution 1970 on February 17, 2011, establishing an arms embargo. This resolution also froze the personal assets of Gaddafi and imposed a travel ban on relevant regimes figures. United Nations Security Council, "In Swift, Decisive Action, Security Council Imposes Tough Measures on Libyan Regime, Adopting Resolution 1970 in Wake of Crackdown on Protesters," February 26, 2011, http://www.un.org/News/Press/docs/2011/sc10187.doc.htm.
13. "UN Security Council Resolution 1973, Libya," *Council on Foreign Relations*, n.d., http://www.cfr.org/libya/un-security-council-resolution-1973-libya/p24426.
14. "London Conference on Libya: Chair's Statement," n.d., http://www.fco.gov.uk/en/news/latest-news/?id=574646182&view=News.
15. "Timeline: Libya's Uprising Against Muammar Gaddafi," *Reuters*, August 22, 2011, http://www.reuters.com/article/2011/08/22/us-libya-events-idUSTRE77K2QH20110822.
16. Ediciones El País, "La suerte de los dictadores de la 'primavera árabe,'" *EL PAÍS*, June 2, 2012, http://internacional.elpais.com/internacional/2012/06/02/ actualidad/1338641961_271002.html.
17. Melissa Bell and Elizabeth Flock, "Video Said to Show a Wounded Gaddafi After His Capture," *The Washington Post—Blogs*, October 21, 2011, http://www.washingtonpost.com/blogs/blogpost/post/sirte-fall-rumors-swirl-of-gaddafi-capture-but-all-unconfirmed/2011/10/20/gIQA5wM7zL_blog.html.

18. "Nato Ends Military Operations in Libya," *The Guardian*, October 31, 2011, http://www.guardian.co.uk/world/2011/oct/31/nato-ends-libya-rasmussen.
19. "Egypt Unrest: Day 10 as It Happened," *BBC*, February 4, 2011, sec. UK Politics, http://news.bbc.co.uk/2/mobile/uk_news/politics/9387166.stm.
20. "G20 Should Back Tunisia, Egypt Transitions-Sarkozy," *Reuters*, February 18, 2011, http://af.reuters.com/article/egyptNews/idAFLDE71H23Y20110218.
21. David Levitz, "Germany Presses Egypt to Strengthen Its Commitment to Democracy," *Deutsche Welle*, April 19, 2011, http://www.dw.de/dw/article/0,,15001657,00.html.
22. Steven Lee Myers, "Tumult of Arab Spring Prompts Worries in Washington," *The New York Times*, September 17, 2011, sec. World / Middle East, http://www.nytimes.com/2011/09/18/world/middleeast/tumult-of-arab-spring-prompts-worries-in-washington.html.
23. Ediciones El País, "Zapatero pide una 'transición pacífica' en Egipto y Túnez," *EL PAÍS*, January 31, 2011, http://elpais.com/diario/2011/01/31/internacional/1296428404_850215.html.
24. "William Hague Arrives in Tunisia to Meet New Regime," *The Guardian*, February 8, 2011, http://www.guardian.co.uk/politics/2011/feb/08/william-hague-visits-tunisia.
25. "Cairo, Uccisi Manifestante e Poliziotto A Suez Alle Fiamme Palazzo Governativo," *Il Corriere Della Sera*, January 26, 2011.
26. Barry Moody, "Italy Supports Egypt's Mubarak but Urges Reform," *Reuters*, January 27, 2011, http://af.reuters.com/article/egyptNews/idAFLDE70Q2L820110127.
27. "Press Conference Given by Alain Juppé, Ministre d'Etat, Minister of Foreign and European Affairs," March 6, 2011, http://www.diplomatie.gouv.fr/en/country-files/egypt-288/visits-3467/article/press-conference-given-by-alain.
28. Ibid.
29. "Remarks by the President on the Middle East and North Africa | The White House," n.d., http://www.whitehouse.gov/the-press-office/2011/05/19/remarks-president-middle-east-and-north-africa.
30. Steven Erlanger, "Europe's Foreign Policy Chief Struggles for Footing," *The New York Times*, February 10, 2011, sec. World / Europe, http://www.nytimes.com/2011/02/11/world/europe/11europe.html.
31. "'Everyone, Including the Muslim Brotherhood, Must Be Involved,'" *Spiegel Online*, February 15, 2011, http://www.spiegel.de/international/europe/eu-foreign-policy-chief-ashton-on-egypt-everyone-including-the-muslim-brotherhood-must-be-involved-a-745522.html.
32. Ibid.
33. European Commission, "The European Neighbourhood Policy (ENP)," 2004, http://ec.europa.eu/world/enp/welcome_en.htm.
34. Ibid. The ENP was proposed to 16 neighboring countries: Algeria, Armenia, Azerbaijan, Belarus, Egypt, Georgia, Israel, Jordan, Lebanon, Libya, Moldova, Morocco, the Occupied Palestinian Territory, Syria, Tunisia and Ukraine. However, only 12 of them agreed. Given their refusal, the EU has not activated the ENP with Algeria, Belarus, Libya and Syria.
35. The German Marshall Fund, "Transatlantic Trends: Immigration," December 15, 2011, http://www.integrazionemigranti.gov.it/Documenti/Documents/Documenti%20da%20newsletter%20gennaio%202012/TTImmigration_final_web.pdf.
36. Ibid.
37. "Charlemagne: Another Project in Trouble," *The Economist*, April 28, 2011, http://www.economist.com/node/18618525.

38. "France and Italy in Call to Close EU Borders in Wake of Arab Protests," *The Guardian*, April 26, 2011, http://www.guardian.co.uk/world/2011/apr/26/eu-borders-arab-protests.

39. "The EU Has Failed the Arab World," *Spiegel Online*, February 28, 2011, http://www.spiegel.de/international/world/europe-s-favorite-dictators-the-eu-has-failed-the-arab-world-a-748074-2.html.

40. "Berlusconi: Permessi Validi, C'è L'ok Europeo," *Il Sole 24 ORE*, n.d., http://www.ilsole24ore.com/art/notizie/2011-04-14/berlusconi-permessi-validi-europeo-063923.shtml?uuid=AaD0WnOD.

41. "Tunisini in Francia Con i Permessi Ma Parigi Nega: Nessun Ingresso," *LaStampa.it*, n.d., http://www3.lastampa.it/cronache/sezioni/articolo/lstp/398184/.

42. "Italy Protests as France Blocks Train Carrying Migrants from Tunisia," *The Guardian*, April 17, 2011, http://www.guardian.co.uk/world/2011/apr/17/italy-protests-france-tunisia-migrant-train.

43. "France and Italy in Call to Close EU Borders in Wake of Arab Protests | EUTimes.net," n.d., http://www.eutimes.net/2011/04/france-and-italy-in-call-to-close-eu-borders-in-wake-of-arab-protests/.

44. Ibid.

45. Debbi Wilgoren and William Branigin, "Boehner Elected House Speaker as 112th Congress Convenes," *The Washington Post*, January 5, 2011, sec. Politics, http://www.washingtonpost.com/wp-dyn/content/article/2011/01/05/AR2011010501936.html.

46. Mark Mazzetti and Helene Cooper, "Bin Laden Captured Through Detective Work," *The New York Times*, May 2, 2011, sec. World / Asia Pacific, http://www.nytimes.com/2011/05/02/world/asia/02reconstruct-capture-osama-bin-laden.html.

47. Evan Perez, "Obama Letter to Congress on Libya Sparks Protests," *Wall Street Journal*, March 22, 2011, http://online.wsj.com/article/SB10001424052748704355304576215073989153598.html.

48. "Remarks by the President on the Middle East and North Africa | The White House."

49. Ibid.

50. Ibid.

51. Ibid.

52. The G-8 is an informal grouping of advanced industrialized nations that meets annually to discuss issues of political and economic relevance. It was created in the 1970s. Initially, the United States, France, the United Kingdom, Germany, Japan and Italy formed the Group of Six (G-6). Canada and Russia were added later (respectively 1976 and 1997) creating the Group of Eight (G-8). The European Union also joins the meeting of the G8 and is represented by the presidents of the European Council and the European Commission.

53. NEXINT, "Declaration of the G8 on the Arab Springs," n.d., http://www.g8-g20.com/g8-g20/g8/english/live/news/declaration-of-the-g8-on-the-arab-springs.1316.html. See also Juan Manuel Bellver, "Los Líderes Europeos Piden Que Se Respete La Tregua En Yemen," *El Mundo*, June 7, 2011, http://www.elmundo.es/elmundo/2011/06/06/internacional/1307388170.html.

54. The G-8 Summit of Deauville also launched the "Deauville Partnership." The partnership is substantially based on two pillars: a political process to support the democratic transition and promote governance reforms and an economic framework for sustainable growth. NEXINT, "Declaration of the G8 on the Arab Springs."

55. Ibid.

56. Sebastian Moffett, Nathalie Boschat, and William Horobin, "G-8 Pledges $40 Billion for 'Arab Spring,'" *Wall Street Journal*, May 28, 2011, http://online.wsj.com/article/SB10001424052702304520804576348792147454956.html.
57. Uri Dadush and Michele Dunne, "American and European Responses to the Arab Spring: What's the Big Idea?" *The Washington Quarterly*, Fall 2011, http://carnegieendowment.org/2011/09/01/american-and-european-responses-to-arab-spring-what-s-big-idea/5sim.
58. Ibid., p.133.
59. Ibid., p.136.
60. Barry Buzan, *People, States, and Fear: The National Security Problem in International Relations* (Sussex: Wheatsheaf Books, 1983).

NOTES TO CHAPTER 8

1. www.un.org 2011.
2. Timothy Garton Ash. "France Plays Hawk, Germany Demurs. Libya Has Exposed Europe's Fault Lines." *The Guardian*, March 24, 2011.
3. Steven Lee Kirkpatrick and D. David Myers, "Allies Split on Goal and Exit Strategy in Lybia." *New York Times*, March 24, 2011.
4. AlJazeera. "New Libya Contact Group to Meet in Qatar." http://english.aljazeera.net. 3 29, 2011.
5. Steven Lee Kirkpatrick and D. David Myers, "Allies Split on Goal and Exit Strategy in Lybia." *New York Times*, March 24, 2011.
6. Mark Landler and Elisabeth Bumiller. "Washington in Fierce Debate on Arming Lybyan Rebels." *New York Times*, March 29, 2011.
7. Foreign & Commonwealth Office. March 29, 2011. www.fco.gov.uk.
8. Al-Jazeera. "New Libya Contact Group to Meet in Qatar." http://english.aljazeera.net. March 29, 2011.
9. Al-Jazeera. "New Libya Contact Group to Meet in Qatar." http://english.aljazeera.net. March 29, 2011.
10. Mark Landler and Elisabeth Bumiller. "Washington in Fierce Debate on Arming Lybyan Rebels." *New York Times*, March 29, 2011.
11. Mark Landler and Elisabeth Bumiller. "Washington in Fierce Debate on Arming Lybyan Rebels." *New York Times*, March 29, 2011.
12. Mark Landler and Elisabeth Bumiller. "Washington in Fierce Debate on Arming Lybyan Rebels." *New York Times*, March 29, 2011.
13. Mark Landler and Elisabeth Bumiller. "Washington in Fierce Debate on Arming Lybyan Rebels." *New York Times*, March 29, 2011.
14. Operation Unified Protector was the NATO operation that had the goal of implementing UNSC resolutions 1970 and 1973.
15. NATO. www.nato.int. March 14, 2011.
16. Bruno Waterfield and Thomas Harding. "Libya: NATO Calls for All Its Members to Help Oust Gaddafi." *The Telegraph*, March 3, 2011. http://telegraph.co.uk.
17. The seven countries were the United States, Canada, United Kingdom, France, Norway, Italy and Denmark.
18. Spetalnick Matt and David Brunnstrom. "NATO States Buck French, British Call over Libya." *Reuters*, April 14, 2011. http://www.reuters.com.
19. Spetalnick Matt and David Brunnstrom. "NATO States Buck French, British Call over Libya." *Reuters*, April 14, 2011. http://www.reuters.com.
20. Spetalnick Matt and David Brunnstrom. "NATO States Buck French, British Call over Libya." *Reuters*, April 14, 2011. http://www.reuters.com.

21. Spetalnick Matt and David Brunnstrom. "NATO States Buck French, British Call over Libya." *Reuters.*, April 14, 2011. http://www.reuters.com.

22. Allegra Strutton. "Obama, Cameron and Sarkozy: No Let-Up in Libya until Gaddafi Departs." *The Guardian*, April 14, 2011.

23. Sarkozy, Cameron, and Obama. "Libya's Pathway to Peace." *The New York Times*, April 14, 2011.

24. Roland Nelles and Gregor Peter Schmitz. "Blow Out Party for a Relationship of Waning Importance." *Der Spiegel*, June 8, 2011.

25. Ian Traynor. "Libya Conflict: EU Awaits UN Approval for Deployment of Ground Troops." *The Guardian*, April 18, 2011.

26. The ICC Prosecutor Moreno-Ocampo reported to the UNSC that he would apply to the ICC's pre-court trial chamber to issue arrest warrants for three people who, he said, seemed to be responsible for crimes against humanity committed in Libya since mid-February. Moreno said that "The evidence collected establishes reasonable grounds to believe that widespread and systematic attacks against the civilian population have been and continue to be committed in Libya, including murder and persecution as crimes against humanity" (UN News Centre 2011).

27. C. J. Chivers. "Inferior Arms Hobble Rebels in Libya War." *The New York Times*, April 20, 2011.

28. Gilbert Achcar. "The Libyan Insurrection between Gaddafi's Hammer, NATO's Anvil and the Left's Confusion: Results and Prospects." *Le Monde Diplomatique*, April 25, 2011.

29. Richard Norton-Taylor. "Libya Conflict Escalates as Ministers Admit It Could Drag on for Months." *The Guardian*, May 24, 2011.

30. BBC. "Libya Crisis: Doha Meeting Seeks to Raise $2.5bn aid." BBC. August 24, 2011.

31. Chris McGreal. "Barack Obama: US Not in Breach of Law Over Role in Libyan Conflict." *The Guardian*, June 16, 2011.

32. H. Philip Gordon. "Statement Before the Subcommittee on European Affairs of the Senate Foreign Relations Committee." Department of State. May 18, 2011.

33. La Republica. *La Ashton a Bengasi Apre la Rappresentanza UE.* Rome, May 22, 2011.

34. M Gonzalez and M.R. De Rituerto. *El Pais.* June 9, 2011. http://international.elpais.com.

35. Jiménez said "La presión política es la mejor que podemos hacer. Significa intensificar los contactos y negociaciones con Gadafi para que deje el poder. Porque tiene que dejarlo. Ya nunca más podrá regir el destino de su país". Genteactiva. *Gente Active.* June 9, 2011. http://genteactive.net.

36. New York Times. "Russia Says France Is Violating Embargo." *The New York Times*, July 1, 2011.

37. Daily News. "Libya Contact Group Recognizes Libya's Revels." *The Daily News*, July 15, 2011.

38. BBC. "Libya: Contact Group Creates Fund for Rebels." London, May 5, 2011.

39. French Ministry of Foreign Affairs. "Friends of Libya Conference." *France Diplomatie*, September 1, 2011. http://www.diplomatie.gouv.fr.

40. Despite its opposition to the NATO bombing campaign, Russia recognized the rebel government. Russia's Foreign Minister Sergei Lavrov said that Russia "established and has maintained diplomatic relations with Libya since Sept. 4, 1955, and has never broken them, regardless of what kind of government was in power in Tripoli." This statement opens a new phase in the Russian position on Libya. Moscow had previously claimed that it would

have withheld official recognition until it was evident that the rebels could unite Libya under their leadership (Erlanger, Russia Recognizes Libya Rebels as World Leaders Meet 2011).

41. Erlanger, Steven. "Russia Recognizes Libya Rebels as World Leaders Meet." September 2011.

NOTES TO CHAPTER 9

1. "The New Transatlantic Agenda," 1995, http://eeas.europa.eu/us/docs/new_transatlantic_agenda_en.pdf.
2. Ibid.
3. Ibid.
4. Ibid.
5. Organization for Economic Cooperation and Development, "Development: Aid to Developing Countries Falls Because of Global Recession" (OECD, April 4, 2012), http://www.oecd.org/document/3/0,3746,en_21571361_44315115_50058883_1_1_1_1,00.html.
6. The OECD defines ODA as "grants or loans to countries and territories on the DAC list of ODA recipients (developing countries) and to multilateral agencies which are: (a) undertaken by the official sector; (b) with promotion of economic development and welfare as the main objective; (c) at concessional financial terms." http://www.oecd.org/dac/dacglossaryofkeytermsandconcepts.htm#ODA.
7. Japan was also a major donor, but it is outside the transatlantic area.
8. Gross National Income (GNI) is the total monetary value of all goods and services produced in a country over a period of time, usually a year.
9. "DAC Members: Dates of Membership and Websites," n.d., http://www.oecd.org/dac/dacmembersdatesofmembershipandwebsites.htm.
10. This goal was based on individual targets of 0.7% for the EU 15 and 0.33% for the 12 countries that joined the EU in 2004 and 2007.
11. "Value of OECD Aid Drops for First Time in 15 Years," *The Guardian*, April 4, 2012, http://www.guardian.co.uk/global-development/2012/apr/04/value-oecd-aid-drops-15-years.
12. European Commission, "In Times of Crisis, the EU Must Not Forget the Poorest in the World," says Commissioner Piebalgs. "EU Confirms Its Position as the World's Largest Aid Donor in 2011," n.d., http://ec.europa.eu/commission_2010–2014/piebalgs/headlines/news/2012/04/20120410_en.htm.
13. Interview, June 9th, 2011.
14. European Commission, "In Times of Crisis, the EU Must Not Forget the Poorest in the World," says Commissioner Piebalgs. "EU Confirms Its Position as the World's Largest Aid Donor in 2011."
15. Jack Treddenick quoted in Stephen J. Flanagan and Guy Ben-Ari, *A Diminishing Transatlantic Partnership?: The Impact of the Financial Crisis on European Defense and Foreign Assistance Capabilities* (Center for Strategic & International Studies, 2011), p.15.
16. I am using the term "military expenditure" (% of GDP) as defined by the World Bank: "Military expenditures data from SIPRI are derived from the NATO definition, which includes all current and capital expenditures on the armed forces, including peacekeeping forces; defense ministries and other government agencies engaged in defense projects; paramilitary forces, if these are judged to be trained and equipped for military operations; and

military space activities. Such expenditures include military and civil personnel, including retirement pensions of military personnel and social services for personnel; operation and maintenance; procurement; military research and development; and military aid (in the military expenditures of the donor country). Excluded are civil defense and current expenditures for previous military activities, such as for veterans' benefits, demobilization, conversion, and destruction of weapons. This definition cannot be applied for all countries, however, since that would require much more detailed information than is available about what is included in military budgets and off-budget military expenditure items. (For example, military budgets might or might not cover civil defense, reserves and auxiliary forces, police and paramilitary forces, dual-purpose forces such as military and civilian police, military grants in kind, pensions for military personnel, and social security contributions paid by one part of government to another.)" http://data.worldbank.org/indicator/MS.MIL.XPND.GD.ZS.

17. Stockholm International Peace Research Institute, "Recent Trends in Military Expenditure" (Stockholm International Peace Research Institute, 2012), http://www.sipri.org:9090/research/armaments/milex/resultoutput/trends.

18. Ibid.

19. It is also important to remember that in July 2011, Congress passed military spending cuts of $487 billion over the next 10 years. These cuts, combined with the withdrawal of U.S. forces from Iraq and Afghanistan, are likely to diminish the total of U.S. military spending over the coming years.

20. Stockholm International Peace Research Institute, "Recent Trends in Military Expenditure."

21. "NATO—The New Strategic Concept: Active Engagement, Modern Defence"—Speech by NATO Secretary General Anders Fogh Rasmussen at the German Marshall Fund of the United States (GMF), Brussels," *NATO*, n.d., http://www.nato.int/cps/en/natolive/opinions_66727.htm.

22. Quoted in Joyner, "NATO's Identity Crisis. NATO in an Age of Austerity," *World Politics Review* (October 26, 2010): 1–4.

23. O'Donnell, ed., "The Implications of Military Spending Cuts for NATO's Largest Members" (Brookings, July 2012), http://www.brookings.edu/research/papers/2012/07/military-spending-nato-odonnell.

24. "Denmark Delays Fighter Purchase up to 4 Years," *Defense News*, n.d., http://www.defensenews.com/article/20100324/DEFSECT01/3240310/Denmark-Delays-Fighter-Purchase-up-4-Years.

25. Christian Molling in O'Donnell, "The Implications of Military Spending Cuts for NATO's Largest Members."

26. Robert M. Gate, "The Security and Defense Agenda (Future of NATO)," June 10, 2011, http://www.defense.gov/speeches/speech.aspx?speechid=1581.

27. Christian Molling in O'Donnell, "The Implications of Military Spending Cuts for NATO's Largest Members," p. 6.

NOTES TO CHAPTER 10

1. For references on U.S. and European relations post 2001, see Francis Fukuyama, "The West May be Cracking Europe and America," *International Herald Tribune*, August 9, 2002, pp. 4–10; John Leech, *Whole and Free: NATO, EU Enlargement and Transatlantic Relations* (Federal Trust for Education & Research, 2002); Philip H. Gordon, "*Bridging the Atlantic Divide*," *Foreign Affairs*, (January/February 2003), vol. 82, no. 1, p. 70; James B. Steinberg,

"An Elective Partnership: Salvaging Transatlantic Relations," *Survival* (June 2003), vol. 45, no. 2; p. 113; Christopher Layne and Thomas Jefferson, "America as European hegemon," *The National Interest* (Summer 2003) vol. 13, no. 72, p. 17–30; Ivo H. Daalder, "The End of Atlanticism," *Survival* (June 2003), vol. 45, no. 2; p. 147; Hall Gardner, *NATO and the European Union: New World, New Europe, New Threats* (Burlington, VT: Ashgate Publishing, 2004); Phillip Gordon and Jeremy Shapiro, *Allies at War: America, Europe, and the Crisis Over Iraq* (New York: McGraw-Hill, 2004); Jaap de Hoop Scheffer, "New Trans-Atlantic Unity," *NATO's Nations and Partners for Peace*, 2004, pp. 20–24; William Wallace, "Broken Bridges," *The World Today* (December 2004), vol. 60, no. 12; pp. 13–16; Daniel Hamilton and Daniel Sheldon, *Conflict and Cooperation in Transatlantic Relations* (Baltimore, MD: Johns Hopkins University Press, 2004); Tod Lindberg, "We. A Community in Agreement on Fundamentals," *Policy Review* (December 2004/January 2005), no. 128, pp. 3–19; Elizabeth Pond, *Friendly Fire: The Near-Death of the Transatlantic Alliance* (European Union Studies Association, 2004); Werner Weidenfeld, *From Alliance to Coalitions: The Future of Transatlantic Relations* (Bertelsmann Foundation Publishers, 2004); E.A. Turpen, "Free World: America, Europe, and the Surprising Future of the West," *Choice* (June 2005), vol. 42, no. 10; p. 1895; Ivo Daalder, *Crescent of Crisis : U.S.-European Strategy for the Greater Middle East* (Washington, DC: Brookings Institution Press, 2006); Matthew Evangelista, ed., *Partners or Rivals?: European-American Relations after Iraq* (Milan, Italy: V&P Publishing, 2005); Vittorio Emanuele Parsi, *The Inevitable Alliance : Europe and the United States beyond Iraq* (New York: Palgrave Macmillan, 2006); Massimo D'Alema, "Diplomacy Al Dente," *Wall Street Journal*, Jun 14, 2006, p. 14; Pierangelo Isernia, Philip P Everts, "European Public Opinion on Security Issues," *European Security*, Dec 2006, vol. 15, no. 4, p. 451; Thomas Ilgen, *Hard Power, Soft Power, and the Future of Transatlantic Relations* (Burlington, VT: Ashgate, 2006); Jeremy Poulter, "NATO as a Security Organization: Implications for the Future Role and Survival of the Alliance," *RUSI Journal*, 2006, vol. 151, no. 3; pp. 58–62; Andrew A Michta, "Transatlantic Troubles," *The National Interest* (November/December 2006), pp. 62–67; Ryan C Hendrickson, "The Miscalculation of NATO's Death," *Parameters* (Spring 2007), vol. 37, no. 1, pp. 98–115; Daniel Dombey, "Transatlantic Climate Shift," *Financial Times*, 4th June 2007, p. 2; Richard Haass, "The Atlantic Becomes a Little Wider," *Financial Times*, December 19, 2007, p. 2; Lance Smith, "Is the Transatlantic Relationship Still Important?," *Vital Speeches of the Day* (June 2007), vol. 73, no. 6; pp. 249–252.

2. Vittorio Parsi, *L'Alleanza Inevitabile: Europa e Stati Uniti oltre l'Iraq* (Milano: Univesita' Bocconi Editore, 2003). Ted Hopf, *Putin and Bush, Perfect Together: Yet Russia's Alliance with Europe is Inevitable . . . Eventually.* Policy Memo 300 of the Program on New Approaches to Russian Security, November 2003 in Evangelista, *Partners or Rivals?*

3. Tony Blair, "Speech to the Economic Club of Chicago," April 22, 1999, and Ulbrich, Associated Press, "Atlantic Alliance Expanding Its Horizons."

4. Sovereignty is traditionally the most important norm. In principle, states can do what they want on their territory. See Stephen Krasner, *Problematic Sovereignty* (New York: Columbia University Press, 2001).

5. As explained in chapter 4, the European Council declared that the Rome Statute, even though limiting state sovereignty, was "fully in line" with the principles and objectives of the European Union. See European Council Common Position, June 11, 2001. It should be noted that many European countries have gradually accepted limitations to their sovereignty in order to be part of European institutions, which are supranational structures. In essence,

EU countries have, to some extent, learned to trade off part of their sovereignty because European common institutions can impose decisions and rules on member states. In this sense, see Walter Mattli, *The Logic of Regional Integration: Europe and Beyond* (Cambridge: Cambridge University Press, 1999). On European integration, see also Antje Wiener and Thomas Diez, *European Integration Theory* (Oxford: Oxford University Press, 2004).

6. European Council Common Position, June 11, 2001 and June 16, 2003. See also Lindley-French, *Terms of Engagement*.

7. In my personal interviews, Richard Ben-Veniste, commissioner on the 9/11 Commission, as well as Marisa Lino, U.S. senior negotiator who drafted the text of Article 98 Agreements (i.e., the bilateral non-surrender agreements protecting American citizens from the ICC) suggested that both Republicans and Democrats were equally concerned with limits to sovereignty that could impinge on the protection of American servicemen and women. See also Bolton, Hearing Committee on International Relations, July 25–26, 2000; Grams, Hearing Committee on Foreign Relations, June 14, 2000. Stephan M. Minikes, U.S. ambassador to the Organization for Security and Cooperation in Europe summarizes the American position on the ICC concisely as follows: "The United States strongly objects to the ICC's claims of jurisdiction over the nationals, including government officials and service members, of states not party to the treaty. We are concerned that the lack of accountability over the ICC and its prosecutors will result in politically motivated attempts to investigate and prosecute U.S. service members and other government officials. We strongly object to the ICC's claim to be able to unilaterally decide whether an U.S. investigation or prosecution was adequate. We think the treaty provides an opening for the ICC to undermine the role of the UN Security Council in determining when a state has committed an act of aggression." Minikes, U.S. Views Regarding the International Criminal Court, July 4, 2002. http://www.state.gov/p/eur/rls/rm/2002/11726.htm (last accessed 3/15/2008).

8. Barbara Crossette, "Helms Vows to Make War on UN Court," *The New York Times*, March 27, 1998. This article can be found online at: www.nyt.com (last accessed 3/15/2008).

9. Mearsheimer, "Back to the Future," pp. 5–56. Harries, "The Collapse of 'The West,'" pp. 41–53. Kupchan, "Reviving the West," pp. 92–104. Walt, "The Ties that Fray," pp. 3–11. Kupchan, "Reviving the West," pp. 92–104. Kagan, "Power and Weakness," pp. 3–28. Kagan, *Of Paradise and Power*.

10. For example, in the cases of the Kyoto global warming treaty (Kyoto Protocol, 1997), the Convention on the Prohibition of the Use, Stockpiling, Production and Transfer or Anti-Personnel Mines and on Their Destruction (Ottawa Treaty, 1997), and the Rome Statute of the International Criminal Court Treaty (Rome Statute, 1998).

11. Elles, "Towards a New Transatlantic Relationship"; Duffield, "NATO's Functions after the Cold War." Robert Blackwill, *The Future of Transatlantic Relations*; Deudney and Ikenberry, "The Logic of the West"; Nye, "The US and Europe"; McCalla, "NATO's Persistence after the Cold War"; Anthony Blinken, "The False Crisis Over the Atlantic."

12. As shown in chapter 4, different interpretations of these concepts induced and amplified tensions among the transatlantic partners.

13. Pew Survey, *U.S. Image Up Slightly, But Still Negative*. June 23, 2005. On this point see also Euro-barometer, *The European Citizens and the Future of Europe. Qualitative Study in 25 Member States*. May 2006.
    This study shows that European citizens view the protective character of the EU as a factor for peace, stability and security, as well as for making it capable of being influential and strong on the world stage in the face of the other major countries or groups of countries (like the United States).

14. Pew Survey, *U.S. Image Up Slightly*.
15. Pew Survey, *U.S. Image Up Slightly*.
16. Katrin Bennhold, "Obama Grabs the Spot Light, in Europe Too," *International Herald Tribune*, March 20, 2008.
17. Von Torsten Krauel, "Der Nue Kennedy," *Berliner Morgenpost*, January 5, 2008; and Von Markus Günther, "Umjubelte Rede über Rassismus in den USA," Frankfurter Rundschau, March 19, 2008.
18. Fabrice Rousselot, "Occasion," *Libération*, January 5, 2008.
19. http://pewresearch.org/pubs/2441/europe-obama-reelection-transatlantic-values-gap-popularity-presidency-confidence
20. On the role of traditional and secular values, see Inglehart, Basañez and Moreno, *Human Values and Beliefs*.

Bibliography

Achcar, Gilbert. "The Libyan Insurrection between Gaddafi's Hammer, NATO's Anvil and the Left's Confusion: Results and Prospects." *Le Monde Diplomatique*, April 25, 2011.

Agence France Presse. "Albright Told That NATO and Europe's Defense are Complementary." December 10, 1998.

Agence France Presse. "Chirac Threatens Pull-Back from NATO Over Southern Command: Report." Bonn. September 28, 1996.

Agence France Presse. "NATO Begins Talks on Bosnia, Reform of the Alliance." Brussels. June 13, 1996.

Agence France Presse. "Sticks to Its Guns Over NATO Southern Command." December 17, 1996.

"Aid from OECD Countries—Who Gives the Most and How Has It Changed?" *The Guardian*, April 6, 2011. http://www.guardian.co.uk/news/datablog/2011/apr/06/aid-oecd-given.

Alderman, Liz. "Aid Pledge by Group of 8 Seeks to Bolster Arab Democracy." *The New York Times*, May 27, 2011, sec. World / Europe.

Al-Jazeera. "New Libya Contact Group to Meet in Qatar." http://english.aljazeera.net. 3 29, 2011.

Andrews David, Randall Henning, and Luis Pauly, eds., *Governing the World's Money*. Ithaca, NY: Cornell University Press, 2002.

Ash, Timothy Garton. "France Plays Hawk, Germany Demurs. Libya Has Exposed Europe's Fault Lines." *The Guardian*, March 24, 2011.

Ashton, Catherine. "The European Union Response to the Arab Spring: A Statesman's Forum with Catherine Ashton." *The Brookings Institution*, July 12, 2011. http://www.brookings.edu/events/2011/07/12-ashton-arab-spring.

Associated Press. "French Defense Minister Visits Pentagon." *Washington*, March 25, 1997.

"Bahrain: a Special Case Among the Arab Spring Uprisings." *The Guardian*, June 19, 2012. http://www.guardian.co.uk/world/2012/jun/19/bahrain-special-case-arab-spring.

Baldwin, David A., ed., *Neorealism and Neoliberalism*. New York: Columbia University Press, 1993.

Barnett, Michael. "Social Constructivism." In *Introduction to Global Politics*, 252–270. Oxford: Oxford University Press, 2010.

BBC. Libya: Contact Group Creates Fund for Rebels. London, May 5, 2011.

BBC. "Libya Crisis: Doha Meeting Seeks to Raise $2.5bn aid." August 24, 2011. http://www.bbc.co.uk.

BBC. "Thatcher's Fight Against German Unity." September 11, 2009, sec. Europe, http://news.bbc.co.uk/2/hi/8251211.stm.

Bell, Melissa, and Elizabeth Flock. "Video Said to Show a Wounded Gaddafi After His Capture." *The Washington Post—Blogs*, October 21, 2011. http://www. washingtonpost.com/blogs/blogpost/post/sirte-fall-rumors-swirl-of-gaddafi-capture-but-all-unconfirmed/2011/10/20/gIQA5wM7zL_blog.html.

Bellver, Juan Manuel. "Los Líderes Europeos Piden Que Se Respete La Tregua En Yemen." *El Mundo*, June 7, 2011. http://www.elmundo.es/elmundo/2011/06/06/internacional/1307388170.html.

Ben-Ari, Guy, Joachim Hofbauer, David Berteau, Roy (CON) Levy, and Gregory (CON) Sanders. *European Defense Trends: Budgets, Regulatory Frameworks, and the Industrial Base: A Report of the Defense-Industrial Initiatives Group.* Center for Strategic & International Studies, 2010.

Berger, Thomas. "Norms, Identity, and National Security in Germany and Japan," pp. 317–356, in Katzenstein, ed., *The Culture of National Security: Norms and Identity in World Politics.* New York: Columbia University Press, 1996.

"Berlusconi: Permessi Validi, C'è L'ok Europeo." *Il Sole 24 ORE*, n.d. http://www.ilsole24ore.com/art/notizie/2011–04–14/berlusconi-permessi-validi-europeo-063923.shtml?uuid=AaD0WnOD.

Biersteker, Thomas. *Distortion or Development? Contending Perspectives on the Multinational Corporation.* Cambridge, MA: MIT Press, 1978, p. 1.

Blackwill, Robert. *The Future of Transatlantic Relations.* Council for Foreign Relations Press, 1999.

Blair, Tony "Speech to the Economic Club of Chicago," April 22, 1999.

Blair, Tony, and Jacques Chirac. "Franco-British Summit. Joint Declaration on European Defense." n.d. http://www.atlanticcommunity.org/Saint-Malo%20Declaration%20Text.html.

Blinken, Anthony. "The False Crisis Over the Atlantic." *Foreign Affairs* (May/June, 2001), pp. 35–48.

Blitz, James. "Mitterrand Feared Emergence of 'Bad' Germans." *Financial Times*, September 9, 2009. http://www.ft.com/cms/s/0/886192ba-9d7d-11de-9f4a-00144feabdc0.html#axzz1wAy4qrGi.

Bronner, Ethan, and Isabel Kershner. "For Palestinians, U.N. Is Best Chance to Change Conflict's Dynamics." *The New York Times*, September 17, 2011, sec. World / Middle East. http://www.nytimes.com/2011/09/18/world/middleeast/palestinians-see-united-nations-appeal-as-best-option-available.html.

Bronner Jr., Michael, and John Farmer. "In Bahrain, a Reformer Who Needs Our Help." *The Washington Post*, May 8, 2011, sec. Opinions. http://www.washingtonpost.com/opinions/in-bahrain-a-reformer-who-needs-our-help/2011/05/08/AFuuQOTG_story.html.

Brown, Neville "Climate, Ecology and International Security." *Survival*, 31:6 (1989), pp. 519–532.

Brussels, European Union. *A Secure Europe in a Better World. European Security Strategy.* December 12, 2003.

Bull, Hedley. *The Anarchical Society: A Study of Order in World Politics.* New York: Columbia University Press, 1977.

Burchill, Scott, Richard Devetak, and Jack Donnelly. *Theories of International Relations.* New York: St. Martin's Press, 1996.

Buzan, Barry. *People, State and Fear: An Agenda for Security Studies in the Post-Cold War Era.* Boulder: Lynne Rienner, 1991, 2nd ed.

Buzan, Barry, Ole Weaver, and Jaap De Wilde, *Security. A New Framework of Analysis.* Boulder, CO: Lynne Rienner, 1998.

Cabos, Carsten Volkery in Los. "Euro-Zone Leaders Tired of Criticism from Abroad." *Spiegel Online*, June 19, 2012. http://www.spiegel.de/international/europe/european-leaders-tired-of-criticism-at-the-g-20-summit-a-839724.html.

"Cairo, Uccisi Manifestante e Poliziotto A Suez Alle Fiamme Palazzo Governativo." *Il Corriere Della Sera*, January 26, 2011.

Center for History and New Media. "Zotero Quick Start Guide." n.d. http://zotero. org/support/quick_start_guide.

"Charlemagne: Another Project in Trouble." *The Economist*, April 28, 2011. http:// www.economist.com/node/18618525.

Checkel, Jeffrey T. *International Institutions and Socialization in Europe.* Cambridge: Cambridge University Press, 2007.

Chivers, C. J. "Inferior Arms Hobble Rebels in Libya War." *The New York Times*, April 20, 2011.

Christiansen, Thomas, and Jack Snyder. 1990. "Chain Gangs and Passed Bucks: Predicting Alliance Patterns in Multipolarity. *International Organization*, vol. 44, no.4, pp. 137–168.

Clinton, William. Letter to Senator Daschle on NATO Enlargement, March 14, 1998.

Clinton, William. "Reforming the UN," *Vital Speeches of the Day*, vol. 60 (October 15, 1993), p. 10.

Clinton, William. The President's News Conference with Visegrad Leaders in Prague, January 12, 1994.

"Clinton Urges NATO Expansion in 1999—New York Times." *New York Times*, n.d. http://www.nytimes.com/1996/10/23/us/clinton-urges-nato-expansion-in-1999.html.

CNN News. "European Security Check—NATO's Future Role," March 19, 1996.

Coker, Christopher. *Twilight of the West.* Boulder, CO.: Westview Press, 1998.

Conforti, Benedetto. *Diritto Internazionale.* Napoli: Editoriale Scientifica, 1997.

"Confrontation In The Gulf; The Oilfield Lying Below the Iraq-Kuwait Dispute— New York Times." *New York Times*, n.d. http://www.nytimes.com/1990/09/03/ world/confrontation-in-the-gulf-the-oilfield-lying-below-the-iraq-kuwait-dispute.html.

"Contact Group to Meet in Qatar." http://english.aljazeera.net. March 29, 2011.

Cook, Robin. Foreign Secretary, Robin the House of Commons, March 25, 1999.

Cooper, Helene, and Matthew Rosenberg. "NATO Formally Agrees to Transition on Afghan Security." *The New York Times*, May 21, 2012, sec. World. http:// www.nytimes.com/2012/05/22/world/nato-formally-agrees-to-transition-on-afghan-security.html.

Cooper, Helene, and Matthew Rosenberg. "Supply Lines Cast Shadow at NATO Meeting on Afghan War." *The New York Times*, May 20, 2012, sec. World. http://www.nytimes.com/2012/05/21/world/two-critical-ties-in-play-for-obama-at-nato-meeting.html.

Cornish, Paul. *Partnership in Crisis: The US, Europe and the Fall and Rise of NATO.* London: Royal Institute of International Affairs, 1997.

Correspondent, By David Blair, Chief Foreign. "Yemen's President Steps down After 33 Years." *Telegraph.co.uk*, November 23, 2011, sec. worldnews. http://www. telegraph.co.uk/news/worldnews/middleeast/yemen/8910946/Yemens-president-steps-down-after-33-years.html.

Cox, Michael. "Martians and Venutians in the New World Order." *International Affairs*, vol.79, n.3 (2003).

"Croatia Votes for Sovereignty and Confederation—New York Times." *New York Times*, n.d. http://www.nytimes.com/1991/05/20/world/croatia-votes-for-sovereignty-and-confederation.html.

Crowford, Neta "Once and Future Security Studies." *Security Studies*, 1:2 (1991), pp. 283–316.

Cummings, Bruce Richard Falk, Stephen Walt, and Micheal C. Desch. "Commentary: Is There a Logic of the West?" *World Policy Journal*, Spring 1994, 11, 1; p. 113.

Daalder, Ivo. *Crescent of Crisis : U.S.-European Strategy for the Greater Middle East.* Washington, DC: Brookings Institution Press, 2006.

Daalder, Ivo. "Europe: Rebalancing the U.S.-European Relationship." *The Brookings Institution*, (Summer 1999), pp. 22–25.

Daalder, Ivo. *Getting to Dayton: The Making of America's Bosnia Policy*. Washington, DC: Brookings Institution Press, 1999.

Daalder, Ivo H. "The End of Atlanticism," *Survival* (June 2003), vol. 45, no. 2; p. 147.

"DAC Members: Dates of Membership and Websites." n.d. http://www.oecd.org/dac/dacmembersdatesofmembershipandwebsites.htm.

Dadush, Uri, and Michele Dunne. "American and European Responses to the Arab Spring: What's the Big Idea?" *The Washington Quarterly*, Fall 2011. http://carnegieendowment.org/2011/09/01/american-and-european-responses-to-arab-spring-what-s-big-idea/5sim.

Daily News. "Libya Contact Group Recognizes Libya's Revels." *The Daily News*, July 15, 2011.

D'Alema, Massimo. "Diplomacy Al Dente," *Wall Street Journal*, June 14, 2006, p.14.

"Declaration of the G8 on the Arab Springs." n.d. http://www.g20-g8.com/g8-g20/g8/english/live/news/declaration-of-the-g8-on-the-arab-springs.1316.html.

"Denmark Delays Fighter Purchase Up to 4 Years." *Defense News*, n.d. http://www.defensenews.com/article/20100324/DEFSECT01/3240310/Denmark-Delays-Fighter-Purchase-up-4-Years.

Der Derian, James. *On Diplomacy. A Genealogy of Western Estrangement*. Oxford: Basil Blackwell, 1987, p. 4.

Deudney, Daniel, and John Ikenberry. "The Logic of the West." *World Policy Journal*, vol. 10, no. 4 (Winter, 1993), pp. 17–25.

Deutsche Press Agentur. "Bonn Throws Weight behind France in NATO Dispute on Fleet." *Paris*. July 3, 1997.

Deutsche Presse-Agentur. "NATO Holds 16 + 1 talks with Russia in Berlin," May 29, 1996.

Devetak, Richard. "Postmodernism." In *Theories of International Relations*, p. 197. New York: St. Martin's, 1996.

DeYoung, Karen, and Scott Wilson. "As Obama Opens NATO Summit in Chicago, Focus Is on Winding Down Afghanistan War." *The Washington Post*, May 21, 2012, sec. World. http://www.washingtonpost.com/world/world-politics/obama-karzai-meet-before-nato-summit-opens/2012/05/20/gIQAFGCLdU_story.html?hpid=z4.

DeYoung, Karen. "In Arab Spring Speech, Clinton Defends U.S. Stance on Syria, Bahrain." *The Washington Post*, November 8, 2011, sec. World. http://www.washingtonpost.com/world/national-security/clinton-defends-us-stance-on-syria-bahrain/2011/11/07/gIQAsAJ9xM_story.html.

Dombey, Daniel. "Transatlantic Climate Shift." *Financial Times*, June 4, 2007, p. 2.

Dorman, Andrew, and Joyce Kaufman. *The Future of Transatlantic Relations: Perceptions, Policy and Practice*. Palo Alto, CA: Stanford University Press, 2010.

Dorsey, James M. "Demonstrations in Libya and Jordan Put Tunisian Model to the Test," January 17, 2011. http://www.dw.de/dw/article/0,,6407406,00.html.

Duffield, John "NATO's Functions after the Cold War." *Political Science Quarterly* (1994–95), 109(5): 763–788.

Eckstein, Harry. "Case Studies and Theories in Political Science," in Fred Greenstein and Nelson Polsby, eds., *Handbook of Political Science, vol. 7. Political Science: Scope and Theory*. Reading, MA: Addison-Wesley, 1975, pp. 94–137.

Egbert, Jahn, Pierre Lemaitre, and Ole Waever, *European Security: Problems of Research on Non-Military Aspects*. Copenhagen: Copenhagen Papers of the Centre for Peace and Conflict Research, 1987.

"Egypt Braced for 'Day of Revolution' Protests." *The Guardian*, January 24, 2011. http://www.guardian.co.uk/world/2011/jan/24/egypt-day-revolution-protests.

" 'Egypt's Uprising Now Seems Like Historical Hiccup.' " *Spiegel Online*, June 19, 2012. http://www.spiegel.de/international/world/german-commentators-slam-egyptian-military-council-power-grab-a-839742.html.

"Egypt Unrest: Day 10 as It Happened." *BBC*, February 4, 2011, sec. UK Politics. http://news.bbc.co.uk/2/mobile/uk_news/politics/9387166.stm.

Eichengreen Barry. *Globalizing Capital: A History of the International Monetary System*. Princeton, NJ: Princeton University Press, 1996.

Elles, James. "Towards a New Transatlantic Relationship." *European Business Journal*, 5(3): 34–41.

Embassy, U.S. "New Transatlantic Agenda." October 20, 2011. http://useu.usmis sion.gov/new_transatlantic_agenda.html.

Erlanger, Steven. "Europe's Foreign Policy Chief Struggles for Footing." *The New York Times*, February 10, 2011, sec. World / Europe. http://www.nytimes.com/2011/02/11/world/europe/11europe.html.

Erlanger, Steven. "Libya's Supporters Gather in Paris to Help Ease New Government's Transition." *New York Times*. September 1, 2011. http://www.nytimes.com.

Erlanger, Steven. "Russia Recognizes Libya Rebels as World Leaders Meet." *The New York Times*, September 1, 2011, sec. World / Africa. http://www.nytimes.com/2011/09/02/world/africa/02nato.html.

European Commission. " 'In Times of Crisis, the EU Must not Forget the Poorest in the World,' Says Commissioner Piebalgs." EU Confirms Its Position as The World's Largest Aid Donor In 2011." n.d. http://ec.europa.eu/commission_2010–2014/piebalgs/headlines/news/2012/04/20120410_en.htm.

European Commission. "The European Neighborhood Policy (ENP)," 2004. http://ec.europa.eu/world/enp/welcome_en.htm.

European Council Common Position. June 2001 on the International Criminal Court (2001/443/CFSP). *Official Journal of the European Communities* 12.6.2001. L. 155/19.

"Europe's Dilemma: Immigration and the Arab Spring." *FPIF*, n.d. http://www.fpif.org/articles/europes_dilemma_immigration_and_the_arab_spring.

Evangelista, Matthew. *Partners or Rivals?: European-American Relations after Iraq*. Milano: V&P Publishing, 2005.

Evens, Peter, Harold Jacobson, and Robert Putnam, eds., *Double-Edged Diplomacy: International Bargaining and Domestic Politics*. Berkeley: University of California Press, 1993.

" 'Everyone, Including the Muslim Brotherhood, Must Be Involved.' " *Spiegel Online*, February 15, 2011. http://www.spiegel.de/international/europe/eu-foreign-policy-chief-ashton-on-egypt-everyone-including-the-muslim-brotherhood-must-be-involved-a-745522.html.

"Evolution in Europe; Germanys Sign Pact Binding Economies—New York Times." *New York Times*, n.d. http://www.nytimes.com/1990/05/19/world/evolution-in-europe-germanys-sign-pact-binding-economies.html.

"Evolution in Europe; The German-NATO Drama: 9 Fateful Months—New York Times." *New York Times*, n.d. http://www.nytimes.com/1990/07/17/world/evolution-in-europe-the-german-nato-drama-9-fateful-months.html.

Fahim, Kareem. "As Hopes for Reform Fade in Bahrain, Protesters Turn Anger on United States." *The New York Times*, June 23, 2012, sec. World / Middle East. http://www.nytimes.com/2012/06/24/world/middleeast/as-hopes-for-reform-fade-in-bahrain-protesters-turn-anger-on-united-states.html.

Fahim, Kareem. "Slap to a Man's Pride Set Off Tumult in Tunisia." *The New York Times*, January 21, 2011, sec. World / Africa. http://www.nytimes.com/2011/01/22/world/africa/22sidi.html.

Fichtner, Ullrich. "Why the World Can't Stop the Killing in Syria." *Spiegel Online*, May 6, 2012. http://www.spiegel.de/international/world/commentary-on-failure-of-international-community-to-stop-the-killing-in-syria-a-836881.html.

Finnemore, Martha. "Constructing Norms of Humanitarian Intervention," pp. 153–185, in Katzenstein, ed., *The Culture of National Security: Norms and Identity in World Politics*. New York: Columbia University Press, 1996.

Finnemore, Martha. *National Interests in International Society*. Ithaca, NY: Cornell University Press, 1996.

Finnemore, Martha. *The Purpose of Intervention: Changing Beliefs about the Use of Force*. Ithaca, NY, Cornell University Press, 2004.

Fischer, Sebastian, and Matthias Gebauer. "NATO Leaders Focus on Funding in Chicago." *Spiegel Online*, May 21, 2012. http://www.spiegel.de/international/world/money-the-key-issue-as-nato-meets-in-chicago-a-834206.html.

Fitchett, Joseph. "Albright Takes Some Heat For Rambouillet 'Success.' " *The New York Times*, March 5, 1999, sec. News. http://www.nytimes.com/1999/03/05/news/05iht-yugo.2.t_0.html.

Fitchett, Joseph. "A More United Europe Worries about Globalizing NATO." *International Herald Tribune*, December 31, 1998.

Flanagan, Stephen J., and Guy Ben-Ari. *A Diminishing Transatlantic Partnership? The Impact of the Financial Crisis on European Defense and Foreign Assistance Capabilities*. Washington, DC: Center for Strategic and International Studies, May 2011.

"For Arab Nations In Transition, U.S. Emphasizes Trade?: NPR." *NPR.org*, n.d. http://www.npr.org/2011/11/16/142325445/for-arab-nations-in-transition-u-s-emphasizes-trade.

Foreign & Commonwealth Office. March 29, 2011. www.fco.gov.uk (accessed January 3, 2012).

"France and Italy in Call to Close EU Borders in Wake of Arab Protests." *The Guardian*, April 26, 2011. http://www.guardian.co.uk/world/2011/apr/26/eu-borders-arab-protests.

French Ministry of Foreign Affairs. "Friends of Libya Conference." *France Diplomatie*, September 1, 2011. http://www.diplomatie.gouv.fr.

Fukuyama, Francis. "The West May Be Cracking." *International Herald Tribune*, August 9, 2002, p. 4.

"G20 Should Back Tunisia, Egypt Transitions-Sarkozy." *Reuters*, February 18, 2011. http://af.reuters.com/article/egyptNews/idAFLDE71H23Y20110218.

Gardner, Hall. *NATO and the European Union: New World, New Europe, New Threats*. Burlington, VT: Ashgate Publishing, 2004.

Garton Ash, Timothy. "Obama Can Now Define the Third Great Project of Euro-Atlantic Partnership." *The Guardian*, May 18, 2011. http://www.guardian.co.uk/commentisfree/2011/may/18/obama-define-great-euro-atlantic-project.

Gate, Robert M. "The Security and Defense Agenda (Future of NATO)." June 10, 2011. http://www.defense.gov/speeches/speech.aspx?speechid=1581.

Genteactiva. *Gente Active*. June 9, 2011. http://genteactive.net.

George, Alexander, and Andrew Bennett. *Case Studies and Theory Development in the Social Sciences*. Cambridge, MA: MIT Press, 2004.

"George Bush, Meet Woodrow Wilson—New York Times." *New York Times*, n.d. http://www.nytimes.com/1990/11/20/opinion/george-bush-meet-woodrow-wilson.html?pagewanted=all&src=pm.

Gerring, John. *Case Study Research. Principles and Practices*. Cambridge: Cambridge University Press, 2007.

Giddens, Anthony. *The Consequences of Modernity*. Palo Alto, CA: Stanford University Press, 1990.

Gladstone, Rick. "U.N. Votes to End Libya Intervention on Monday." *The New York Times*, October 27, 2011, sec. World / Middle East. http://www.nytimes.com/2011/10/28/world/middleeast/security-council-ends-libya-intervention-mandate.html.

Glain, Stephen. "Muslim Brotherhood Official Says West Is Neglecting Egypt." *The Washington Post*, February 4, 2012, sec. World. http://www.washingtonpost.com/world/middle_east/muslim-brotherhood-official-says-west-is-neglecting-egypt/2012/02/02/gIQA9Tc7mQ_story.html.

Goff, Patricia M., and Kevin C. Dunn. *Identity and Global Politics: Empirical and Theoretical Elaborations*. New York: Palgrave Macmillan, 2004.

Goldgeier, James M. *Not Whether But When: The U.S. Decision to Enlarge NATO*. Washington, DC: Brookings Institution Press, 1999

Gompert David C., and F. Stephen Larrabee, eds., *America and Europe: A Partnership for a New Era*. New York: Cambridge University Press, 1997.

Gonzalez, M., and M. R. De Rituerto. *El Pais*. June 9, 2011. http://international.elpais.com.

Gordon, Philip. *Allies at War*. Blacklick, OH: McGraw-Hill, 2004.

Gordon, Philip H. "Bridging the Atlantic Divide." *Foreign Affairs* (January/February 2003), vol. 82, no. 1, p. 70

Gordon, Philip H. "Statement Before the Subcommittee on European Affairs of the Senate Foreign Relations Committee." Department of State. May 18, 2011. http://www.state.gov/p/eur/rls/rm/2011/163616.htm (accessed February 11, 2012).

Gordon, Phillip, and Jeremy Shapiro. *Allies at War: America, Europe, and the Crisis over Iraq*. New York: McGraw-Hill, 2004.

"Govt Scuttles Talk of France Aircraft Carrier Share." *Google News*, n.d. http://www.google.com/hostednews/afp/article/ALeqM5gpUdv0B-QbaxL_e1ZJJK3iABheUw.

Gowa, Joanne. *Allies Adversaries, and International Trade*. Princeton, N.J: Princeton University Press, 1993.

Greenfield, Danya, and Rosa Balfour. "Arab Awakening: Are the US and EU Missing the Challenge?" Atlantic Council, June 28, 2012. http://www.acus.org/files/publication_pdfs/403/95825_ACUS_arab_awakening_us_eu.pdf.

Greenwood, Christopher. "Is There a Right of Humanitarian Intervention?" *The World Today*, (February, 1993), vol. 49, no. 2, p. 38.

Grieco, Joseph. "Anarchy and the Limits of Cooperation: A Realist Critique of the Newest Liberal Institutionalism," in *Neorealism and Neoliberalism: The Contemporary Debate*, ed. D. Baldwin. New York: Columbia University Press, 1993.

Grieco, Joseph. *Cooperation among Nations: Europe, American and Non-Tariff Barriers to Trade*. Ithaca, NY: Cornell University Press, 1990.

Guicherd, Catherine. "International Law and the War in Kosovo." *Survival*, vol. 41, no. 2 (1999), pp. 26–27.

Gunther, Hellmann, and Reinhard Wolf. "Neorealism, Neoliberal Institutionalism, and the Future of NATO." *Security Studies*, 1993, vol.3, pp. 3–43.

Habermas, Jürgen. *L'Occidente Diviso*. Bari, Italy: Laterza, 2005.

Haftendorn, Helga, and Christian Tuschhoff, eds. *America and Europe in an Era of Change*. Boulder, CO: Westview Press, 1993.

Hall, Rodney Bruce. *National Collective Identity: Social Constructs and International Systems*. New York: Columbia University Press, 1999.

Hamilton, Daniel, and Daniel Sheldon. *Conflict and Cooperation in Transatlantic Relations*. Baltimore, MD: Johns Hopkins University Press, 2004.

Hammer, Joshua. "The Contenders." *The New Yorker*, April 5, 2010. http://www.newyorker.com/reporting/2010/04/05/100405fa_fact_hammer.

Hampson, Olster. *Madness in the Multitude. Human Security and World Disorder.* Oxford: Oxford University Press, 2002.

Harries, Owen. "The Collapse of 'The West.' " *Foreign Affairs*, September/October 1993, pp. 41–53.

Hass, Richard N. "The Atlantic Becomes a Little Wider." *Financial Times*, December 19, 2007, p. 2.

Hass, Richard N., ed., *Transatlantic Tensions: The United States, Europe, and Problem Countries.* Washington, DC: Brookings Institution Press, 1999.

Heclo, Hugh. *Modern Social Politics in Britain and Sweden.* New Haven, CT: Yale University Press, 1974.

Helga Haftendorn. "The Security Puzzle: Theory-Building and Discipline-Building in International Security." *International Studies Quarterly*, 35:1 (1991), pp. 3–17.

Hendrickson, Ryan C. "The Miscalculation of NATO's Death." *Parameters* (Spring 2007), vol. 37, no. 1, pp. 98–115.

Herman, Robert. "Identity, Norms and National Security: The Soviet Foreign Policy Revolution and the End of the Cold War," pp. 271–316, in Katzenstein, ed., *The Culture of National Security: Norms and Identity in World Politics.* New York: Columbia University Press, 1996.

Heuser, Beatrice. *Transatlantic Relations: Sharing Ideals and Costs.* London: Royal Institute of International Affairs, 1996.

Hodge, Carl C., ed., *Redefining European Security.* London: Garland Science, 1999.

Hoekman, Bernard, and Michel Kostecki. *The Political Economy of the World Trading System: From GATT to WTO.* Oxford: Oxford University Press, 1999

Hogan, Michael. *The Marshall Plan: America, Britain, and the Reconstruction of Western Europe, 1947–1952.* Cambridge: Cambridge University Press, 1987.

Holbrooke, Richard. *To End a War.* New York: Random House, 1998.

Homer-Dixon, Thomas, and Roger Karapin. "Graphical Argument Analysis: A New Approach to Understanding Arguments, Applied to a Debate about the Window of Vulnerability." *International Studies Quarterly* (1989), vol. 33, no. 4, p. 389.

Hopf, Ted. *Social Construction of International Politics: Identities & Foreign Policies, Moscow, 1955 and 1999.* Ithaca, NY: Cornell University Press, 2002.

Hopf, Ted. "The Promise of Constructivism in International Relations Theory." *International Security* (Summer 1998), vol. 23, no. 1, pp. 175–176.

Huntington, Samuel. "The Clash of Civilization?" *Foreign Affairs*, 72 (Summer 1993).

Huntington, Samuel. *The Clash of Civilization. Remaking of World Order.* New York: Touchtone, 1996.

Hurd, Ian. "Constructivism," in *The Oxford Handbook of International Relations.* New York: Oxford University Press, 2008.

Ignatius, David. "A Transition for Arab Economies." *The Washington Post*, March 10, 2011, sec. Opinions. http://www.washingtonpost.com/wp-dyn/content/article/2011/03/09/AR2011030904334.html.

Ilgen, Thomas. *Hard Power, Soft Power, and the Future of Transatlantic Relations.* Burlington, VT: Ashgate, 2006.

Inglehart, Ronald, and Christian Welzel. *Modernization, Cultural Change, and Democracy.* Cambridge: Cambridge University Press, 2005.

Inglehart Ronald, Miguel Basañez, and Alejandro Moreno, eds., *Human Values and Beliefs: A Cross-Cultural Source.* Ann Arbor: University of Michigan Press, 1993.

International Herald Tribune. "Clinton Offers Paris Compromise on NATO; US to Endorse a New French-led Force." Paris. March 14, 1997.

"In Tunisia, Clinton Cites Promise of Arab Spring." *USATODAY.COM*, n.d. http://www.usatoday.com/news/world/story/2012–02–25/Clinton-Tunisia-2–25/53247438/1.

"Iraq Army Invades Capital of Kuwait in Fierce Fighting—New York Times." *New York Times*, n.d. http://www.nytimes.com/1990/08/02/world/iraq-army-invades-capital-of-kuwait-in-fierce-fighting.html.

Isaacson, Walter. "Madeleine's War," *Time Magazine*, May 9, 1999.

Isernia, Pierangelo and Philip P Everts. "European Public Opinion on Security Issues." *European Security*, Dec. 2006. vol. 15, no. 4, p. 451.

"Is the 0.7% Aid Target Still Relevant?" *The Guardian*, August 2, 2012. http://www.guardian.co.uk/global-development/poverty-matters/2012/aug/02/is-aid-target-still-relevant.

"Is the Arab Spring Good or Bad for the U.S.?" *NPR.org*, n.d. http://www.npr.org/2012/01/09/144799401/is-the-arab-spring-good-or-bad-for-the-u-s.

"Italy Protests as France Blocks Train Carrying Migrants from Tunisia." *The Guardian*, April 17, 2011. http://www.guardian.co.uk/world/2011/apr/17/italy-protests-france-tunisia-migrant-train.

James, Barry. "U.S. Outlines Shift in Criteria for Providing Development Aid." *The New York Times*, October 25, 2002, sec. Archive. http://www.nytimes.com/2002/10/25/news/25iht-aid_ed3__0.html.

Joffe, Josef. "The Alliance Is Dead. Long Live the New Alliance." *New York Times*, September 29, 2002.

Joyner, Daniel H. "NATO's Identity Crisis. NATO in an Age of Austerity." *World Politics Review*, October 26, 2010, pp. 1–4.

Joyner, Daniel H. "The Kosovo Intervention: Legal Analysis and a More Persuasive Paradigm." *European Journal of International Law*, 2002, 13(3), p. 597.

Judah, Tim. *Kosovo: War and Revenge, Second Edition*. New Haven, CT: Yale University Press, 2002.

Judt, Tony. "The Way We Live Now." *New York Review of Books*, March 27, 2003, vol. 50, no. 5, p. 6.

Kagan, Robert. *Of Paradise and Power: America and Europe in the New World Order*. New York: Alfred A. Knopf, 2003.

Kagan, Robert "Paradise and Power." *Policy Review* (June and July 2002).

Katzenstein, Peter J., ed. *The Culture of National Security: Norms and Identity in World Politics* New York: Columbia University Press, 1996.

Keck, Margaret E., and Kathryn Sikkink. *Activists Beyond Borders: Advocacy Networks in International Politics*. Ithaca, NY: Cornell University Press, 1998.

Keohane, Robert. *After Hegemony: Cooperation and Discord in the World Political Economy*. Princeton, NJ: Princeton University Press, 1984.

Keohane, Robert O. "Reciprocity in International Relations." *International Organization* 40, no. 1, (1986), pp. 1–27.

Keohane, Robert, and Lisa Martin. "The Promise of Institutionalist Theory." *International Security*, vol. 20, no. 1 (Summer 1995), pp. 39–51.

Keohane, Robert, and Joseph Nye. *Power and Interdependence*, 3rd ed. New York: Longman, 2001.

"Key Findings." *Transatlantic Trends*, n.d. http://trends.gmfus.org/immigration/key-findings/.

Keylor, William. R. *The Twentieth-Century World and Beyond*. Oxford: Oxford University Press, 2006, p. 244.

King, Gary, Robert Owen Keohane, and Sidney Verba. *Designing Social Inquiry: Scientific Inference in Qualitative Research*. Princeton, NJ: Princeton University Press, 1994.

Kirkpatrick, David D. "Mohamed Morsi of Muslim Brotherhood Declared as Egypt's President." *The New York Times*, June 24, 2012, sec. World / Middle East. http://www.nytimes.com/2012/06/25/world/middleeast/mohamed-morsi-of-muslim-brotherhood-declared-as-egypts-president.html.

Kirkpatrick, David D. and Steven Lee Myers. "Allies Split on Goal and Exit Strategy in Libya." *New York Times*, March 24, 2011.

Kissinger, Henry A., and James A. Backer III. "Grounds for U.S. Military Intervention." *The Washington Post*, April 8, 2011, sec. Opinions. http://www.washingtonpost.com/opinions/grounds-for-us-military-intervention/2011/04/07/AFDqX03C_story.html.

Klotz, Audie. *Norms in International Relations: The Struggle Against Apartheid.* Ithaca, NY: Cornell University Press, 1999.

Klotz, Audie, and Cecelia Lynch. *Strategies for Research in Constructivist International Relations.* Armonk, NY: M. E. Sharpe, 2007.

Kofi, Annan. UN Secretary General, Report of the Secretary-General Pursuant to Resolution 836 (1993) (S/25939).

"Kohl and Mitterrand Renew Pact." *The Independent*, n.d. http://www.indepen dent.co.uk/news/world/europe/kohl-and-mitterrand-renew-pact-1479953.html.

Krasner, Stephen D. *Sovereignty: Organized Hypocrisy.* Princeton, NJ: Princeton University Press, 1999.

Kratochwil, Friedrich V. *Rules, Norms, and Decisions: On the Conditions of Practical and Legal Reasoning in International Relations and Domestic Affairs.* Cambridge: Cambridge University Press, 1991.

Krauthammer, Charles. "Reimagining NATO." *Washington Post*, May 24, 2002.

Kupchan, Charles. "Rethinking Europe." *The National Interest* (Summer 1999) vol. 56, p. 78.

Kupchan, Charles. "Reviving the West." *Foreign Affairs*, May/June, 1996, pp. 92–104.

Kupchan, Charles. "The Alliance Lies in the Rubble." *Financial Times*, April 10, 2003.

Kupchan, Charles. *The End of the American Era: U.S. Foreign Policy and the Geopolitics of the Twenty-First Century.* New York: Knopf, 2002.

Kupchan, Charles. "The End of the West." *The Atlantic Monthly*, November 2002, vol. 290, no. 4, p. 43.

Lamy, Steven L., John Baylis, Steve Smith, and Patricia Owens. *Introduction to Global Politics.* Oxford: Oxford University Press, 2010.

Landler, Mark, and Elisabeth Bumiller. "Washington in Fierce Debate on Arming Libyan Rebels." *New York Times*, March 29, 2011.

Lapid, Yosef, and Friedrich V. Kratochwil, eds. *The Return of Culture and Identity in IR Theory.* Boulder, CO: Lynne Rienner, 1996.

Larrabee, F. Stephen, and Peter A. Wilson. "NATO's Shrinking Resources." *The New York Times*, May 16, 2012, sec. Opinion. http://www.nytimes.com/2012/05/17/opinion/natos-shrinking-resources.html.

"La suerte de los dictadores de la 'primavera árabe.'" *EL PAÍS*, June 2, 2012. http://inter nacional.elpais.com/internacional/2012/06/02/actualidad/1338641961_271002.html.

Layne, Christopher, and Thomas Jefferson. "America as European Hegemon." *The National Interest*, (Summer 2003) vol. 13, no. 72, pp. 17–30.

Leech, John. *Whole and Free: NATO, EU Enlargement and Transatlantic Relations.* London: Federal Trust for Education & Research, 2002.

"Legitimacy and Authority in International Politics." *International Organization* 53, no. 2 (Spring 1999): 379–408.

Legro, Jeffrey. *Rethinking the World: Great Power Strategies and International Order.* Ithaca, NY: Cornell University Press, 2005.

Leigh, Karen. "Bahrain: Caught Between Saudi Arabia and Iran." *Time*, March 15, 2011. http://www.time.com/time/world/article/0,8599,2058992,00.html.

Levinson, Charles. "Muslim Brotherhood Looks West in Bid to Revive Egyptian Economy." *Wall Street Journal*, February 17, 2012, sec. Asia Business. http://online.wsj.com/article/SB10001424052970204062704577220454030969184.html.

Levitz, David. "Germany Presses Egypt to Strengthen Its Commitment to Democracy." *Deutsche Welle*, April 19, 2011. http://www.dw.de/dw/article/0,,15001657,00.html.

"Liam Fox Challenges Cameron's Overseas Aid Pledge." *The Guardian*, May 17, 2011. http://www.guardian.co.uk/politics/2011/may/17/liam-fox-challenge-pm-overseas-aid-targets.

"Libyan Army Calls for Benghazi to Surrender as Saif Gaddafi Says Town Will Fall Within 48 Hours." *Telegraph.co.uk*, March 16, 2011, sec. worldnews. http://www.telegraph.co.uk/news/worldnews/africaandindianocean/libya/8385250/Libyan-army-calls-for-Benghazi-to-surrender-as-Saif-Gaddafi-says-town-will-fall-within-48-hours.html.

Lijphard, Arend. "The Comparable Cases Strategy in Comparative Research." *Comparative Political Studies*, vol. 8, July 1975, pp. 158–177.

Lindberg, Tod. "We. A Community in Agreement on Fundamentals." *Policy Review* (December 2004/January 2005), no. 128, pp. 3–19.

Lindberg, Tod, ed. *Beyond Paradise and Power: Europe, America, and the Future of a Troubled Partnership*. New York: Routledge, 2005.

Lizza, Ryan. "The Consequentialist." *The New Yorker*, May 2, 2011. http://www.newyorker.com/reporting/2011/05/02/110502fa_fact_lizza.

London, James Blitz, in "Mitterrand Feared Emergence of 'Bad' Germans." *Financial Times*, September 9, 2009. http://www.ft.com/cms/s/0/886192ba-9d7d-11de-9f4a-00144feabdc0.html#axzz1wAy4qrGi.

"London Conference on Libya: Chair's Statement." n.d. http://www.fco.gov.uk/en/news/latest-news/?id=574646182&view=News.

Londoño, Ernesto, and Karin Brulliard. "Islamist Mohamed Morsi Is Sworn in as President of Egypt." *The Washington Post*, July 1, 2012, sec. World. http://www.washingtonpost.com/world/middle_east/islamist-morsi-is-sworn-in-as-president-of-egypt/2012/06/30/gJQA84vZDW_story.html.

Luenen, Chris. "Europe Must Engage the Muslim Brotherhood to Re-Engage the Arab World." *World Politics Review* (October 21, 2011). http://www.worldpoliticsreview.com/articles/10416/europe-must-engage-the-muslim-brotherhood-to-re-engage-the-arab-world.

Lundestad, Geir. *The United States and Western Europe Since 1945: From "Empire" by Invitation to Transatlantic Drift: From "Empire" by Invitation to Transatlantic Drift*. Oxford: Oxford University Press, 2005.

Macfarquhar, Neil. "At U.N., Syria Blames Foes for Conflict and Refugee Crisis." *The New York Times*, October 1, 2012, sec. World / Middle East. http://www.nytimes.com/2012/10/02/world/middleeast/at-united-nations-syria-blames-foes-for-conflict.html.

Macfarquhar, Neil. "Russia and China Block United Nations Resolution on Syria." *The New York Times*, October 4, 2011, sec. World / Middle East. http://www.nytimes.com/2011/10/05/world/middleeast/russia-and-china-block-united-nations-resolution-on-syria.html.

Mackinnon, Angus. "US Clashes with European Allies over Future NATO Strategy." *Agence Freance Presse*, December 8, 1998.

Mahbubani, Kishore. "The West and the Rest." *The National Interest*, Washington, Summer 1992, no. 28, p. 3.

Mahncke, Dieter, Wyn Rees, and Wayne C. Thompson, *Redefining Transatlantic Security Relations: The Challenge of Change*. Manchester, NY: Manchester University Press, 2004.

Mannion, Jim. "US-France Dispute Clouds NATO Defense Ministers Meeting." Agence France Presse, December 16, 1996.

Mansfield, Edward D., and Brian Pollins. *Economic Interdependence and International Conflict: New Perspectives on an Enduring Debate*. Ann Arbor: University of Michigan Press, 2003.

Marx Karl and Friedrich Engels. The German Ideology (1845).

Matt, Spetalnick, and David Brunnstrom. "NATO States buck French, British call over Libya." *REUTERS*. April 14, 2011. http://www.reuters.com.

Matthews, Jessica Tuchman. "Redefining Security." *Foreign Affairs* (1989), vol. 68, no. 2, pp. 162–177.

Maxwell, Joseph. *Qualitative Research Design*. Newbury Park, CA: Sage, 1996.

Mazzetti, Mark, and Helene Cooper. "Bin Laden Captured Through Detective Work." *The New York Times*, May 2, 2011, sec. World / Asia Pacific. http://www.nytimes.com/2011/05/02/world/asia/02reconstruct-capture-osama-bin-laden.html.

McCalla, Robert. "NATO's Persistence After the Cold War." *International Organization*, Summer 1996, pp. 445–475.

McGreal, Chris. "Barack Obama: US Not in Breach of Law Over Role in Libyan Conflict." *The Guardian*, June 16, 2011.

Mearsheimer, John. "Back to the Future: Instability in Europe After the Cold War," *International Security*, vol. 15, no. 1 (Summer, 1990), pp. 5–56.

Mearsheimer, John J. *The Tragedy of Great Power Politics*. New York: W. W. Norton & Company, 2003.

Merkel, Peter H. *The Distracted Eagle: The Rift between America and old Europe*. New York: F. Cass, 2005.

Michta, Andrew A. "Transatlantic Troubles." *The National Interest* (November/December 2006), pp. 62–67.

"Military Expenditure (% of GDP) | Data | Graph." n.d. http://data.worldbank.org/indicator/MS.MIL.XPND.GD.ZS/countries/1W-US-DE-FR-GR-ES-AT?display=graph.

Moffett, Sebastian, Nathalie Boschat, and William Horobin. "G-8 Pledges $40 Billion for 'Arab Spring.'" *Wall Street Journal*, May 28, 2011. http://online.wsj.com/article/SB10001424052702304520804576348792147454956.html.

Molling, Christian, and Sophie-Charlotte Brune. "The Impact of the Financial Crisis on European Defense." *European Parliament*, April 2011. http://www.europarl.europa.eu/committees/en/sede/studiesdownload.html?languageDocument=EN&file=40671.

Monar, Jörg, ed., *The New Transatlantic Agenda and the Future of the EU-US Relations*. London: Kluwer Law International, 1998.

Moody, Barry. "Italy Supports Egypt's Mubarak but Urges Reform." *Reuters*, January 27, 2011. http://af.reuters.com/article/egyptNews/idAFLDE70Q2L820110127.

Morgenthau, Hans. *Politics Among Nations: The Struggle for Power and Peace*. New York: McGraw Hill, 1993.

"Mubarak 'Lent French PM a Plane.'" *BBC*, February 8, 2011, sec. Europe. http://www.bbc.co.uk/news/world-europe-12397397.

Myers, Steven Lee. "Tumult of Arab Spring Prompts Worries in Washington." *The New York Times*, September 17, 2011, sec. World / Middle East. http://www.nytimes.com/2011/09/18/world/middleeast/tumult-of-arab-spring-prompts-worries-in-washington.html.

NATO. "Financial and Economic Data Relative to NATO Defense," March 10, 2011.

NATO. *www.nato.int*. March 14, 2011. http://www.nato.int/cps/en/natolive/news_72775.htm (accessed January 7, 2012).

"NATO Allies Grapple with Shrinking Defense Budgets." *The Washington Post*, January 30, 2012, sec. World. http://www.washingtonpost.com/world/national-security/nato-allies-grapple-with-shrinking-defense-budgets/2012/01/20/gIQAK-Bg5aQ_story_1.html.

"NATO—Financial and Economic Data Relating to NATO Defence—Defence Expenditures of NATO Countries (1990–2011) (Rev1)." *NATO*, n.d. http://www.nato.int/cps/en/natolive/news_85966.htm.

"NATO Ends Military Operations in Libya." *The Guardian*, October 31, 2011. http://www.guardian.co.uk/world/2011/oct/31/nato-ends-libya-rasmussen.

"NATO's Cousin Organization will Meet on Crisis—New York Times." *New York Times*, n.d. http://www.nytimes.com/1990/08/21/world/nato-s-cousin-organization-will-meet-on-crisis.html.

"NATO's Future: Reconnecting Means with Ends." *AICGS*, n.d. http://www.aicgs.org/issue/natos-future-reconnecting-means-with-ends/.

"NATO's Role in Kosovo. Press Conference by the Secretary General of NATO, Mr Javier Solana and the Spanish Prime Minister, Mr Aznar." n.d. http://www.nato.int/kosovo/press/p990525a.htm.

"NATO—The New Strategic Concept: Active Engagement, Modern Defence"—Speech by NATO Secretary General Anders Fogh Rasmussen at the German Marshall Fund of the United States (GMF), Brussels." *NATO*, n.d. http://www.nato.int/cps/en/natolive/opinions_66727.htm.

Nelan, Bruce W. "Men of the Year 1990–TIME." *Time*, n.d. http://www.time.com/time/specials/packages/article/0,28804,2030812_2030809_2030719,00.html.

Nelles, Roland, and Gregor Peter Schmitz. "Blow Out Party for a Relationship of Waning Importance." *Der Spiegel*, June 8, 2011.

Neumann, Iver B. *Russia and the Idea of Europe: A Study in Identity and International Relations*. New York: Routledge, 1996.

New York Times. "Evolution in Europe; The German-NATO Drama: 9 Fateful Months—New York Times," http://www.nytimes.com/1990/07/17/world/evolution-in-europe-the-german-nato-drama-9-fateful-months.html.

New York Times. "Russia says France Is Violating Embargo." *New York Times*, July 1, 2011.

New York Times. "Upheaval in the East; Gorbachev Voices New Reservations On German Unity." n.d., http://www.nytimes.com/1990/02/21/world/upheaval-in-the-east-gorbachev-voices-new-reservations-on-german-unity.html?pagewanted=all&src=pm.

NEXINT. "Declaration of the G8 on the Arab Springs." n.d. http://www.g8-g20.com/g8-g20/g8/english/live/news/declaration-of-the-g8-on-the-arab-springs.1316.html.

"North Atlantic Treaty Organization—NATO and the Post-Cold War World." n.d. http://www.americanforeignrelations.com/E-N/North-Atlantic-Treaty-Organization-Nato-and-the-post-cold-war-world.html#b.

Norton-Taylor, Richard. "Libya Conflict Escalates as Ministers Admit It Could Drag on for Months." *The Guardian*. London, May 24, 2011.

Nye, Joseph. "The Contribution of Strategic Studies: Future Challenges," Adelphi Paper no.35 (1989). London: International Institute for Strategic Studies (IISS);

Nye, Joseph. "The US and Europe: Continental Drift?" *International Affairs*, vol. 76, no. 1, 2000, pp. 51–59.

Nye, Joseph, and Sean Lynn-Jones. "International Security Studies." *International Security*, 12:4, pp. 5–27.

O'Brien, Conor Cruise. "The Future of 'the West.'" *The National Interest*, Winter 1992/93, no. 30, p. 3.

O'Donnell, ed. "The Implications of Military Spending Cuts for NATO's Largest Members." *Brookings*, July 2012. http://www.brookings.edu/research/papers/2012/07/military-spending-nato-odonnell.

Onuf, Nicholas. *World of Our Making: Rules and Rule in Social Theory and International Relations*. Columbia: University of South Carolina Press, 1989.

"On the Media: A Response to the Critics." *Review of International Studies* 26 (2000): 165–180.

Organization for Economic Cooperation and Development. "Development: Aid to Developing Countries Falls Because of Global Recession." OECD, April 4, 2012.

http://www.oecd.org/document/3/0,3746,en_21571361_44315115_50058883_1_1_1_1,00.html.

Orum Anthony, Joe Feagin, and Gideon Sjoberg. "Introduction: The Nature of the Case Study," in Orum, Feagin and Sjoberg, eds., A Case for the Case Study. Chapman Hill: University of North Carolina Press, 1991, pp. 1–21.

Owen, David. *Bosnia and Herzegovina–the Vance Owen Peace Plan.* Liverpool: Liverpool University Press, 2012.

Owen, Harries. "The Collapse of 'The West.'" *Foreign Affairs*, September/October 1993, pp. 41–53.

Oye, Kenneth A. *Cooperation Under Anarchy.* Princeton, NJ: Princeton University Press, 1986.

País, Ediciones El. "La 'primavera árabe': una visión personal." *El País*, December 17, 2011. http://elpais.com/diario/2011/12/17/opinion/1324076411_850215.html.

Parsi, Vittorio Emanuele. *The Inevitable Alliance : Europe and the United States Beyond Iraq.* New York: Palgrave Macmillan, 2006.

Peel, Quentin. "Ruhe's Mission to Europeanise NATO: German Defence Minister Is Recruiting Support for Reduced US Role in Alliance." *The Financial Times.* February 23, 1996, p. 2.

Perez, Evan. "Obama Letter to Congress on Libya Sparks Protests." *Wall Street Journal*, March 22, 2011. http://online.wsj.com/article/SB10001424052748704355304576215073989153598.ht.l

Perrin de Brichambaut, Marc. "The Indivisibility of Euro-Atlantic Security." *OSCE*, February 4, 2010. http://www.osce.org/sg/41452.

Polgreen, Lydia. "Arab Spring Reveals International Court Flaws." *The New York Times*, July 7, 2012, sec. World / Middle East. http://www.nytimes.com/2012/07/08/world/middleeast/arab-spring-reveals-international-court-flaws.html.

Pollard, Robert. *Economic Security and the Origins of the Cold War.* New York: Columbia University Press, 1985.

Pond, Elizabeth. *Friendly Fire: The Near-Death of the Transatlantic Alliance.* Pittsburgh, PA: European Union Studies Association, 2004.

Popper Karl Raimund. *The Logic of Scientific Discovery.* London: Hutchinson, 1968.

Poulter, Jeremy. "NATO as a Security Organization: Implications for the Future Role and Survival of the Alliance." *RUSI Journal*, 2006. vol. 151, no. 3; pp. 58–62.

"President Obama Executive Order Gives Treasury Authority to Freeze Yemeni Assets in U.S." *The Washington Post*, May 17, 2012, sec. World. http://www.washingtonpost.com/world/national-security/president-obama-executive-order-will-give-treasury-authority-to-freeze-us-based-assets-in-yemen/2012/05/15/gIQALWPUSU_story.html.

"Press Conference Given by Alain Juppé, Ministre d'Etat, Minister of Foreign and European Affairs." March 6, 2011. http://www.diplomatie.gouv.fr/en/country-files/egypt-288/visits-3467/article/press-conference-given-by-alain.

"Press Information." *Transatlantic Trends*, n.d. http://trends.gmfus.org/transatlantic-trends/press-information/.

"Protest in Egypt: Another Arab Regime Under Threat." *The Economist*, January 27, 2011. http://www.economist.com/node/18013760.

Ragin, Charles. *The Comparative Method: Moving Beyond Qualitative and Quantitative Strategies.* Berkeley: University of California Press, 1987.

Rawls, John A. *Theory of Justice.* Cambridge, MA: Harvard University Press, 1971.

"Remarks by the President on the Middle East and North Africa | The White House." n.d. http://www.whitehouse.gov/the-press-office/2011/05/19/remarks-president-middle-east-and-north-africa.

Remnick, David. "Behind the Curtain." *The New Yorker*, September 5, 2011. http://www.newyorker.com/talk/comment/2011/09/05/110905taco_talk_remnick.

Reus-Smit, Christian, and Duncan Snidal. *The Oxford Handbook of International Relations*. New York: Oxford Handbooks Online, 2008.

Reus-Smit, Christian. *The Moral Purpose of the State: Culture, Social Identity, and Institutional Rationality in International Relations*. Princeton, NJ: Princeton University Press, 2009.

Rodrigo, Fernando. "Spain and NATO's Enlargement," October 7, 1997. http://www.nato.int/acad/conf/enlarg97/rodrigo.htm.

Romero, Simon, and John M. Broder. "Rio+20 Summit Overshadowed by Global Economy." *The New York Times*, June 18, 2012, sec. World / Americas. http://www.nytimes.com/2012/06/19/world/americas/rio20-summit-overshadowed-by-global-economy.html.

Ropp, Steve C., and Kathryn Sikkink. *The Power of Human Rights: International Norms and Domestic Change*. Cambridge: Cambridge University Press, 1999.

Rosenthal, Andrew. "U.S. And Allies Open Air War on Iraq; Bomb Baghdad and Kuwaiti Targets; 'No Choice' But Force, Bush Declares." *The New York Times*, n.d. http://www.nytimes.com/learning/general/onthisday/big/0116.html#article.

Ruggie, John Gerard. "Continuity and Transformation in the World Polity: Toward a Neorealist Synthesis." *World Politics* 35, no. 2 (January 1983), pp. 261–285.

"Russia Recognizes Libya Rebels as World Leaders Meet." *The New York Times*, September 1, 2011, sec. World / Africa. http://www.nytimes.com/2011/09/02/world/africa/02nato.html.

Sarkozy, Cameron, and Obama. "Libya's Pathway to Peace." *The New York Times*, April 14, 2011.

Sayare, Scott, and Cowell Alan. "France Expels 14 Libyan Officials." *The New York Times*, May 6, 2011.

Scheffer, Jaap de Hoop. "New Trans-Atlantic Unity," *NATO's Nations and Partners for Peace*, vol. 49, No 4; 2004, pp. 20–23.

Schnabel, Albrecht, and Ramesh Chandra Thakur. *Kosovo and the Challenge of Humanitarian Intervention: Selective Indignation, Collective Action, and International Citizenship*. New York: United Nations University Press, 2000.

Schweller, R. L. "Neorealism's Status-Quo Bias: What Security Dilemma?," *Security Studies* 5, no. 3, pp. 90–121.

"Serb-Led Presidency Drafts Plan for New and Smaller Yugoslavia—New York Times." *New York Times*, n.d. http://www.nytimes.com/1991/12/27/world/serb-led-presidency-drafts-plan-for-new-and-smaller-yugoslavia.html.

Shadid, Kareem Fahim, Anthony, and Rick Gladstone. "Qaddafi Dies in Libya, Marking an Era's Violent End." *The New York Times*, October 20, 2011, sec. World / Africa. http://www.nytimes.com/2011/10/21/world/africa/qaddafi-is-killed-as-libyan-forces-take-surt.html.

Shane, Scott. "Fast-Changing Arab World Is Upending U.S. Assumptions." *The New York Times*, July 9, 2012, sec. World / Middle East. http://www.nytimes.com/2012/07/10/world/middleeast/fast-changing-arab-world-is-upending-us-assumptions.html.

Simma, Bruno. "NATO, the UN and the Use of Force: Legal Aspects." *European Journal of International Law*, 1999, vol. 10, no. 1., p. 12.

Simoni, Serena. "Transatlantic Relations: A Theoretical Framework." In *The Future of Transatlantic Relations*, pp. 16–32. Palo Alto, CA: Stanford University Press, 2011.

Sly, Liz, and Ernesto Londono. "Obama Speech Greeted with Wariness, Apathy in Mideast." *The Washington Post*, May 28, 2011, sec. World. http://www. washingtonpost.com/world/middle-east/obama-speech-greeted-with-skepticism-yawns-in-mideast/2011/05/19/AFfVhI7G_story.html.

Smith, Lance. "Is the Transatlantic Relationship Still Important?," *Vital Speeches of the Day*. (June 2007), vol. 73, no. 6; pp. 249–252.

Social Theory of International Politics. Cambridge: Cambridge University Press, 1999.

Solana, Javier, Speech. Russian Council on Foreign and Security Policy, March 20, 1996.

Spetalnick, Matt, and David Brunnstrom. "NATO States Buck French, British Call over Libya." *Reuters*. Berlin.

Speth, James Gustave. "Wake Up, OECD: Concerted Development Assistance Isn't Optional." *The New York Times*, May 19, 1995, sec. Opinion. http://www.ny times.com/1995/05/19/opinion/19iht-edspeth.html.

Spiegel Online. "Thatcher and Kohl 'Quarreled Terribly,'" September 14, 2009, http://www.spiegel.de/international/spiegel/0,1518,648927,00.html.

Steele, John. "Learning to Live with Milosevic." *Transitions*, 5. p. 20.

Steinberg, James B. "An Elective Partnership: Salvaging Transatlantic Relations." *Survival* (June, 2003), vol. 45, no. 2, p. 113.

Stockholm International Peace Research Institute. "Recent Trends in Military Expenditure." Stockholm: Stockholm International Peace Research Institute, 2012. http://www.sipri.org:9090/research/armaments/milex/resultoutput/trends.

Stoecker, Randy. "Evaluating and Rethinking the Case Study." *The Sociological Review*, vol. 39, February 1991, pp. 88–112.

Strutton, Allegra. "Obama, Cameron and Sarkozy: No Let-Up in Libya until Gaddafi Departs." *The Guardian*, April 14, 2011. http://www.guardian.co.uk/world/2011/apr/15/obama-sarkozy-cameron-libya.

Supply Lines Cast Shadow at NATO Meeting on Afghan War." *The New York Times*, May 20, 2012, sec. World. http://www.nytimes.com/2012/05/21/world/two-critical-ties-in-play-for-obama-at-nato-meeting.html.

Taylor, Charles. "Interpretation and the Sciences of Man," in Paul Rabinow and William M. Sullivan, eds., *Interpretative Social Science: A Second Look*. Berkeley: University of California Press, 1987, pp. 33–81.

"Thatcher and Kohl 'Quarreled Terribly.'" *Spiegel Online*, September 14, 2009. http://www.spiegel.de/international/spiegel/0,1518,648927,00.html.

"Thatcher's Fight Against German Unity." *BBC*, September 11, 2009, sec. Europe. http://news.bbc.co.uk/2/hi/8251211.stm.

"The Arab Spring and Europe's Turn." n.d. http://www.aljazeera.com/indepth/opin ion/2011/06/20116113211917794.html.

"The Birth of Two Plus Four: An Inside Look at the Reunification Negotiations." *Spiegel Online*, September 29, 2010. http://www.spiegel.de/international/ger many/germany-s-unlikely-diplomatic-triumph-an-inside-look-at-the-reunifica tion-negotiations-a-719848–6.html.

"TheCabin.net,", n.d. http://thecabin.net/stories/122998/opE_1229980059.html.

"The Constructive Turn in International Relations Theory." *World Politics* 50, no. 02 (1998): 324–348.

"The EU Has Failed the Arab World." *Spiegel Online*, February 28, 2011. http:// www.spiegel.de/international/world/europe-s-favorite-dictators-the-eu-has-failed-the-arab-world-a-748074–2.html.

"The EU's Response to the 'Arab Spring,'" December 16, 2011. http://europa.eu/rapid/pressReleasesAction.do?reference=MEMO/11/918.

"The European Neighbourhood Policy (ENP)," 2004. http://ec.europa.eu/world/enp/welcome_en.htm.

The Economist. "The Aging Alliance," October 23, 1999.

The German Marshall Fund. "Transatlantic Trends: Immigration," December 15, 2011. http://www.integrazionemigranti.gov.it/Documenti/Documents/Documenti%20da%20newsletter%20gennaio%202012/TTImmigration_final_web.pdf.

"The Iraqi Invasion; West Europeans Join U.S. in Condemning Invasion—New York Times." *New York Times*, n.d. http://www.nytimes.com/1990/08/03/world/the-iraqi-invasion-west-europeans-join-us-in-condemning-invasion.html.

"The New Transatlantic Agenda," 1995. http://eeas.europa.eu/us/docs/new_transatlantic_agenda_en.pdf.

"The President on Libya: 'We Have Already Saved Lives' | The White House." n.d. http://www.whitehouse.gov/blog/2011/03/22/president-libya-we-have-already-saved-lives.

The Purpose of Intervention: Changing Beliefs about the Use of Force. Ithaca, NY: Cornell University Press, 2003.

The White House. Washington: *The National Security Strategy of the United States of America.* September 17, 2002.

"Three Factions in Bosnia Begin Talks in London—New York Times." *New York Times*, n.d. http://www.nytimes.com/1992/07/28/world/three-factions-in-bosnia-begin-talks-in-london.html.

Tickner, Ann. *Gender in International Relations: Feminist Perspectives on Achieving Global Security.* New York: Columbia University Press, 1992.

"Timeline: Break-up of Yugoslavia." *BBC*, May 22, 2006, sec. Europe. http://news.bbc.co.uk/2/hi/europe/4997380.stm.

"Timeline: Libya's Civil War." *The Guardian*, November 19, 2011. http://www.guardian.co.uk/world/2011/nov/19/timeline-libya-civil-war.

"Timeline: Libya's Uprising Against Muammar Gaddafi." *Reuters*, August 22, 2011. http://www.reuters.com/article/2011/08/22/us-libya-events-idUSTRE77K2QH20110822.

"Towards a Post-American Europe: A Power Audit of EU-U.S. Relations." n.d. http://www.brookings.edu/research/reports/2009/11/02-europe-shapiro.

"Transatlantic Declaration of 1990." October 20, 2011. http://useu.usmission.gov/1990transatlantic_declaration.html.

"Transatlantic Trends: Immigration," December 15, 2011. http://www.integrazionemigranti.gov.it/Documenti/Documents/Documenti%20da%20newsletter%20gennaio%202012/TTImmigration_final_web.pdf.

Traynor, Ian. "Libya Conflict: EU Awaits UN Approval for Deployment of Ground Troops." *The Guardian*, April 18, 2011.

"Treaty of Maastricht on European Union." n.d. http://europa.eu/legislation_summaries/institutional_affairs/treaties/treaties_maastricht_en.htm.

"Tunisia Elections 2011: Ennahda Islamist Party Official Winner." *Huffington Post*, October 27, 2011. http://www.huffingtonpost.com/2011/10/27/tunisia-elections-2011-ennahda_n_1062709.html.

"Tunisini in Francia Con i Permessi Ma Parigi Nega: Nessun Ingresso." *LaStampa.it*, n.d. http://www3.lastampa.it/cronache/sezioni/articolo/lstp/398184/.

Turpen, E. A. "Free World: America, Europe, and the Surprising Future of the West." *Choice* (June 2005), vol. 42, no. 10, p. 1895.

"UK Expels Gaddafi Diplomats and Recognises Libya Rebels." BBC. July 27, 2011. http://www.bbc.co.uk.

Ulbrich, Jeffrey. Associated Press. "Atlantic Alliance expanding its horizons," June 22, 1998.

Ullman, Richard H., ed., *The World and Yugoslavia's War.* Washington, DC: Council of Foreign Relations, 1996.

"U.N. Details Its Failure to Stop '95 Bosnia Massacre—New York Times." *New York Times*, n.d. http://www.nytimes.com/1999/11/16/world/un-details-its-failure-to-stop-95-bosnia-massacre.html.

United Nations Security Council. "In Swift, Decisive Action, Security Council Imposes Tough Measures on Libyan Regime, Adopting Resolution 1970 in Wake of Crackdown on Protesters." February 26, 2011. http://www.un.org/News/Press/docs/2011/sc10187.doc.htm (accessed February 6, 2013).

United Nations. Security Council Resolution 770 (August 13, 1992).

United Nations. Security Council Resolution 794. 1992.

UN News Centre. *UN News Centre.* May 4, 2011. http://www.un.org/apps/news/story.asp?NewsID=38270 (accessed February 6, 2012).

UN Resolution 2014 Security Council Condemns Human Rights Violations by Yemeni Authorities, Abuses by 'Other Actors', After Months of Political Strife,, October 21, 2011. http://www.un.org/news/press/docs/2011/sc10418.doc.htm.

"UN Security Council Resolution 1973, Libya." *Council on Foreign Relations*, n.d. http://www.cfr.org/libya/un-security-council-resolution-1973-libya/p24426.

"Upheaval in the East; Gorbachev Voices New Reservations on German Unity—New York Times." n.d. http://www.nytimes.com/1990/02/21/world/upheaval-in-the-east-gorbachev-voices-new-reservations-on-german-unity.html?pagewanted=all&src=pm.

U.S. Congress, Senate. Committee on Foreign Relations. *The International Criminal Court: Protecting American Servicemen and Officials from the Threat of International Prosecution:* Hearing before Committee on Foreign Relations. 106th Cong., 1st sess., June 14, 2000.

U.S. Embassy. "New Transatlantic Agenda," /new_transatlantic_agenda.html, October 20, 2011, http://useu.usmission.gov/new_transatlantic_agenda.html;

"U.S. Recognizes 3 Yugoslav Republics as Independent—New York Times." *New York Times*, n.d. http://www.nytimes.com/1992/04/08/world/us-recognizes-3-yugoslav-republics-as-independent.html.

"Value of OECD Aid Drops for First Time in 15 Years." *The Guardian*, April 4, 2012. http://www.guardian.co.uk/global-development/2012/apr/04/value-oecd-aid-drops-15-years.

Van Evera, Stephen. *Guide to Methods for Students of Political Science.* Ithaca, NY: Cornell University Press, 1997.

Verschuren, Piet. "Case Study as a Research Strategy: Some Ambiguities and Opportunities," in *Social Research Methodology*. Newbury Park, CA: Sage, 2001.

Walker, R.B.J. "East Wind, West Wind: Civilizations, Hegemonies, and World Orders," in Walker, ed., *Culture, Ideology and World Order.* Boulder, CO: Westview Press, 1984.

Walker, R.B.J. "World Politics, and Western Reason: Universalism, Pluralism, Hegemony," in Walker, *Culture, Ideology and World Order.* Boulder, CO: Westview Press, 1984.

Wallace, William. "Broken Bridges." *The World Today* (December 2004), vol. 60, no. 12; pp. 13–16.

Wallerstein, Immanuel Maurice. *The Capitalist World-Economy: Essays.* Cambridge: Cambridge University Press, 1979.

Wallerstein, Immanuel Maurice. *World-Systems Analysis: An Introduction.* Durham, NC: Duke University Press, 2004.

Walt, Stephen M. *The Origins of Alliances.* Ithaca, NY: Cornell University Press, 1987.

Walt, Stephen. "The Precarious Partnership: America and Europe in a New Era." In *Atlantic Security: Contending Visions*, in Charles Kupchan, ed. (New York: Council on Foreign Relations, 1998), p. 8.

Walt, Stephen. "The Renaissance of Security Studies." *International Studies Quarterly*, vol. 35, no. 2 (1991), p. 212.

Walt, Stephen. "The Ties That Fray." *The National Interest* (Winter 1998–1999), pp. 3–11.

Walt, Stephen "Why Alliances Endure or Collapse." *Survival*, Spring 1997, vol. 39, Iss.1; p. 156.

Waltz, Kenneth. *Theory of International Politics*. Redding, MA: Addison-Wesley, 1979.

Waterfield, Bruno, and Thomas Harding. "Libya: NATO Calls for All Its Members to Help Oust Gaddafi." *The Telegraph,* March 3, 2011. http://telegraph.co.uk.

Weaver Ole, Barry Buzan, Morten Kelstrup, and Pierre Lemaitre. *Identity, Migration and the New Security Agenda in Europe*. London: Pinter, 1993.

Weidenfel, Werner [et.al.]. *From Alliance to Coalitions: The Future of Transatlantic Relations*. Gütersloh, Germany: Bertlsmann, 2004.

Weidenfeld, Werner. *America and Europe: Is the Break Inevitable?* Gütersloh, Germany: Bertlsmann, 1996.

Weidenfeld, Werner. *From Alliance to Coalitions: The Future of Transatlantic Relations*. Washington, DC: Bertelsmann Foundation Publishers, 2004.

Wendt, Alexander. "Anarchy Is What States Make of It: The Social Construction of Power Politics." *International Organization* 46, no. 2 (Spring 1992), pp. 391–425.

Wendt, Alexander. "On the Media: A Response to the Critics." *Review of International Studies* 26 (2000), pp. 165–180.

Wendt, Alexander. *Social Theory of International Politics*. Cambridge: Cambridge University Press, 1999.

Wheeler, Nicholas J. *Saving Strangers. Humanitarian Intervention in International Society*. Oxford: Oxford University Press, 2000.

Whitlock, Craig. "Mubarak Steps Down, Prompting Jubilation in Cairo Streets." *The Washington Post*, February 12, 2011, sec. World. http://www.washington post.com/wp-dyn/content/article/2011/02/11/AR2011021102386.html.

Whitlock, Craig. "NATO Allies Grapple with Shrinking Defense Budgets." *The Washington Post*, January 30, 2012, sec. World. http://www.washingtonpost. com/world/national-security/nato-allies-grapple-with-shrinking-defense-bud gets/2012/01/20/gIQAKBg5aQ_story_1.html.

"Why Comply? Social Learning and European Identity Change." *International Organization* 55, no. 03 (2001): 553–588.

Wiegrefe, Klaus. "An Inside Look at the Reunification Negotiations." *Spiegel Online*, September 29, 2010. http://www.spiegel.de/international/germany/germany-s-unlikely-diplomatic-triumph-an-inside-look-at-the-reunification-negotiations-a-719848.html.

Wiegrefe, Klaus. "The Birth of Two Plus Four: An Inside Look at the Reunification Negotiations." *Spiegel Online*, September 29, 2010. http://www.spiegel.de/international/germany/germany-s-unlikely-diplomatic-triumph-an-inside-look-at-the-reunification-negotiations-a-719848–6.html.

Wiener, Jarrod, ed., *The Transatlantic Relationship*. New York: St. Martin's Press, 1996.

Wilgoren, Debbi, and William Branigin. "Boehner Elected House Speaker as 112th Congress Convenes." *The Washington Post*, January 5, 2011, sec. Politics. http://www.washingtonpost.com/wp-dyn/content/article/2011/01/05/AR2011010501936. html.

"William Hague Arrives in Tunisia to Meet New Regime." *The Guardian*, February 8, 2011. http://www.guardian.co.uk/politics/2011/feb/08/william-hague-visits-tunisia.

Wilson, Scott, Joby Warrick, and Liz Sly. "Obama Says Assad Must Go, but Crackdown Continues." *The Washington Post*, August 19, 2011, sec. World.

http://www.washingtonpost.com/world/middle-east/obama-says-assad-must-go-but-crackdown-continues/2011/08/19/gIQApc8jPJ_story.html.

Wolfke, Karol. *Custom in Present International Law*, 2nd rev. ed. Dordrecht: Martinus Nijhoff Publishers, 1994.

World-Systems Analysis: An Introduction. Durham, NC: Duke University Press, 2004.

www.un.org. *Security Council Approves "No-Fly Zone" over Libya*, March 17, 2011. http://www.un.org/News/Press/docs/2011/sc10200.doc.htm (accessed January 7, 2012).

Xinhua News Agency. "Kohl Cautions NATO about Eastward Expansion," February 3, 1996.

"Yemen President Saleh Steps Down." *BBC*, February 27, 2012, sec. Middle East. http://www.bbc.co.uk/news/world-middle-east-17177720.

"Yemen's Ali Abdullah Saleh Resigns—But It Changes Little." *The Guardian*, November 24, 2011. http://www.guardian.co.uk/commentisfree/2011/nov/24/yemen-ali-abdullah-saleh-resigns.

Yin, Robert. *Case Study Research: Design and Methods.* Newbury Park, CA: Sage, 1994.

"Yugoslav Republic Of Croatia Declares Independent Nation—New York Times." *New York Times*, n.d. http://www.nytimes.com/1991/05/30/world/yugoslav-republic-of-croatia-declares-independent-nation.html.

Zakaria, Fareed. *From Wealth to Power: The Unusual Origins of America's World Role.* Princeton, NJ: Princeton University Press, 1999.

"Zapatero pide una 'transición pacífica' en Egipto y Túnez." *EL PAÍS*, January 31, 2011. http://elpais.com/diario/2011/01/31/internacional/1296428404_850215.html.

Index

Made in the USA
Middletown, DE
26 August 2021